INDIGENOUS PEOPLES AND POLITICS

Edited by

Franke Wilmer
Montana State University

A ROUTLEDGE SERIES

INDIGENOUS PEOPLES AND POLITICS

FRANKE WILMER, *General Editor*

NEGOTIATING CLAIMS

The Emergence of Indigenous Land Claim Negotiation Policies in Australia, Canada, New Zealand, and the United States

Christa Scholtz

Routledge
New York & London

Published in 2006 by
Routledge
Taylor & Francis Group
270 Madison Avenue
New York, NY 10016

Published in Great Britain by
Routledge
Taylor & Francis Group
2 Park Square
Milton Park, Abingdon
Oxon OX14 4RN

© 2006 by Taylor & Francis Group, LLC
Routledge is an imprint of Taylor & Francis Group

Printed in the United States of America on acid-free paper
10 9 8 7 6 5 4 3 2 1

International Standard Book Number-10: 0-415-97690-1 (Hardcover)
International Standard Book Number-13: 978-0-415-97690-9 (Hardcover)
Library of Congress Card Number 2005031153

Library of Congress Cataloging-in-Publication Data

Scholtz, Christa Sieglinde, 1970-
      Negotiating claims : the emergence of indigenous land claim negotiation policies in Australia, Canada, New Zealand, and the United States / Christa Scholtz.
            p. cm. -- (Indigenous peoples and politics)
      Includes bibliographical references and index.
      ISBN 0-415-97690-1
      1. Indigenous peoples--Land tenure. 2. Indigenous peoples--Claims. 3. Negotiation. 4. Land tenure--Cross - cultural studies. I. Title. II. Series.

K738. S336 2006
346.04'32089--dc22   2005031153

Taylor & Francis Group
is the Academic Division of Informa plc.

Visit the Taylor & Francis Web site at
http://www.taylorandfrancis.com

and the Routledge Web site at
http://www.routledge-ny.com

Contents

Acknowledgments

At the foundation of this project are the writings and musings of policymakers as captured and organized in archives around the world. I begin, then, by paying homage to those professionals who catalogue errant bits of paper so that these documents may become accessible building blocks for scholarship. My thanks to the National Archives of Australia, Canada, New Zealand, and the United States. Particular thanks to New Zealand's Department of Prime Minister and Cabinet for allowing access to official documents less than 25 years old, and to Canada's Privy Council Office for expediting my Access to Information requests.

My gratitude to all those directly involved in and affected by indigenous land claim policies who agreed to an interview. These individuals shared their time, thoughts, speculations, and convictions when all I had to offer in return was a free cup of coffee, an opportunity to reflect, and the promise not to distort their words.

Thanks also to those organizations that provided funding, without which my wanderings could not have strayed so far. These are: the Social Sciences and Humanities Research Council of Canada (Doctoral Fellowship Program), the MacArthur Foundation, the Center for International Studies (Princeton University), the Center for Regional Studies (Princeton University), and the Brookings Institution.

Heartfelt thanks to those centers of learning that made comparative research not just practicable, but delightful. These are the School of Business and Public Management at Victoria University of Wellington, and the Political Science Program of the Research School of the Social Sciences (Australian National University).

For the important role that each played in the development of this book, I especially thank Elizabeth Bloodgood Ames, Elisabeth Barot, Nancy

Bermeo, Katharina Coleman, Anne-Marie Gardner, Laura McMaster, Mary Moreland, Tom Romer, Kathryn Stoner-Weiss, and Deborah Yashar.

Vielen Dank to my parents, Eberhard and Elisabeth Scholtz, whose support began with my first breath and continues to this day. And thanks to my husband Lyle, with whom I plan to ride over many roads.

Chapter One
Introduction

WHY NEGOTIATION?

Since World War Two, there has been a global trend of increasing political activism of indigenous peoples. This resurgence has sustained an important dialogue in the post-war global rights revolution[1] that explores the tensions inherent in the recognition by liberal individualist states of the collective rights of indigenous peoples to self-determination. At the core of this resurgence, there is a demand for a decolonization of relations between indigenous peoples, the "nations within," and settler states. The global narrative in this decolonization of relations is to achieve an internal reconfiguration of power where collective rights of indigenous peoples are recognized and given force within philosophical and legal regimes that give normative priority to individual rights.

At the heart of indigenous grievances, there is a call for a reallocation of power on the basis of collective rights. These grievances must be put in real world terms, in the form of political demands that can at once mobilize indigenous energies and be processed and understood within the real world political context. This requires policy demands that are actionable. The challenge for indigenous activism is to operationalize a demand for power sharing and a recognition of collective rights that simultaneously mobilize indigenous peoples and elicit a supportive (or at least benign) response from the broader society. This challenge is to move demands from the lofty realm of political theory to the grubby world of policy. How these narratives are told is not without consequence. Care must be taken in how claims are packaged, since "whatever else might be said about the character of indigenous rights, they are 'mediated rights': the recognition of indigenous interests in land as legal or political rights inevitably transforms those interests."[2] The challenge for indigenous activists is to make an actionable claim for recognition to governments in the form of a reasonable policy alternative that the state can understand, digest, accept, and institute.

In this study, I focus on how policy-makers respond to the critical actionable demand made by indigenous peoples worldwide to recognize their land rights and resolve their land claims. These are claims regarding both historical dispossession and continuing land ownership and use. This study asks the following question: *Why do governments choose to negotiate land claims rather than resolve claims through some other means?* In this study, I am not concerned with why a government might choose to negotiate one claim at a given time. Rather, I am interested in exploring why a government would choose to implement a negotiation *policy*, committing itself to a long-run strategy of negotiation over a number of claims and over a significant course of time. Answering this question requires an analysis of policy options open to a government at a given opportunity and of the conditions which facilitate or mitigate its choice to negotiate. This study examines the emergence of a particular type of policy response and the institutions that support it.

Why is the negotiation outcome interesting? If policy-makers are to choose a negotiation policy, they must reach two prior conclusions: 1) that they will recognize indigenous special land and political rights claims by enshrining the principle of indigenous consent in the policy process, and 2) that policy-makers will not divorce themselves politically from the outcomes of negotiation by delegating their decision-making power to another party. To negotiate is to recognize collective rights while inviting possible blame for policy outcomes that will likely prove unpopular. Therefore, negotiation is actually a politically risky strategy. After all, " . . . indigenous peoples' claims to continued sovereignty over their territories question the source and legitimacy of state authority."[3] To some degree, engaging in a negotiation process legitimizes the claim that the authority of the state rests on shaky ground, and opens up the Pandora's Box of historical wrongs perhaps best left undisturbed. In other respects, policy-makers' usual pay-offs for engaging with social groups are arguably too minimal to be worth the potential costs: little opportunity to win over a significant set of voters in return for some risk of electoral backlash, and a high risk of creating uncertainty among well-entrenched property interests over the ability of the state to act as their guarantor.

To understand what drives policy-makers to the negotiating table, I base my analysis on its normative underpinnings. The recognition of indigenous collective rights, at the heart of the negotiation choice, challenges deeply held notions of national citizenship. The western liberal ideal has been that all citizens in a political community should be equal members of that community, where equality is defined by a common parcel of rights which every citizen shares. At any given point in time, the story of indigenous land claims shows that policy responses are reflections of how government actors believe aboriginal people and the rights they claim can fit within a national dialogue on citizenship. In discussing land claims, policy-makers stake out the conditions under which collective cultural or property rights can coexist within a national citizenship regime. The key to understanding the emergence of negotiation policies is to trace the factors that push and prod this dialogue about citizenship within governments.

In this study, I lay out policy-makers' conceptual frameworks, and I examine how their predispositions on the issues of civilization and citizenship color their evaluations of a negotiation policy's political acceptability and administrative feasibility. This focuses on whether and how policy-makers' conceptual underpinnings shift prior to a negotiation choice being made, and before the point where concrete outcomes of the policy become clear. I also take care to understand how ideology is constrained by the more practical pressures that lead policy-makers to privilege one policy option over another. This calls for an analysis of relative risks, costs, and benefits across policy options. Policy-makers may be ideologically predisposed to accept some policy choices but be jostled by circumstances to institute others. To gain a firm grasp on policy change generally, and on the emergence of negotiation policies specifically, one must examine how policy-makers' expectations about future policies develop. Herein lies the challenge of pressure politics for any social group: to engage with state actors not only to persuade and effect a profound attitudinal change, but also to create conditions where state actors respond in a manner in line with that group's policy preferences.

This project reaches out to address questions of interest to political scientists who may have never cast an interested eye on the politics of indigenous peoples. An important objective of this research is to understand how politically and economically marginalized communities engage the state to achieve policy outcomes that threaten entrenched norms, economic interests and the interests of the state itself. The project speaks to the effectiveness and the limitations of political and judicial strategies available to these communities in seeking leverage over government action. In contexts where groups have limited electoral resources or opportunities to build coalitions with other groups in order to pursue smaller and more targeted policy goals, the ability of social groups to build communities of interests within and across the state is critically important.

The Cases: Australia, Canada, New Zealand and the United States

The development of indigenous land claims politics is examined in four countries, primarily since the Second World War: Australia, Canada, New Zealand, and the United States. A wide comparative analysis necessarily takes the eye away from important nuances; however, by widening the geographic scope of this study, I achieve key methodological aims. First, variation on the dependent variable is maximized. Just as indigenous peoples have always pressed for recognition of their land rights and claims, states have always responded. States have experienced three broad stages in indigenous policy development, ranging from dispossession, assimilation, to self-determination. The responses of states have varied in form, timing, intent, and effects. Governments in each of the countries noted above faced key decision-making opportunities at different times, and only by widening the study's perspective to include countries around the globe can one appreciate the full range of options theoretically available to policy-makers. I ask what factors in each country truncated the set of considered policy options, and whether the negotiation option was among them. I examine the legacies of previous policy choices in light of the set of options available at later choice opportunities. Also, when looking at negotiation outcomes, a wider scope provides an appreciation of both intra- and inter-national variation.

How do these cases array on the dependent variable? Who has implemented a negotiation policy and who has not? Both Canada and New Zealand have embraced land claim negotiation policies that have included a wide range of claimant groups and involved all regions of the country. These policies are national in scope and are considered institutionalized alternatives to litigation. Canada adopted its negotiation policy in 1973, with New Zealand following in 1989. Prior to its negotiation policy and after 1951, Canada allowed Indians to pursue land claims in the courts. In New Zealand prior to 1989, there was little effective remedy for claims until the creation, in 1975, of a strictly advisory body called the Waitangi Tribunal. From 1975 until 1989, the New Zealand government engaged in some negotiations on an ad hoc basis, but it was not until 1989 that the formal negotiation policy was implemented.

Canada and New Zealand stand in contrast to the other two cases. Australia represents a case of halted and gradual negotiation. The Australian

Commonwealth instituted a negotiation policy in 1976, but this effort was limited to the one area of the continent where the Commonwealth has exclusive jurisdiction—the Northern Territory. An attempt by the Hawke Labor government to extend the negotiation policy to the States failed in the mid 1980s. However, in 1993, a limited national negotiation policy was implemented under the Commonwealth's Native Title Act. Only recently, since approximately 2000, have attempts at regional agreement-making begun to emerge. Finally, there is the United States. The United States represents the non-negotiation case. Since the formal end of treaty-making in 1871, the United States has preferred litigation and special-party arbitration to negotiation. From 1863 to 1946, Indian tribes were allowed to sue the United States in the Court of Claims once they petitioned Congress and received a special jurisdictional act. In 1946, Congress created the Indian Claims Commission to litigate a backlog of historical claims, while allowing tribes to bring claims arising from actions after 1946 to the Court of Claims. With the closure of the Indian Claims Commission in 1978, the courts have once again been the arena in which claims resolution is pursued. While a few claims have been negotiated on an ad hoc basis and after protracted litigation (e.g. Maine and Florida settlement agreements), no formal or institutionalized alternative to litigation has emerged.

These cases form a useful universe for comparison. First, each is a settler state with a history of British colonialism. Each has a developed common law legal system with independent judiciaries. Each is a developed industrialized state with administrative capacity and has shared similar assimilationist philosophies regarding indigenous peoples. However, the situation varies as to when courts became active players in developing indigenous rights jurisprudence. In each case, except the United States, indigenous people had mobilized politically before key judicial decisions examining the status of their rights under the common law were made. These four countries also vary in key institutional respects. The three federal states and one unitary state (New Zealand) have different jurisdictional rules governing the roles of national and sub-national governments in indigenous affairs. Also, in the cases of Canada and Australia, the federal government is the sole sovereign over internal territories (the Northwest, Yukon, Nunavut, and Northern Territories), creating an interesting situation where unitary "islands" exist within the boundaries of federal states. Only the United States has a presidential system of separated powers, where both the legislative and executive branches play significant roles in policy formulation and implementation.

CONCLUSIONS

A critical task of this study is to parse out the relative weight of judicial versus other arguments in explaining executive negotiating behavior.
Scholars point to the judicialization of politics as one of the "most significant trends in the late-twentieth and early-twenty-first century government."[4] Catalytic court decisions recognizing indigenous property
rights for the first time are most often identified as the primary causal
force behind the advent of land claim negotiations. While I explore the
important role that courts play, I insist on explaining the emergence of
negotiation policies in conjunction with the ability of indigenous groups
to leverage potential and actual judicial changes into political gains. I
explain the emergence of negotiation policies by the interaction between
judicial change and indigenous political mobilization, and not judicial
change alone. Specifically, the sequencing of political mobilization *prior*
to judicial determinations of indigenous land rights significantly changes
policy-makers' evaluations of their policy alternatives. Political mobilization before significant court decisions means that policy-makers must
make policy choices in a context where indigenous people can credibly
threaten to impose future political costs. Political mobilization changes
policy-makers' long-run payoffs, and this increases the likelihood that
negotiation will emerge.

Before the political mobilization and organized public protest of
indigenous peoples that began seriously in the mid 1960s, the aboriginal
policy agenda in these four polities was largely defined by non-indigenous
advocates firmly wedded to an assimilationist or integrationist agenda.
While non-indigenous advocates for aboriginal policy reform were important supporters for the extension of equal citizenship rights to indigenous
individuals, their support did not extend to the recognition of special
indigenous rights. Policy-makers, most markedly in Canada and the United
States, believed that delegation of land grievances to the courts was appropriate because all citizens, indigenous or not, should have recourse to the
judicial branch. Policy-makers reasoned that they would win some and
lose some in the courts, and should the courts deny a claim, that there
would be no subsequent political repercussions. Delegation to the courts
was not so much a blame-avoidance strategy as a means of inculcating
indigenous people to act as proper citizens. Use of the courts served assimilationist principles, and was associated with a greater dialogue of equal
and undifferentiated citizenship that held little sympathy for indigenous
peoples' special rights.

Examination of cabinet memoranda and records of cabinet discussions reveal that land rights were forced onto the cabinet agenda only through the representations of indigenous peoples. The mid-1960s marked an important qualitative change in indigenous political history across all the countries in this study. During this decade of the civil rights movement, indigenous political organizations expanded their repertoires to include collective action through public protest. Land rights became the central symbol around which disparate indigenous groups could unite. Once indigenous peoples demonstrated publicly that they could unite behind a common agenda, indigenous peoples began to matter in the policy process as never before. The key effect of indigenous political mobilization, in the mid 1960s, was to make policy-makers aware for the first time that indigenous peoples could be political entities on their own terms, and could impose potential costs on policy-makers in the future.

The engine behind the emergence of negotiation policies is political mobilization before judicial change. I demonstrate how this argument applies across all four countries. However, this study's cross-national design has allowed me to identify two variables which condition policy-makers' evaluations of the negotiation option. These variables are: 1) political norms that affect policy-makers' underlying preference for delegation; and 2) federalism, specifically the allocation of legislative competence over aboriginal affairs and resource management.

Even in the presence of judicial change and political mobilization, policy-makers may be restrained from delegating political decisions to courts by internal norms over the appropriateness of judicial policy-making and review. I find the effect of this political norm in the two extreme cases: the United States (pro-delegation) and New Zealand (anti-delegation). In the United States, a fundamental narrative in the American political project is the role of the judiciary in ensuring the Constitution's integrity. The Supreme Court, not Congress nor the President, is the ultimate arbiter of justice. In this political culture, to provide a policy alternative outside of the court system is to risk thwarting fundamental justice. This norm privileges the delegation of policy-making functions to the judiciary. In contrast, the norm of parliamentary sovereignty as it is expressed in New Zealand holds the opposite. In New Zealand, governments traditionally view judicial review as fundamentally undemocratic, and resist the delegation of policy-making functions from Parliament to the courts. In the New Zealand political dialogue, the legitimacy of non-judicial dispute resolution mechanisms is much higher, and a negotiation policy is, *ceteris paribus,* more likely to emerge.

This study also explores how one particular institutional variable, federalism, impacts the probability that a negotiation policy will emerge and diffuse across state borders. Federalism matters in so far as it involves a sub-national government, as the owner of public lands and the government in charge of natural resource development, as a party to the negotiations.[5] In the context of modern land claim negotiations, this assignment of jurisdictions between the federal and sub-national governments means that to conclude a land claims settlement involving more than strictly cash compensation, sub-national governments are necessary parties to the agreement and, as such, are veto players. I conclude that on balance, federalism hinders the development of policies that recognize and protect indigenous rights. Indigenous people are, in almost all cases, intra-state minorities. Sub-national states are much more likely than central governments to protect established economic interests in the context of indigenous protest. Land and resource management is important to sub-national governments. They jealously guard their power in this jurisdiction and are disinclined to impose costs on concentrated interests due to fears of inter-state economic competition.[6] Attempts by central governments to impose negotiation policies on sub-national governments will, almost certainly, meet staunch resistance. Therefore, central governments weigh the benefits of protecting indigenous rights at the cost of risking intergovernmental relations. This calculation is serious, and often the protection of indigenous rights is lost.

CONTRIBUTIONS TO THE LITERATURE

A contribution of this study is the focus on decision-making in the executive branch (as well as the legislative branch in the American case) in the development of a negotiation response to indigenous land claims. The literature on indigenous land rights policies betrays a fragmented treatment of the state. This study is an effort to redress that fragmentation by turning a concerted eye to the workings of key public policy decision-makers. This fragmentation of the state in land rights literature is due, in part, to the theoretical preoccupations of the intellectual disciplines most involved with this subject area: law and anthropology.

Any academic discipline approaches a subject with a given set of questions or biases about what is of interest. From the law perspective, it is natural to consider land claims politics on the basis of the judicial branch in order to understand the development of an indigenous rights jurisprudence. Legal scholars have focused on how a received body of law, grounded in a Western theory of liberal rights and state sovereignty, can be reconciled with the aspirations and legal structures of indigenous peoples and their organizations.[7] Within this literature, the non-judicial branches of the state feature only occasionally, and if their appearance is requested, it is to prevail upon them to use their policy-making powers in the interests of greater justice. The analysis is usually limited to exhorting executives and legislators to incorporate developing judicial principles within their policy frameworks.

Even in recent work, which attributes significant changes in land claims policy to the catalytic power of judicial decisions, the view of executive action is simplistically treated. The causal chain presented is that only when courts find favorably for indigenous land rights are policy-makers provoked to deliver negotiation policies. A closer look at key judicial decisions quickly indicates that court judgments often yield unclear and contradictory signals from which policy-makers could hope to chart a new course. More often than not, judicial judgments raise more questions than they answer. While judicial decisions may spur governments past inertia, these decisions do not provide the whole story of how governments respond. There is little analysis done within the legal treatment of indigenous land rights issues to understand how policy-makers within the executive branch view the risks that judicial developments place in front of existing policy choices. Critically, more attention needs to be given to how they weigh the relative risks of their policy options, given changes within the judicial branch and other constraints within the political landscape. How executives and their administrators go about doing this (or not) is left under-explored.

From within anthropology, the interest in land claims politics has primarily been to document historical patterns of indigenous social structure and land tenure as well as indigenous strategies of resistance to state domination. The role of anthropology in the development of land claims jurisprudence has been substantial, and giving evidence in court of historical indigenous land use tenure systems has been its particular preserve. Interest in the development of land claims policies from within the policy-making structures has been tangential to the core pursuits of this discipline as well. However, in the instances anthropologists have turned their skills to look at the administrative state itself, the products of their efforts demonstrate the worth of the enterprise.[8] The influence of a sustained academic interest in indigenous politics by law and anthropology has certainly resulted in a rich set of literatures, but greater attention needs to be allocated to the decision-making environments of executive and administrative actors.

The contemporary study of the state has also been conditioned by the dominant conceptual framework for the analysis of indigenous-state relations: colonialism. This conceptual framework cuts across academia's disciplinary boundaries. Indigenous-settler relationships have been characterized by patterns of colonial domination and resistance. The colonialism literature has been used to convey the role of the state in the oppression and attempted assimilation of indigenous communities the world over. It has been a powerful paradigm used to good effect in the international mobilization and resurgence of indigenous activism over the last thirty years.[9] One consequence, however, of this intellectual tradition has been a privileging of state power. The view of the state in this intellectual tradition is one of almost overwhelming force. What is emphasized is the degree to which all parts of the state speak with the same voice and work to reinforce the colonial and paternalistic patterns of the other. A danger of this tradition is to neglect looking at the state in a critical and differentiated way to find contestation within it. It is arguable that, prior to welfare state expansionism of the post-war era, the relatively small size of governments and limited scope for administrative action facilitated ideological uniformity and limited contestation of policy goals across the state itself, hence limiting the usefulness of a more concerted look at the executive branch. This, however, is no longer the case. The executive deserves renewed attention.

OUTLINE

From September 2000 to December 2001, I conducted the fieldwork on which this analysis is based. I rely on a variety of sources, including approximately 60 interviews with policy-makers and indigenous activists in Canada, New Zealand, and Australia. Individuals were assured of their personal confidentiality, and the references in the following chapters are based on my notes of those interviews. Much of the work is historical, and as much as possible I have drawn my conclusions from primary sources. I relied heavily on the collections of the National Archives of Canada (Ottawa), Archives New Zealand (Wellington), the National Archives of Australia (Canberra), and the National Archives and Records Administration (Washington D.C.). I have also used the Taos Blue Lake archival collection at Princeton University's Seeley-Mudd Library.

Chapter Two gives a detailed examination of the study's theoretical background. I delve more closely into the literatures on institutional emergence, bargaining, and social movements within comparative politics. Chapters Three through Five are empirical case studies of cabinet decision-making in Canada, New Zealand, and Australia respectively. Each of these chapters ends with the implementation of a negotiation policy. Chapter Six is an examination of the non-negotiation case: the United States. In Chapter Seven, I conclude with final thoughts on the outcomes of the land claims negotiation process.

Chapter Two
Negotiation: Of Recognition and Delegation

INTRODUCTION

A politics of recognition reflects a change from a politics of equal dignity among individuals to a politics of difference based on the need to recognize explicit cultural and collective rights.[1] The demand is made on the basis that a politics of equal dignity, while important and hard fought, is insufficient to rectify institutionalized patterns of cultural delegitimation. Therefore, the demand for recognition is highly normative, and is often framed in terms of historic oppression and injustice. Minority cultural groups the world over justify a demand for recognition on the basis that to withhold such recognition perpetuates their oppression and thus inflicts collective harm.[2] Indigenous people, as first occupants, have been a key constituency in the global politics of recognition. Many indigenous people argue that the recognition of their collective rights is a prerequisite for a truly post-colonial relationship with the state. The larger project of indigenous politics has been for countries to recognize indigenous peoples as legitimate self-determining and sovereign communities. As part of this larger post-colonial political project, indigenous peoples have demanded that governments recognize their land rights and engage in a dialogue to resolve historic and continuing grievances. The demand that the state recognize indigenous land rights makes it clear that the recognition sought involves not only a state's symbolic approval of collective rights, but also the recognition of a fundamental and enforceable property right to land.

Theorists have focused primarily on the philosophical and historical roots of the emergence of a demand for recognition from "below." Important debates have flourished on the challenges facing those demanding recognition, particularly on the strategic dilemmas that arise when groups wish to pursue potentially competing goals, such as cultural recognition versus economic distribution.[3] However, the normative literature on recognition has devoted comparatively little attention to the *supply* side of the recognition equation.[4] If recognition by the state of collective rights is indeed a public good, then one may ask why, and under what conditions, do states supply the recognition that some groups demand? Like any other public good that holds real consequences for people's lives, recognition must have an impact on the distribution of social, economic, or ideological resources across social groups. To this distribution of social power the state is rarely neutral. If one accepts the central notion that recognition by the state distributes good as well as harm, then one must ask whether the state itself has an interest in whether, and how, this distribution occurs. In the specific case of indigenous land rights, the state has never shown itself to be a disinterested player. The rights in question relate to possibly the most central of its economic assets and involve peoples often economically and socially marginalized.

This study examines a key policy choice in this politics of recognition. It examines the emergence of land claim negotiations, a policy choice where governments explicitly recognize the validity of indigenous collective claims to land as well as indigenous communities' equal standing as parties to an agreement. These negotiations provide settings where indigenous peoples engage the executive outside of the usual institutional spaces that have regulated indigenous-settler relations. Unlike other institutional spaces where indigenous-state relations are fashioned, such as courts or social service agencies, land claim negotiations accord indigenous peoples and indigenous authority structures an explicit recognition of their role as strategic political actors involved in a dialogue with the government. Hence, land claim negotiations are both symbolically and substantively important. They are also controversial. At best, land claim negotiations are bargaining sites where the state and an indigenous group enter into a good faith effort to address past wrongs and build an enduring basis for a beneficial future. At worst, they make a mockery of good relationship building, where one party is forced by a lack of bargaining strength to accept a bad deal that will taint future prospects for good relations. However, these negotiations are always about testing the practical worth of legal rights and hard fought political protest, and refashioning the political linkages between indigenous and settler societies. Thus, land claim negotiations are critical venues for the negotiation of " . . . the nature and extent of [indigenous peoples'] ongoing membership in provincial or territorial communities and the nature of their citizenship in the [national] community."[5]

Negotiation is an important outcome in a politics of recognition, but its theoretical relevance is not limited to this normative dimension. Negotiation is also interesting since, by entering into a public process of bargaining with indigenous communities as co-signatories to a mutual agreement, governments, in effect, deny themselves whatever future political deniability might come by allowing others, such as a court or an arbitrator, to make decisions in their stead. On this normative dimension referred to in this study as the delegation dimension, negotiation is a policy choice where governments spurn the political value of insulating themselves from future political outcomes of a controversial process.

For a negotiation decision to occur, the executive must come to two prior conclusions. First, the executive will recognize *collective* indigenous rights and not simply guarantee indigenous *individuals* the array of civil liberties that citizens in modern democracies have come to expect. Second, the executive will sit at the bargaining table with indigenous groups, and thereby not insulate itself from future blame should settlement agreements either not be reached or become politically unpopular in the future. To negotiate indigenous land rights is a risky strategy that gives credence to controversial rights claims, while accepting a clear measure of political responsibility for policy outcomes which may threaten established economic interests. In this study, I ask: *Why do governments, particularly the executive branch, choose to negotiate in lieu of other ways of resolving indigenous land disputes?* Why would an executive choose to negotiate indigenous land claims instead of implementing other policy alternatives? These alternatives include doing nothing, pursuing active litigation, choosing arbitration, or simply legislating away indigenous land rights.

This study focuses primarily on the executive branch of the state. As the state is not a unitary actor, branches of the state of particular interest must be identified. I focus on the executive because it is both democratically accountable and ultimately responsible for the overall direction of state policy-making. It is the leading agent within the state for policy change and implementation.[6] This is particularly true in parliamentary systems, but is also true in presidential systems, except in the rare circumstances of legislative override. The executive is elected with a mandate to drive the policy agenda and, within the limits of constitutional review, can overrule the judiciary. Therefore, the executive branch's role in the provision of public goods is central.

This study addresses the recognition indigenous land rights by the executive branch in Australia, Canada, and New Zealand. On the basis of an in-depth analysis of these three cases, I conclude by examining the generalizability of my findings to the United States, where both the legislative and executive branches are involved in policy formulation. To summarize, Canada chose to implement a full national negotiation policy in 1973; New

Zealand followed in 1989. Australia adopted a limited and partial negotiation response in 1976 that did not expand to address all of Australia's aboriginal claims until 1993. Australia's is a case of halting and hesitant negotiation. The United States adopted an arbitration model in 1946, but aside from a few isolated and *ad hoc* negotiations in the 1970s and 1980s, has not implemented a land rights negotiation policy in the modern era. In Australia, Canada, and New Zealand, each executive had a number of prior opportunities to implement a negotiation policy and deliberately chose not to. Those "missed" opportunities provide valuable insights into the intranational timing of negotiation responses.

The polities are also interesting for what they have in common. They are each developed industrialized democracies with independent judiciaries. The presence of a legitimate independent judiciary is an important characteristic of the executive's policy-making environment. Executives in each of these countries make policy decisions knowing that indigenous people have the choice of pursuing grievances in the courts. In polities with legitimate and independent judiciaries, the executive has an alternative to pursuing a negotiation policy. The executive may choose to litigate every indigenous rights grievance that comes its way. The executive's choice to negotiate land claims is interesting precisely when negotiation is a departure from the common method of resolving grievances between the state and its citizens: the courts. Courts do not have to be *neutral* arbiters, but they must be seen by all possible litigants to reach judicial conclusions without concern that their *independence* will be eroded in the future. The lack of an independent court system would severely undermine the comparison of negotiation strategies across polities, as the dynamic interplay between the judicial and executive branches would be different.

These polities are similar in that the indigenous population is in the minority. While the relative size of the indigenous minority varies across the four polities, the common dynamic remains one where a culturally and historically defined minority demands the majority to recognize a particular collective property right that may redistribute economic power from a larger number of people. The provision of recognition in these four countries is one where the majority recognizes collective indigenous rights at some immediate cost to itself. Therefore, the majority must grapple with a demand for recognition that challenges a simplistic view of democracy. The minoritarian dynamic makes the land claims context in Canada and Australia significantly different from that, for instance, in Zimbabwe, Bolivia, or Guatemala.

In this chapter, I undertake the following tasks. First, to fully characterize the study's dependent variable, I lay out the range of dispute resolution policies from which governments can choose, outlining the key distinctions between them according to the normative dimensions of recognition and delegation. Second, I engage the literature in political science in order to generate a series of plausible explanatory variables. Departing from the literature on the politics of recognition, I reinsert the question of land claims politics within the larger debate on institutional change and emergence within comparative politics. Normative theories of recognition politics offer and evaluate the arguments on which an executive or legislative or judicial branch may justify a choice to provide recognition. However, normative political theory alone cannot explain why, when, or how a branch of the state provides the recognition as demanded. Just as the demand for racial equality was necessary, but insufficient, to procure policies of racial desegregation, a demand for indigenous recognition cannot sufficiently explain a government's decision to recognize indigenous land rights. Normative political theory cannot explain how policy-makers evaluate the merit of recognition demands, or how policy-makers make tradeoffs between recognition and other imperatives, including the incentive to delegate decision-making authority. We must look to the literature on institutional change and emergence to explore the provision of recognition policies and the institutions which underpin them. Underneath this theoretical umbrella of institutional change and emergence, I engage literatures specific to courts, collective action, federalism, and bargaining.

This chapter presents the arguments I demonstrate in the empirical chapters that follow. I argue that executive policy-makers implemented land claim negotiation policies once indigenous peoples demonstrated they were capable of acting as players in a game theoretic sense. Once indigenous peoples mobilized politically, were able to demonstrate the ability to commit collectively to a political strategy, and were able to demonstrate the ability to change the political environment by influencing mainstream opinion, policy-makers grudgingly accepted or were otherwise persuaded that an aboriginal policy based on the denial of aboriginal collective rights would incur future and long-run political costs. The credible threat, that aboriginal people could exact future political costs, decreased executives' long-run utility for a delegation strategy, since legal or arbitrated solutions would not fix the larger political problem. I argue that key court decisions, whether they legitimate aboriginal rights claims or not, predict the timing of significant policy change because they motivate policy-makers to re-examine policy. However, court decisions do not in and of themselves determine the kind of policy solutions that executives ultimately choose.

THE DEPENDENT VARIABLE:
NEGOTIATION AND ITS POLICY COMPETITORS

A land claim is a dispute over the rights of indigenous people to the use, enjoyment, and ownership of particular lands, and these rights are defined and resolved in relation to the rights of other property rights holders. A key normative question facing the government, when it considers a response to a land claim, is how to deal with this underlying dispute. The range on the dependent variable, or the type of response, is the set of options available to the executive branch to resolve the issue of competing land rights. Since the executive branch is a key landowner as well as a creator of property rights in land, the selection of a dispute resolution option is important because the government has an interest in how the dispute is handled.

Policy options for dispute resolution vary in important ways. Policy options rest on normative foundations. Consequently, the emergence of policy institutions cannot be divorced from the norms that underpin them. Dispute resolution has two dimensions: recognition and delegation. The recognition dimension asks whether the executive will recognize indigenous collective rights in future policies. It also relates to the formal status accorded the indigenous party vis-à-vis the executive and the symbolic credence given to indigenous peoples' fundamental political claims. For instance, a dispute resolution process that casts the indigenous party as the executive's equal symbolically recognizes the fundamental political claim that indigenous people are collective (and potentially sovereign) political actors. In contrast, an executive who is not willing to recognize indigenous peoples' collective claims is better served by those policy options that cast the indigenous claimant in a role as a non- sovereign player.

Options that delegate decision-making authority to another party, such as courts or third-party arbitration, have the disputing parties cede a measure of control over the resolution process. The basic trade off is ceding a measure of control in return for resolution by an independent party. The independence of a third party may help legitimize an outcome, and it may also provide disputants with the cover of plausible deniability should the imposed solution prove unpopular or controversial. Delegation is what Kent Weaver calls the "pass the buck" blame avoidance strategy.[7] Figure 1 presents my view of a policy-maker's decision tree, making it visually clear how policy-makers would arrive at a negotiation decision. This is not a game in the strict sense, since there is no second player interacting with the executive in a specified series of moves. The decision tree does show, however, that in some series of potential and unspecified

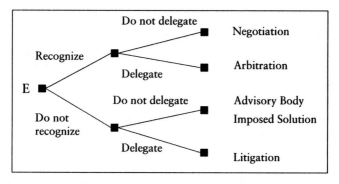

Figure 1. The Executive's Choices

moves with other actors, the executive's essential choices amount to the following two main questions:

1. *Recognize / Do not delegate.* This is the negotiation option, where the parties bargain to reach a settlement which is endorsed by each party. All parties to a negotiated agreement "own" the outcome to an extent which cannot be replicated through other policy options. The accordance of veto status to indigenous actors in this choice option renders negotiation the highest on the symbolic recognition scale. There is important potential that by pursuing a negotiation choice, the recognition conferred goes beyond a nod to indigenous peoples as holding particular property rights to implicitly acknowledging them as sovereign actors acting for a defined community. The negotiation outcome suggests that policy-makers came to accept the reversal, symbolically if not always in substance, of long-held assimilationist norms. These assimilationist norms hold that a government's recognition of indigenous collective rights will impede indigenous integration into the body politic.

The degree to which the negotiation option is institutionalized and formalized by governments varies. At its most simple, a government negotiates with groups in an ad hoc manner and on a case by case basis. Few institutional structures may be established to distinguish negotiation from reaching an out of court settlement. This is the example of the east coast land claim settlements (e.g. Maine and Rhode Island) in the United States during the mid-1980s. In other cases, governments may develop overarching negotiation principles and procedures which normalize the bargaining process across negotiation tables and cement the perception that a government's negotiation policy is a real alternative to a court based solution. This institutionalized negotiation policy is the dependent variable on which I focus in this study. An institutionalized negotiation policy has occurred in Canada since 1973 and in New Zealand since 1989. The Australian Commonwealth implemented a partial negotiation policy in 1976 that was limited to the Northern Territory. The status of negotiation across Australia has varied since the implementation of the Native Title Act (1993).

2. *Recognize / Delegate.* Governments have a choice to provide institutional mechanisms for the resolution of grievances outside the regular court system. Special third-party arbitration is the closest alternative to a court based model. An arbitrator makes a binding decision for the disputing parties. However, the full array of judicial rules and practices do not apply to restrict either the process by which the grievance is presented or the process by which the decision is made. Indeed, flexibility in the rules governing the institutional environment is one of the great reasons and advantages for providing this institutional mechanism versus allowing the court to remain the default arbitrator. The closest example of this option was the American Indian Claims Commission, which operated from 1946 to 1976. New Zealand's Waitangi Tribunal also operates as a special third-party arbitrator for a limited number of claims since 1987.

On a symbolic level, the creation of a special arbitration mechanism recognizes that a group's grievances merit special attention and their resolution is better achieved outside normal judicial procedures. The existence of a third party imposing binding decisions on both parties allows either party to point to an independent actor as the source of any outcomes, while exercising more control over procedural questions than is afforded in a regular court of law.

3. *Do not recognize / Do not delegate.* These options have executives retaining control over policy outcomes while treating the indigenous party as any other social group. The option which completely sidelines indigenous voices is the imposed solution, where an executive may respond to a land claim by introducing legislation to impose a policy response. This response is legislative fiat, where the indigenous party has no formal role other than as an on-looker. One example is the attempt by the Western Australian State government to legislate away indigenous land rights in 1995.

An executive may not choose such a hostile tactic, and may instead choose to do nothing. Doing nothing is essentially a choice to neglect indigenous demands to deal constructively with their claims. However, the do nothing option may not be cost or risk free, particularly in cases where indigenous people have the ability to test the validity of their rights claims in court. In countries with institutionalized and independent judiciaries, an executive's choice to do nothing is essentially an invitation to bring on litigation and to allow delegation (to courts) through passive means.

The executive may also choose to create a consultative body. In the game of institutional supply, executives have the choice of providing institutions that address indigenous grievances while reserving the discretion to act on those grievances. Examples include the Canadian Indian Claims Commissioner (1969–1976) and New Zealand's Waitangi Tribunal (1975). While a third party may be given the responsibility of addressing the legitimacy of indigenous grievances and making recommendations for government action, the recommendations remain non-binding on the government. The government protects its discretion and control over the outcomes of the process while according minimal recognition of indigenous grievances. The formal role of indigenous peoples in this model is limited to one of consultation, where the final discretion over outcomes is out of their hands.

4. *Do not recognize / Delegate.* This is the litigation option. A government can find itself in court either by actively pursuing litigation or if an indigenous party starts legal proceedings. While an executive has privileged access to legal resources and expertise which makes it a dominant party in legal proceedings, it has no greater control over key aspects of the legal environment than any other legal disputant. The government is bound by the same rules, schedule, and procedures as other parties to a legal action. Litigation casts the predominant relationship between the government and the indigenous applicant as legal disputants, as a relationship like any other that can be held between a government and its citizens. Since indigenous peoples are accorded no different role or relationship vis-à-vis the executive than any other citizen or group, this option is in harmony with an ideological commitment to undifferentiated citizenship and the equality of rights under the law. In this regard, litigation is a non-recognition option. A key example of this strategy is the United States before 1946 and since 1976. Prior to 1946, Indian claimants seeking resolution of their historic land grievances needed to seek congressional leave allowing them to pursue their cases in court. After the close of the Indian Claims Commission in 1976, the United States has allowed Indian tribes to continue to use the courts without providing extra-judicial dispute resolution processes.

LAND CLAIM NEGOTIATIONS AND THEORIES OF INSTITUTIONAL EMERGENCE

This study seeks to explain the emergence of a particular kind of policy response: negotiation. I have established that inherently, this policy outcome involves policy-makers addressing two issues: whether to recognize indigenous collective rights and whether to seek political cover from potential blame for resolving indigenous peoples' property rights disputes. By framing the outcome of interest as a product of this simple decision tree, one can appreciate the central task of this study: to understand those factors that drove executive policy-makers to change their thinking at each decision node. The heuristic of the policy-maker's decision tree enforces a basic contention of this study. To understand the emergence of negotiation as an institutionalized policy response, the causal mechanisms must directly address whether and how policy-makers' norms about indigenous collective rights and delegation came to be challenged, and how this challenge produced a change in policy behavior. The study begins with the maxim that " . . . informal rules form the basis for the intentional development of formal institutions . . . as the context in which new formal institutions are established."[8]

By asking why governments choose to resolve indigenous land disputes through negotiation and not through other means, I address the larger literature in comparative politics regarding why some institutions emerge rather than others. In the short survey below, I have chosen theoretical insights which I find compelling, and underline my own contribution to the larger theoretical and methodological questions of explaining institutional emergence.

Punctuated Equilibria and Institutional Change: The Explanatory Limits of Judicial Shocks

The punctuated equilibrium model of institutional change supposes institutional stasis where actors within the state, economy, and society mutually adapt to the institutional incentive structure. They have little reason to challenge these institutions until some exogenous event shocks the system, and upsets the status quo. In this view of institutional change, new institutions arise to solve coordination problems. Actors adapt to a new equilibrium, and once again, adapt to the prevailing incentives. Those hoping for more change must await another exogenous shock. In the field of land claims politics, the closest thing to a punctuated equilibrium model of institutional change is what I call the judicial shock assumption. According to this assumption, governments instituted negotiation policies after high courts recognized the validity of indigenous land rights. Judicial change, in the form of high court decisions, is a key independent variable in explaining the emergence of land rights negotiation policies because the judicial shock spurred governments to accept a negotiation equilibrium.

As iconic evidence of the judicial shock hypothesis, scholars often point to the Canadian and New Zealand cases. Canada publicly announced its new land claims negotiation policy seven months after the Supreme Court's *Calder* decision (1973),[9] in which the court accepted the legal legitimacy of aboriginal property rights. The Canadian aboriginal policy literature draws a clear and strong causal line between the *Calder* decision and the Trudeau government's decision to implement a negotiation policy. The following citation is representative of the literature: " . . . As a result of the [*Calder*] decision, Trudeau redirected federal policy to allow the Nisga'a and other non-treaty groups to negotiate directly with the federal government."[10] Similarly, New Zealand announced its intention to negotiate Maori claims after the Court of Appeal's Lands Case of 1987.[11] Mason Durie writes that " . . . as ordered by the court, the New Zealand Maori Council and the Crown entered into negotiations."[12] The causal logic of the judicial shock thesis is that cabinets choose to recognize aboriginal collective rights and spurn a delegation strategy as a result of judicial activism. The assumption is that above all other variables in the political environment, executives are particularly responsive to direction from the judiciary. The theoretical implication for indigenous peoples wishing to force governments to a bargaining table is that they are best served by allocating their finite energies and resources to a judicial strategy. The assumption posits little complication on the road from judicial victory to negotiation outcome.

The difficulty with the judicial shock story as a causal explanation for the emergence of negotiation policies rests with its causal scope. A solid causal argument needs to meet three conditions. It needs to address timing (X must precede Y), correlation (changes in X must relate to changes in Y), and rival explanations (there is no other variable doing the work). It is not problematic to verify that high court decisions often precede significant policy change, but a wider cross-national survey of the empirical record renders it problematic to assume that negotiation policies (versus its policy competitors) are *destined* to emerge once the judicial dust settles. For instance, in 1941, the United States Supreme Court ruled that an indigenous land claim could be based on land rights not previously recognized through a treaty or other legislative means.[13] In 1946, Congress responded by establishing an arbitration mechanism, the Indian Claims Commission, whose decisions were appealed in the federal Court of Claims. Within the context of the Indian Claims Commission process, the United States refused to negotiate Indian claims and insisted that the Commission rule on every one of the nearly 500 claims that came before it. In the 1992 *Mabo* decision,[14] the Australian High Court recognized for the very first time that aboriginal land rights could exist in the common law, but the Commonwealth's subsequent policy response (the Native Title Act) provided a whole range of policy options: mediation, arbitration to a specialist tribunal, and negotiation. Interestingly, the Australian Commonwealth implemented a negotiation framework in the Northern Territory after a 1971 court decision[15] *refused* to recognize the legal validity of common law aboriginal land rights. There are also instances where policy-makers deliberated and instituted policy change *without* the benefit of a critical court decision. In 1975, the New Zealand government established the Waitangi Tribunal to hear Maori claims, and to make recommendations for claims resolution.

The empirical record suggests that the judicial shock thesis is an insufficient explanation for the emergence of government negotiation policies. Judicial change is a good predictor, but not the sole determinant, of policy change. A reasonable hypothesis explaining why judicial change is a predictor of policy change is that judicial uncertainty over indigenous land rights, by extension, uncertainty over a critical component of a nation's property rights regime, induces risk averse executives to act.[16] However, current thinking on courts and negotiation offers little guidance on the link between court action and subsequent policy outcomes. Little theoretical work asks what type of response a policy-maker would choose in the face of judicial uncertainty. Bargaining theory in labor economics supports the hypothesis that high levels of judicial uncertainty induce parties to reach negotiated decisions outside of court.[17] Unfortunately, for the present research agenda, this literature has not considered the design of extra-judicial decision-making arenas as a function of judicial uncertainty. In the absence of a clear judicial order that "the government shall negotiate," the link between judicial change and policy-makers' choice to negotiate is underspecified. Even if such a bold judicial pronouncement was forthcoming, one must ask why the executive would cast off its discretion over policy and move in lock step with the judicial branch. One must look to non-judicial explanations to understand why governments choose one policy option over others. A more satisfactory approach to understanding the emergence of negotiation policies lies in appreciating the interaction between judicial and non-judicial variables. Attention to the relative causal importance of judicial and non-judicial factors in explaining intra and cross-national policy change allows for a bridge between two literatures normally ignorant of each other: judicial and comparative politics.[18]

With Thelen, I argue that the judicial shock explanation is inherently limited since, like all punctuated equilibrium approaches to institutional change, it theoretically divorces institutional change from institutional stasis by treating institutional change as "extraordinary politics."[19] To do so is to undervalue analytically the degree to which groups continually contest institutional structures. By undervaluing the continuance of contestation, the punctuated equilibrium approach risks hiding from view less apocalyptic opportunities for change, or moments when actors did have a choice to make and perhaps did not, or chose differently. The exogenous shock approach to institutional change also risks undervaluing the degree to which the institutions that emerge are conditioned by those that came before.

Beyond the Judicial Shock Assumption: Alternative Explanations and Arguments

Political Mobilization: Getting Back to Collective Action

Thelen's response to punctuated equilibrium type arguments is to assert that scholars would be more ably served by paying closer empirical attention to the ideational and material bases on which institutions rest.[20] The scholar's task is then to tease out how changes in social structures, other institutions, and attitudes upset these bases in a plausible causal chain. This approach has the advantage of linking theories of institutional stasis with those of change, focusing our comparative gaze not just on one outcome of the dependent variable. It allows one to appreciate when change was possible, did not happen, or did not happen as expected. To link the empirical investigation of institutional change to institutional stasis heightens our awareness that so-called "critical junctures" for change are not only those usually visible forks in the road where institutional change was the outcome, but also those less visible forks where actors' mutual choices led down the path of the status quo.

An important set of explanations linking both the temporal pattern of institutional change and the types of institutions that emerge are rooted in the literature on interest groups and collective action. In policy areas characterized by strong ideological or normative frameworks, how are policy-makers' norms challenged? Do policy-makers abandon a policy principle when the cost of holding onto it rises beyond what they are prepared to pay? An agency based approach to policy-makers' normative change puts political contestation on the front burner. It is hard to imagine how policy-makers came to recognize indigenous rights, and agreed to bargain, without examining the capacity of indigenous peoples to put their land rights on the policy agenda in the first place.

Some hypotheses link the ability of a social or interest group to impact the policy agenda to the group's strength. One indicator of a group's agenda setting power is the size of a group's membership base. The idea is that policy-makers will pay attention to those groups that can deliver electoral support through a large membership base or through coalitions with other groups.[21] Large membership bases are also indicators of group power if a group can tap that base for financial resources, and deliver those resources to political decision-makers. However, the likelihood that indigenous communities can deliver electoral or financial gains to policy-makers is generally low, due to their small size, general geographic remoteness, and persistent economic marginalization. The simple link between the relative size of an indigenous population and its ability to force a government response to its claims is tenuous. In Australia, Canada and the United States, indigenous people represent less than 5% of the national population. In New Zealand, where it can be argued that minority politics is Maori politics, the government only instituted a direct negotiation policy in 1989, almost fifty years after the establishment of the American claims commission process. Given the demographic size of the indigenous populations in question, and their at-times significant reliance on the state to subsidize political organizations, interest group arguments relating political strength to population size are not compelling hypotheses explaining the comparative emergence of negotiation policies.

Instead, interest group or collective action type arguments need to link indigenous political mobilization with policy-makers' changing perceptions of a policy option's relative feasibility. In his theory of institutional emergence, Jack Knight makes this linkage by focusing on the central lesson of sub-game perfection in non-cooperative game theory.[22] Sub-game perfection is the formal term given for the common intuition that one's current choices are conditioned by expectations of what other players would do if they had the opportunity to make choices in the future. By implication, new behaviors or institutions emerge when one can change an opponent's expectation of one's future behavior. Perhaps ironically, a key way to demonstrate the capacity to credibly commit to a future strategy is to demonstrate one's current ability to change. This emphasis on players' ability to change expectations of future behavior grounds institutional emergence not on radical exogenous changes to the structure of the game (i.e. punctuated equilibrium theories), but on the capacities of players to change their own behavior. This is where institutional emergence and theories of collective action come together.

Knight's approach suggests that governments did not change their land claims policies until indigenous groups demonstrated their potential to commit to a future political strategy. The ability to commit to a future political strategy is not necessarily dependent on the size of a group's membership base. This means that a causal explanation in this study may rest on when indigenous political actors were able to act collectively and cohesively. A non-unitary actor's ability to maintain cohesiveness and to make reasoned judgments (conditioned on available information) about the probabilities of future scenarios is the hallmark characteristic of a *player* in the game-theoretic sense. Political mobilization concerns the ability of those organizations claiming to represent indigenous interests to unite, put forward an actionable agenda, and influence others. Paying attention to policy-makers' perceptions of indigenous groups' demonstrated capacity to commit to future strategies also has an important theoretical implication. It implies that in the politics of minority rights, the *most* important resource for minorities to mobilize in the struggle for policy change is their own collective energies; influencing others or winning the approbation of outside groups is important, yet secondary.

Game theory usually accepts players as given, but an empirical study of institutional emergence cannot. Along with judicial explanations of institutional change, this study evaluates the impact of indigenous group variables on policy-makers' acceptance of the negotiation option. The political mobilization of national and regional indigenous lobbies and the ability of indigenous communities to act as cohesive negotiating parties are collective action variables that compete with judicial variables to explain executive negotiation behavior.

The Main Argument:
The Sequencing of Judicial Change and Indigenous Political Mobilization

A critical task of this study is to parse out the relative weight of judicial versus other arguments in explaining executive negotiating behavior. The advent of catalytic court decisions recognizing indigenous property rights for the first time is most often identified as the primary causal force behind the advent of land claim negotiations. While this study explores the important role that courts play, it insists on explaining the emergence of negotiation policies in conjunction with the ability of indigenous groups to leverage potential and actual judicial change into political gain. The primary argument is that the emergence of negotiation policies is explained by the interaction between judicial change and indigenous political mobilization, not judicial change alone. Specifically, negotiation policies are most likely to emerge when indigenous communities are politically mobilized *prior* to the advent of crucial court decisions.

Before serious political mobilization and organized public protest by indigenous people in the mid-1960s, non-indigenous advocates firmly wedded to an assimilationist or integrationist agenda largely defined the aboriginal policy agenda. In many ways, policy-makers' political constituency in aboriginal policy reform were churches, farmers, miners, and others, but rarely indigenous people. While non-indigenous advocates for aboriginal policy reform were important supporters for the extension of equal citizenship rights to indigenous individuals, their support did not extend to the recognition of special indigenous rights.

The mid-1960s marked an important qualitative change in indigenous political history across all the countries considered in this study. During this decade, indigenous political organizations expanded their repertoires to include collective action through public protest. Land rights became the central symbol around which disparate indigenous groups and organizations could unite and find a common voice. The key effect of indigenous political mobilization, starting in the mid-1960s, was to make policy-makers aware for the first time that indigenous peoples could matter. Indigenous political mobilization began to make it clear to policy-makers that any aboriginal policy reform would require some measure of indigenous cooperation, which would come at the price of addressing indigenous land rights. Indigenous political mobilization both challenged the normative underpinnings of assimilationist policies and forced policy-makers to evaluate the political cost of continuing with a non-recognition strategy.

If indigenous political mobilization increases policy-makers' awareness that non-recognition could be costly, it also decreases the attractiveness of delegated policy solutions. The key mechanism linking political mobilization to the attractiveness of delegated solutions is policy-makers' changing evaluations of what would happen should the government win its case in court. In the advent of an adverse decision, a mobilized indigenous group could credibly threaten to impose costs on the government in the political sphere until the claim was settled to some level of satisfaction. In other words, in the presence of a mobilized group, winning in court would provide a government no political resolution. This finding turns the classic blame avoidance thesis on its head, which predicts that as issues become more politically controversial, policy-makers should prefer to delegate decision-making power.

A critical consequence is that when a government faces numerous outstanding claims, political mobilization lowers the long run benefit of engaging in a litigation or arbitration strategy. This effect holds even under conditions of judicial change, which may affect the probability that the government will win in court. However, the most important immediate repercussion of a court decision is whether it sparks further mobilization of indigenous protest.

The main reason why high court decisions were catalytic and ushered policy change is that they eliminated the executive's option to do nothing. In systems that privilege the rule of law, high court decisions cannot be ignored. Just as court decisions can further galvanize social forces, high court decisions galvanize the executive branch to provide a policy response. There are many reasons why policy responses languish within an administration's policy system, including the sheer size of government bureaucracies, and the many competing demands for cabinet attention. In parliamentary systems, one difficulty in achieving significant policy change stems from the doctrine of collective cabinet responsibility. This doctrine puts a premium on reaching a broad consensus at the cabinet table. In instances of deep polarization or normative disagreement across key cabinet members, the executive is more likely to do nothing than push through a policy position that some ministers could not publicly support. The cabinet debate, like the social debate, on indigenous land rights is often polarized, and archival evidence shows that the pressure of a high court decision provided allies (or detractors) of indigenous land rights the opportunity to reach an agreement across the table where otherwise, an agreement would be impossible.

High court decisions appear to predict a negotiation response because in Australia, Canada, and New Zealand, precedent-setting high court rulings on indigenous land rights occurred after indigenous peoples demonstrated their capacity to mobilize and act collectively in the public sphere. The sequencing of pan-tribal political mobilization (and increasing support across mainstream opinion for indigenous land rights) before judicial activism meant that governments were more likely to consider negotiation as a preferred policy than had the reverse scenario held true. The counterfactual is that the United States Supreme Court recognized indigenous land rights in the common law in 1823,[23] far before Native Americans were organized politically and could protect their judicial gains from Congress or the President. When Congress chose to arbitrate native land claims in 1946, it did so partly because Native Americans had no political leverage to impose any serious political costs, or to demand anything other than monetary compensation for their historic losses. The Indian Claims Commission only needed to determine if a claim had merit, and identify a financial award for compensation.

Political Norms and Underlying Preferences over Delegation

Even in the presence of judicial change and political mobilization, policymakers may be restrained from delegating political decisions to courts by internal norms over the appropriateness of judicial policy-making and review. In polities where governments hold judicial review as fundamentally undemocratic, the legitimacy of non-judicial dispute resolution mechanisms is that much higher, and a negotiation policy is more likely to emerge. The effect of this political norm is most evident in the United States and New Zealand. Although debates about the legitimacy of courts as policy-makers are not foreign to the American political psyche, they are far less vociferous than in New Zealand, where the doctrine of parliamentary supremacy holds fast. Thus this study shows that government-held norms regarding the role of courts in a robust democracy go some way in explaining reluctance or willingness to provide negotiation policies, thus linking cross-national variation in such norms to the emergence of particular policies.

Federalism: A Mediating Variable?

Judicial change and political mobilization variables can change relatively quickly, and can account for changes in the dependent variable within countries over time. The value of a cross-national comparison, however, is to evaluate whether largely stable institutional structures and given historical legacies can significantly shape the dance between social forces and key decision-makers. Comparative institutional scholars have often come to the conclusion that stable institutional configurations can account for policy divergence across countries. We should therefore look to institutions as important mediating variables.

Structural opportunities theorists in the social movement literature present the argument that political opportunity structures, such as institutional design, account for cross-national differences in policy outcomes. [25] As such, the ability of interest groups to influence governments to respond to their demands is at least partly a function of institutional variables that are beyond their control. The argument is compelling, but the political opportunity structure argument, if not carefully specified, risks being carried by an amalgam of institutional particularities of any given case, with few *a priori* hypotheses about which institutional variables interact to create an "opportunity structure." The following empirical questions must be resolved: Which domestic institutions shaped policy-makers' evaluations of the relative feasibility of their options? Did institutional legacies shape or truncate the set of feasible policy alternatives in a consistent way across time?

Federalism is one important and unavoidable institutional variable in a cross-national study of land claims negotiation policies. The theoretical literature disagrees on whether one should expect federalism to help or hinder the emergence of negotiation policies. In studies on federalism, a basic theoretical metaphor often used is the "container." Federalism is important because it creates a series of discrete institutional spaces where similar political battles are fought, but other elements are different enough to create more or less fertile environments for political change. This container argument is the root of the federalism as policy laboratory metaphor. It is argued that, by creating different sub-national units where politics over particular policy issues can play out, federalism increases the probability that groups can win gains in these smaller arenas. Thus, federalism may increase the likelihood

that negotiation policies emerge because it may be easier to achieve graduated change than to convince one central government to implement change
on a national scale. In federal states, sub-national governments may act as
policy innovators. Through reputation effects or learning mechanisms, these
policy innovations may spread across the federation.[26] It is assumed that
sub-national states can innovate in their own sphere of competence without
interference from, or even the necessary cooperation with, the national level
government. In the policy fields such as health insurance,[27] the metaphor
has been extensively used whereby sub-national states have the constitutional jurisdiction to innovate, and intergovernmental difficulties turn on
issues of cost-sharing and the role of the national government in enforcing a
set of common standards across all jurisdictions.

However, if one adopts a more strategic point of view, the hypothesis that the division of state power across a geographic space facilitates
the emergence of negotiation policies may be more difficult to sustain. The
division of state power across not only geography, but also policy areas,
can create policy environments where both the emergence and the disper-
sion of certain policies *require* inter-governmental cooperation. When the
resolution of a policy question crosses governments' autonomous spheres
of action, there is cause for governments to engage in strategic play when
deciding whether to implement negotiation policies. The emergence of
negotiation policies can be high-jacked by intergovernmental rivalry. One
hypothesis is that in federal systems where jurisdictional responsibilities
overlap, national governments will shy away from negotiation because
sub-national governments must be included at the bargaining table, making negotiation at least a tripartite affair. Sub-national governments may
impose political costs or withhold cooperation in other policy areas, should
a federal government unilaterally choose to negotiate with indigenous people, when negotiation will impact sub-national governments' capacities to
act within their jurisdictions.

The countries in this study offer great variation in the division of power
across governments. New Zealand is a unitary state, and acts as a control
for the others. In Canada, the federal government has jurisdiction over
"Indians and lands reserved for Indians." The provinces retain constitutional jurisdiction over land and resource management. As a result, any
resolution to indigenous land claims requires the assent and cooperation
of both levels of government. In Australia, the States had exclusive jurisdiction over both aboriginal affairs and land/resource management until
1967, when the Australian electorate amended the constitution to allow the
Commonwealth government the concurrent right to legislate in aboriginal
affairs. Consequently, the Australian states have a stronger role to play in

land claims politics than Canadian provinces. However, in both countries, the federal government can resolve indigenous land claims in their northern territories without the encumbrance of sub-national governments.

Interestingly, key innovators in land claims politics in Canada and Australia were not sub-national governments,[28] but national governments who first implemented negotiation strategies in the Northwest, the Yukon, and the Northern Territories. This leads to a contrary hypothesis: federal governments were able to respond because their federations included unitary "islands" where negotiation was simpler. In systems with relatively strong sub-national governments with respect to their political weight within federal institutions as well as the degree of financial independence from central government coffers, federal governments may have less leverage to coerce sub-national cooperation. Contrary to the first hypothesis, intergovernmental politics may serve only to stymie land claims negotiations. The theoretical view that federalism creates a positive political opportunity structure for political change may be limited when looking at a policy area where negotiated settlement solutions necessarily cross governments' jurisdictional boundaries, and where the ability to achieve negotiated outcomes depends inherently on getting the approval of both levels of government.

At times, federalism's impact on the policy process is weak, but it can also be substantial. On balance, federalism does play a mediating role in the emergence and diffusion of negotiation policies. There is little evidence that federalism supported the diffusion of these policies from the sub-national to the national level. The impact of federalism is most often to hinder the development and diffusion of policies which recognize and protect indigenous land rights. In this particular policy area, federalism fails to accommodate territorially-based minority rights, in contrast to successes elsewhere.[29] Federalism gives economic interests, particularly large players like forestry, mining, oil and agricultural producers, more leverage over sub-national governments' policy preferences, since sub-national governments are more dependent on and more sensitive to land-based resource economies. As a result, sub-national governments are likely to be less accommodating of indigenous interests than central governments. If sub-national governments choose to innovate in aboriginal policy, it is more likely that their innovations would eliminate, weaken, or circumvent the recognition of indigenous land rights rather than protect these rights. Sub-national governments are more likely to innovate tyrannically. The degree to which sub-national governments hold jurisdiction over public lands and resource development, paired with opposition to indigenous claims by economic actors, strongly decreases the likelihood that national negotiation policies will emerge.

In contrast, while a national government may adopt a pro-development position, it must respond to a larger constituency of interests. Ottawa, Wellington or Canberra needs to be mindful of its nation-wide constituency, which may include urban support for indigenous land rights. Central governments have generally been innovators in land claims politics, but the willingness of central governments to implement national negotiation policies is always conditioned on the potential cost of harming intergovernmental relations. National governments tread lightly in the face of intransigent sub-national governments. Sub-national opposition can both stall the expansion of negotiations across the country (the failure to pass national land rights legislation in the 1980s in Australia is largely due to intergovernmental politics), and make it more difficult to reach settlement agreements when sub-national governments do come to the bargaining table. A federal government has a real imperative to constrain its own policies in order to avoid future enforcement costs from combative States and provinces. Unitary governments simply do not face this additional constraint on their behavior.

IMPLICATIONS

By identifying the types of dispute resolution mechanisms supplied by governments in land claims politics, I address larger questions concerning institutional change and the status of minoritarian group rights in democratic polities. Social and policy actors evaluate policy alternatives within temporally embedded processes, illustrating that polities do not always consider the full range of policy alternatives before them. Instead, the range of policy alternatives considered at any critical juncture is historically constructed. Historical comparative policy studies have neglected to examine how advanced democratic governments evaluate their policy options under conditions of high uncertainty regarding the following issues: the political and legal legitimacy of rights that minority groups claim, how favorably courts may review policy alternatives should they be put into place, the outcomes of any given policy in the future, and how policy alternatives will mobilize minorities, majorities, and any number of special interests. Comparative policy studies have not cast a concerted eye on the mechanisms government actors have, or have not, put in place to evaluate the relative merits of policy alternatives in a context of ongoing judicial and political change.

This study brings together more mature literatures in comparative politics regarding institutional change and collective action, with a field of inquiry that comparative politics has at times neglected: law and courts.[30] Institutional change and supply cannot be understood without a nuanced eye to the relative causal weight of political, judicial, and institutional variables in forming policy-makers' evaluations of policy alternatives. If my work calls on comparative politics to be more attuned to the judicial, I call upon the study of indigenous politics to be more mindful of how policy outcomes are products of contexts where judicial and political processes interact.

By engaging in land claim negotiations, governments: 1) validate indigenous peoples as bearing collective property rights (the recognition dimension); 2) accept shared political responsibility for future policy outcomes (the delegation dimension). Negotiation is, therefore, a highly *political* method of resolving an underlying land grievance. At the core of a government's decision to negotiate is an ideological shift, recognizing indigenous groups as politically distinct and legitimate collective actors. By engaging in a negotiation, governments recognize that uncertainty over competing property rights can only be resolved through a larger process of political relationship building. The importance of a negotiations policy is not just to establish clearer rules regulating property disputes, but to establish mechanisms that will regulate the future the political and economic relationships between the state and indigenous groups within its borders. Thus, negotiation as a policy alternative is unique in its requirement that governments foresee a continuing political relationship with its indigenous populations as collective actors, not solely as individuals.

Chapter Three

Indigenous Land Rights and Cabinet Decision-Making in Canada (1945–1973)

INTRODUCTION

This study explores the conditions under which governments establish a negotiation policy with indigenous[1] peoples in order to address their grievances over land. What distinguishes a negotiations policy from a government's ad hoc approach to claim negotiation? An ad hoc approach indicates that a government is addressing a grievance of a particular group; it does not signal a government's commitment to address other grievances of indigenous people at any other time. A negotiation policy is important because the government consciously and explicitly commits itself to a future long-run strategy over a number of claims and across a number of groups. A negotiation policy sends the message that a government is willing to engage in a long-range process which symbolically accepts the legitimacy of indigenous collective property rights and the ability of indigenous people to act as politically self-determining actors.

This chapter provides a historical account of how the Canadian federal government came to adopt a land claim negotiation policy. I concentrate here on setting out the significant moments in time when the Canadian federal government was pressured to redefine its policy goals and reconsider their implementation. By focusing on these critical points in time, I ask why did the Canadian federal government not choose a negotiation policy in 1951, 1964, or 1969, but did finally in 1973? By providing a detailed, sequential account of each opportunity, I show what prevented governments from choosing a negotiation response sooner. I am also able to trace the process whereby key decision-makers perceived changes in their political environments, and determine how these changes impacted their ideological development and subsequent policy decisions. This approach allows me to demonstrate that the sequencing of events, particularly the sequencing of political mobilization and legal change, affected policy-makers' evaluations of the feasible set of policy alternatives at each choice opportunity, and therefore, the relative value of negotiation.

The nerve centre of executive decision-making in Canada's parliamentary system is the cabinet. Governments make the policy decisions in cabinet committees and in full cabinet which collectively bind each minister of the Crown. By combining archival and interview data with secondary sources, I present the key issues which affected cabinet opinion. I am able to identify the proponents, and sometimes the opponents, to the negotiation of indigenous land claims. I am also able to document and analyze the dynamics of internal consensus-building which underpin the doctrine of collective cabinet responsibility.

This chapter examines the internal and external cabinet pressures that lead to policy change. Among the external factors, the political mobilization of indigenous peoples is more important than judicial change in explaining the types of land claims policies implemented by cabinet. The political mobilization of indigenous people prior to the advent of judicial recognition of indigenous property rights makes negotiation much more likely. Two aspects of political mobilization are particularly important. The first is the demonstrated ability of pan-tribal indigenous organizations to act collectively and bring together a coalition of indigenous actors around a particular principle or policy option. The second is the politics of public protest that signals the ability of disparate indigenous groups to oppose government policies, as well as their potential to mobilize wider public opinion. Political mobilization warns policy-makers that the issue of indigenous land rights widens the potential zone of social conflict, and consequently, that the government is dealing with an issue of political, not strictly legal, ramifications. The politicization of indigenous land rights decreases the feasibility of policy mechanisms that delegate decision-making power to courts or arbitrators. The political resurgence of indigenous people diminishes the usefulness to governments of pursuing further litigation, chiefly since governments can no longer assume that indigenous groups will quietly accept a court's adverse decision.

This study challenges the hypothesis that governments prefer to delegate decision-making power to courts precisely when issues become "too hot to handle." The blame avoidance hypothesis attributes policy inaction to a government's calculation that having courts render judgments in difficult cases would allow it to credibly deflect blame or punishment when implementing contentious policies. Governments faced with potentially unpopular policy decisions prefer to point a finger and say "the courts made us do it." While this argument is intuitively compelling, it is not an accurate portrayal of the thinking around cabinet tables, at least as recorded in archival and other materials.

What is interesting is the degree to which cabinets are unwilling to delegate meaningful decision-making capacity in the face of politically mobilized groups. This is true of the Canadian, New Zealand and Australian cases, as demonstrated in subsequent chapters. Governments are more likely to do nothing, to appoint non-binding commissioners, or to negotiate rather than delegate to courts or arbitrators in the presence of political mobilization. If these parliamentary governments do not easily forfeit the power to govern, then why are important judicial decisions such important precursors for policy change? The answer lies not in a government's incentives to escape blame, but in the difficulty of achieving consensus around the cabinet table without the additional pressure of a high court decision.

The doctrine of cabinet responsibility has the general effect that in the presence of divided and forceful cabinet opinion, governments are more likely to do nothing than forge ahead with significant policy change. Even forceful Prime Ministers hesitate to push through policy measures when senior cabinet members express strong reservations. As Trudeau remarked, " . . . a prime minister is always dependent on having a cohesive cabinet and caucus. If too many of his colleagues resign, he will cease to be prime minister."[2] In the context of a court decision, proponents to a policy option within cabinet require a lower standard of comfort around the table to obtain the formal buy-in of previously leery cabinet members. Court decisions decrease the size of the minimal winning coalition needed to make any particular decision.

But what type of decision? The critical court judgments on indigenous rights generally do not tell governments what institutional mechanisms to establish. The Canadian, New Zealand, and Australian cases show that the cabinet coalition in favor of a negotiation policy is built over time, and does not magically appear once a court makes a critical ruling. While catalytic court decisions legitimated indigenous property rights (with the exception of the Australian judicial ruling in 1971), this judicial legitimation did not effect a wholesale and immediate transformation of cabinet members' views. The process which allowed cabinets to recognize indigenous land rights and negotiate with indigenous peoples was incremental. In Canada, New Zealand and Australia, the political mobilization of indigenous peoples forced cabinets to re-evaluate longstanding normative goals of assimilation and formal equality. Governments were forced to balance the normative assimilationist goals of their indigenous policies with the achievement of other policy goals. At times, a strict application of the principles of formal equality and the non-recognition of indigenous rights lost out. Previous policy decisions compromised the normative principles of formal equality, and recognized indigenous collective rights. These compromises established a series of precedents that, bit by bit, brought cabinet members to legitimate and finally negotiate land claims.

This chapter also concludes that advisory commissions, usually established to investigate the merit of indigenous claims, played important and unintended roles in the development of a wider public dialogue on the legitimacy of indigenous rights. Advisory commissions in Canada and New Zealand became strong advocates of the resolution of land grievances outside the courts. The commissions became important external and independent voices calling for the political resolution of land claims on the basis of good-faith negotiations and honoring the principle of partnership between the Crown and indigenous peoples. By building positive reputations with indigenous peoples and establishing their independence from governments, these commissions restructured the political environment in favor of negotiation policies. They also provided indigenous groups with important opportunities to build linkages with the executive branch outside of traditional indigenous affairs bureaucracies. These linkages provided additional support for a negotiation response within the administrative state.

Indigenous Land Rights: By Aboriginal Title or by Government Act

In order to understand the politics of indigenous land claims, it is necessary to recognize a key distinction in the legal status of indigenous property rights. Indigenous land claims are part of a larger political project for self-determination, but claims are usually made with regard to specific legal rights. Present day land rights may stem from the legal doctrine of aboriginal title, or from a government act, such as treaties or legislation. The doctrine of aboriginal title holds that indigenous peoples' land rights are grounded in their possession and occupancy of land prior to the era of colonial expansion. Thus, aboriginal title rights stem from indigenous peoples' own systems of customary law, and are not created by the new colonial sovereigns. In title claims, indigenous people argue that their right to commercially harvest timber, extract minerals in a mining venture, or to pass unimpeded through a farmer's field for ceremonial purposes, arise because aboriginal title was never lawfully extinguished. In the politics of recognition, title claims are important because they assert a property right which is derived from different sources of law and continue to exist independent of government approbation.

The second type of land claim relates to a property right created through government action, either by statute, executive order, or treaty.

The validity of these property rights derives from the democratic and sovereign power of a government. In this respect indigenous land rights are the same as any other property right held by a non-indigenous person. Such a land claim may assert that governments have not fulfilled the obligations to which they previously agreed or that they have acted illegally and deprived indigenous peoples of the full enjoyment of such rights. In the politics of recognition, treaty claims are less contentious for governments than title claims, since their legitimacy rests on the operation of one system of law.

Whether aboriginal people can make treaty claims or title claims (or both) defines the language of land claims politics in each country. In Canada, indigenous people in different areas of the country make both treaty and title claims. The case study will show how the Canadian government reacted to both types of claims. In New Zealand, land claims are almost exclusively treaty claims; in Australia, land claims are title claims. Since the Canadian and Australian cases involve title claims, governments in these two federal systems struggled, much more than in New Zealand, with the question of whether aboriginal rights should be recognized. Once the question of recognition was addressed, the secondary question of how to recognize these rights, through negotiation or some other means, became important.

SETTING THE SCENE

Indian Policy in Canada Before 1945

British imperial policy recognized that the New World's original inhabitants had rights to land. Thus, Britain adopted the policy that its colonial representatives would enter into treaty agreements to cede or extinguish aboriginal rights in return for some combination of reserved lands, goods, and a right to continue to hunt and fish on unoccupied Crown land. The constitution of 1867 assigned the federal government jurisdiction over "Indians and lands reserved for Indians," and representatives of the federal Crown engaged in a process of signing land cession agreements with Canada's indigenous peoples from the late 1800s until 1921. Important for modern land claims politics, these land cession agreements did not cover all of what would become Canada. Indigenous peoples in large parts of the northern territories, northern Québec, the Maritimes, and British Columbia did not sign treaties which, according to the goverment, extinguished aboriginal title.[3]

Nonetheless, the federal government transferred ownership of Crown lands and the jurisdiction over their development to the provinces, and Indian communities were segregated onto insufficient and scattered reserved lands.[4] One scholar writes that " . . . today . . . all Canadian Indian reserves combined constitute less than one half of the Navajo reservation in Arizona alone."[5] Reserve size was allotted according to a formula, varying from 120 to 640 acres per family, dependent on land quality for agricultural purposes. Reserves were also allocated based on band sizes at the time of allocation, not projecting to a time when native populations would reverse their decline.[6] In British Columbia, reserve allotments were particularly small. The federal and provincial governments preferred small scattered reserves rather than the concentration of native peoples on larger allocations, since small reserves, it was thought, would speed up the assimilation process and negate the future need for reserves in any case.[7] The key mechanism that defined federal policy over Indian communities and Indian reserved lands was the Indian Act, a federal statute first enacted in 1876. The regulation of Indian reserved lands and of almost every aspect of Indian community life was achieved through the Indian Act.

The legal status of indigenous land rights in Canada was affected by court opinion on the existence of aboriginal title within the common law, and the enforceability of land rights guaranteed under the treaties. These questions were addressed in an early court case. In 1888, Britain's Judicial Committee of the Privy Council[8] ruled in the *St. Catherine's Milling* case[9] that aboriginal title was not a legal right, and that indigenous rights to land were restricted to use and occupancy rights reserved to them in treaty: "The Crown has all along had a present proprietary estate in the land, upon which the Indian title is a mere burden."[10] This decision established both the bedrock legal precedent and the political *modus vivendi* on indigenous land rights in Canada for almost a century: that indigenous rights to land existed only at the government's convenience, and the government could unilaterally change or extinguish these rights through executive or legislative action. Indigenous land rights were subject to the political whims of the day, although whatever rights the government did create under the treaties were enforceable in Canadian courts.

After 1921, indigenous peoples who did not sign treaties had two options: test the judiciary and see whether it would change its mind on the aboriginal title issue; or pressure the federal government to recognize aboriginal title, and prevail on provincial governments to respect these rights in provincial settlement and natural resource policies. Early demands by Indian bands in British Columbia for the government to recognize and address their title claims joined the voices of treaty bands across the country for the government to establish sufficient reserve lands for a reasonable land base. By the mid 1920s, attempts to organize indigenous voices on a regional basis to assert land rights had attracted the attention of Parliament.

The reaction of Parliament in 1927 to Indian land claims was basically to shut down indigenous organizations before they really got off the ground. The government rejected the merit of title claims out of hand, and then made it impossible for nascent Indian organizations or any organizations willing to act on Indians' behalf, to pursue their grievances in the courts. The federal government did so by amending the Indian Act and making it illegal to raise money to pursue a land claim against the Crown.[11] Reconciling land grievances, expanding reserve land bases, and recognizing the special rights of Indian communities did not fit within a global policy goal of assimilation.

The overriding goal of Canada's Indian policy also had great implications for the inclusion of indigenous people within the citizenship regime. Assimilation's great hope was for Indians to turn away from their traditional ways, and through the civilizing influences of agriculture and a religious education, become prepared for the rights and responsibilities of full citizenship. This teleological view of citizenship established a basic tradeoff. For status Indians, the acquisition of equal citizenship rights, such as the federal franchise, came at a price: the relinquishment of rights guaranteed under the Indian Act. Of particular importance to the Canadian government was the right not to be taxed on income earned on reserves. In the Canadian imagination of the time, equal citizenship was undifferentiated citizenship where special Indian rights and Canadian citizenship rights could not co-exist. The dichotomy has had an important impact on Indian identity politics that echoes still today. To become Canadian and to escape many of the punitive measures of the Indian Act meant to turn away from Indian-ness. Some Indian groups had no use for Canadian citizenship, holding instead to a separate and supra-national Indian citizenship; others believed the Indian Act and segregation under the reserve system held more dangers than benefits. Most sought an accommodation between the two views, seeking an equality which could accommodate difference.

The process of shedding Indian status in exchange for the full rights and responsibilities of citizenship was called enfranchisement. To speak of enfranchisement, therefore, has a particular meaning in the Canadian context, and is not simply reducible to gaining the right to vote. By the early 1900s, few status Indians availed themselves of the enfranchisement opportunity, and Canadian policy-makers sought ways to rectify the slow pace of change. In 1920, the Indian Branch pushed for compulsory enfranchisement, so that both individuals and bands that the Branch determined were "ready" for citizenship would be forced to bear their citizenship responsibilities.[12] Although the Branch reportedly never enforced the compulsory enfranchisement provision,[13] its existence was a clear indication of the state's coerciveness in Indian administration. It was not until the end of the Second World War that Canadian policy-makers would confront the idea that voting rights and Indian rights were not necessarily inimical to each other.[14]

In sum, the federal government defined policy progress by the Indians' total assimilation into the dominant society, having shed their cultural ties and linkages to their communities. This global policy goal had no room for recognizing or promoting indigenous collective rights. As the senior public servant of the federal Indian Affairs Branch stated in 1920, " . . . Our object is to continue until there is not a single Indian in Canada that has not been absorbed into the body politic, and there is no Indian question, and no Indian Department."[15] Manifestly, by the outbreak of the Second World War, the Canadian federal government had fully committed itself to an assimilationist policy for Indian people. Any land rights enjoyed by its indigenous populations were minimal and subject to unilateral extinguishment. Indigenous groups and their supporters were also effectively barred from the courts.

THE SECOND WORLD WAR

The Second World War and its aftermath served as a catalyst for the re-examination of Canadian federal Indian policy for a number of critical reasons which do not primarily include land claims. First, by the end of the war, the demographic trend of population decline on Indian reserves had reversed, as the rate of natural increase of the registered Indian population had been climbing since 1936.[16] The immediate issue of concern for the administrators of federal government Indian policy was the prospect of increasing education costs for an increasingly young population which, according to the federal budget, was supposed to disappear. This population growth accentuated the economic and social conditions on reserves already exacerbated by the Depression. The economic marginalization of Indian communities eventually drew the attention of social reformers, already mobilizing to push forth the creation of a modern welfare state. The economic conditions of Indian reserve populations and the extension of pension benefits to Indian war veterans were enough to ensure the interest of new welfare state reformers to the dossier of Indian policy.

The 1930s and early 1940s saw the emergence and consolidation of regional-level Indian associations to address the impact of life on Indian reserves and the overarching issue of aboriginal rights. The Indian Association of Alberta, the Native Brotherhood of British Columbia and the Federation of Saskatchewan Indians were formed during this period. Regional and local networks and organizations were the strongest basis for Indian political action, but the war years also brought with them opportunities for Indian leaders to meet on a national scale. Local and regional Indian leaders congregated in Ottawa in 1943 and 1944 to meet with government officials to discuss a panoply of issues. While discussions with government officials may not have been fruitful, these meetings were important networking opportunities that led some Indian leaders to call for a national political organization and voice. In 1945, Andrew Paull, the engine behind the Native Brotherhood of British Columbia, became President of the North American Indian Brotherhood (NAIB). The NAIB was Andrew Paull's attempt to knit together a national political agenda for Indian communities, though observers and his contemporaries pointed out that in its early years, the NAIB was in practice reducible to a support system for Andrew Paull himself.[17] While the effectiveness of a national Indian organization remained limited for years due to the lack of adequate resources, its foundation marked an important step in the organization of an Indian political voice in Canada.

The social change brought on by the war, the establishment and advocacy of fledgling native rights groups and associations across the country, and internal government concerns about the fiscal implications of Indian policies culminated with the creation, in 1946, of a special joint committee of the House of Commons and Senate. This joint committee was to conduct a review of the federal government's Indian policies. The joint committee held hearings on all aspects of Indian policy until 1948, and it provided Indian leaders with the opportunity to directly present their views and policy agendas to Parliament and a larger public audience than they ever had before. In contrast to parliamentarians' and other witnesses' approval of the fundamental goals of assimilation, Andrew Paull stressed the need for Parliament to investigate and address both treaty-based and title-based grievances. The NAIB supported the creation of a special third-party arbitrator in the form of an independent claims commission which would have the power to investigate treaty violations and settle them. In 1948, the joint committee recommended that the government establish such a commission to examine treaty-based grievances, but sidestepped the issue of aboriginal title claims.

INDIAN POLICY OPPORTUNITIES AFTER WORLD WAR TWO

The St. Laurent Cabinet Reviews the Indian Act, 1948–1951

With the conclusion of the policy review by Parliament, cabinet was faced with the choice of how to respond. The Indian Affairs Branch prepared a memorandum to cabinet in the fall of 1948 to establish the principles for a revised Indian Act. The exercise indicated that the fundamental assimilationist goals of federal policy had not changed, but that the legislation was to give Indians more control over reserve administration so that "they may become more self-sustaining."[18] The proposed revisions to the Indian Act were mostly concerned with other issues in Indian policy (e.g. the legal definition of Indian status, conditions of enfranchisement, and educational provisions). The sole mention of the underlying issues of land grievances was to continue the 1927 prohibition on financially supporting a claim.[19] There was zero support within the Indian Affairs Branch for a treaty claims commission or for any measure supporting a land claims agenda. There is no recorded evidence that other ministers were interested in bringing the land claims issue directly to cabinet.

In any case, this deflection of the core issues in Indian communities' policy agendas was not the issue that served in 1948 to derail further cabinet consideration of Indian policy reform. The proposed secularization of Indian education made an opponent of the then powerful Catholic Church, particularly so in Québec. By the 1940s, the Catholic Church administered the core social service functions of the modern state: education, hospital care, and care for the indigent.[20] The secularization of Indian education provisions was a small part of a larger battle the Church would begin to face in the 1940s: the expansion of the welfare state and the diminution of the Church's role in the public sphere. It was a battle the Church took seriously. In 1942, Church-based hospitals formed an association to fight the initial proposals for a state-run health care insurance program;[21] and one scholar of Québec Catholicism places the 1944 defeat of Québec's Liberal government at the Church's feet.[22] The Catholic Church's willingness to mobilize against the secularization of Indian education provisions must be seen within this wider context of growing institutional threat. In December 1948, cabinet decided the politically safer course of action was to delay the revision of the Indian Act until after the 1949 federal election.[23]

The Liberal government won that election, but did not reconsider Indian policy reform until the spring of 1950. Prime Minister St. Laurent moved Indian Affairs into the portfolio of the Minister of Citizenship and Immigration, clearly signaling the ideological framework that would govern Indian policy for the foreseeable future. In May 1950, the new Minister of Citizenship and Immigration, Walter Harris, reacquainted cabinet with the recommendations of the special joint committee, including the establishment of an Indian claims commission. The Minister noted that the claims commission proposal "[was] not being initiated by the Department,"[24] therefore indicating that the measure enjoyed neither bureaucratic nor his own personal support. With no advocate for land claims at the table, cabinet concluded that "no Indian claims commission [was] to be established at this time."[25] Harris introduced the revised Indian Act, largely unchanged from the draft prepared two years earlier, into Parliament in June. In his speech in the House of Commons, Harris confirmed that " . . . the underlying purpose of Indian administration has been to prepare the Indians for citizenship with the same rights and responsibilities as enjoyed and accepted by other members of the community."[26]

The Indian Act revisions did not meet with unquestioned approval. The legislation came under fire from civil libertarians for not going far enough in pursuing an equal citizenship agenda, as the government still refused to extend the federal vote to those Indians unwilling to waive their tax exemption status. Leslie reports that key cabinet ministers feared an unrestricted franchise would deliver Indian votes to the socialist and left-of-centre party, the Cooperative Commonwealth Federation.[27] As expected, the Catholic Church opposed the education provisions, and the Indian organizations condemned much of the legislation, especially its unwillingness to embrace their special rights and address their land grievances. The opposition of Indian groups was manageable, but the opposition of the Catholic Church was a whole other issue. This sparked the Minister to delay the issue again by ordering another internal review of the legislative revisions before proceeding through Parliament.

In December of 1950, the internal review sparked a minor change of heart with the Minister, and he recommended to cabinet that the 1927 provision restricting the solicitation of contributions to fight land claims in the courts be deleted. The memorandum to cabinet specifies his reasoning:

> There has been widespread criticism of this section. It may be mentioned that this provision was first introduced into the Indian Act in

1927 and, according to Departmental records, no conviction has been obtained under the present Section. The retention of this provision is not considered warranted as it is ineffectual in practice and also considered by the Indians and others as being an unnecessary interference in personal liberty. It is therefore recommended that it be deleted.[28]

In conjunction with this recommendation, the Minister once again brought before cabinet the longstanding Indian demand for a claims commission and for recognition of their aboriginal title claims. The Minister did not see fit to make a recommendation on this issue at that time, only indicating to his cabinet colleagues that they had the option of creating a commission under the new legislation or by executive act. He did, however, echo his recommendation of allowing Indians unfettered access to the courts:

> An alternative method of dealing with Indian claims is to have them brought before courts of competent jurisdiction . . . It is claimed by the Indians, however, that it would be possible for a commission to go into questions which would not be in the jurisdiction of a court.[29]

Cabinet deliberated on the issue in January of 1951. At that point, Walter Harris was ready to make his preference against a commission known, indicating to his colleagues that " . . . it was undesirable to have a commission, and it was recommended that any cases be dealt with on an *ad hoc* basis."[30] Cabinet agreed.

The Minister's preference for litigation over an arbitration strategy is totally in keeping with the civil libertarian approach to Indian land grievances. A special third party arbitrator would legitimate the Indians' special rights agenda, while allowing Indians unrestricted access to the regular court system would reinforce their equality vis-à-vis non-indigenous Canadians. Indeed, in consultation with Indian groups on the Indian Act revisions, Harris indicated that "practical use of the legal system would advance the process of Indian integration into mainstream society."[31] In June 1951, the legislation passed the House of Commons without a claims commission, but it did allow indigenous groups to pursue a litigation strategy if they were able.

The Indian Act reform process represents the first post-World War Two opportunity for the Canadian federal government to respond to Indian land grievances. Cabinet only considered three policy options during this time: do nothing, allow special third-party arbitration, or allow for litigation. Negotiation was not part of the feasible set of alternatives, an omission which is explicable given the federal government's ideological commitment to assimilation and its causal belief that encouraging land rights would delay the assimilation process. There was no support within the federal bureaucracy for a claims commission either at this point, and therefore little likelihood that administrative actors would seek to persuade the lead minister to that course of action. There was also little reason for other cabinet ministers to develop an interest in Indian land claims, since Indian organizational capacities were still minimal, political mobilization was nascent, and nonindigenous support for Indian policy reform did not extend to the Indian special rights agenda. Cabinet opened up the road for land rights litigation precisely because they felt that it would amount to an exercise in civic education. Moreover, Cabinet could be reasonably assured at the time, that in the climate of low political mobilization and judicial restraint, Indian wins in the courts could be easily reversed at the cabinet table.

Adjudication or Consultation? 1961–66

Examination of Indian policy goals languished during the final days of the St. Laurent government. Prospects for change improved in 1957, when the Conservative Party was swept into power under the leadership of John Diefenbaker. A conservative populist from northern Saskatchewan, Diefenbaker made his political reputation in the Opposition trenches as a staunch supporter of individual liberties.[32] He sought also the elimination of "second-class citizenship," to which he had often felt relegated due to his German surname.[33] An avowed civil libertarian and a promoter of equal Canadian citizenship for Canadians of diverse backgrounds, Diefenbaker's approach to Indian policy would be heavily conditioned by these two passions. As a biographer writes, " . . . he saw a place for Native Canadians as individuals within the nation. They were among the neglected and excluded with whom Diefenbaker identified himself."[34] Diefenbaker objected to the arbitrary powers of the Minister included in the Indian Act, bridled against the paternalism of Indian Affairs administration, and supported extending the right to vote to status Indians residing on reserve. The unrestricted extension of the franchise to status Indians was fundamentally intertwined with Diefenbaker's passionate espousal of Canada's first Bill of Rights. It was during the Bill of Right's passage through the House of Commons in 1960 that Diefenbaker extended status Indians the unconditional right to vote.

Diefenbaker's enthusiasm for the indigenous individual's civil rights was real, but neither he nor his cabinet ministers were comfortable with the collectivist nature of Indian land rights agendas. All felt that focusing on a special rights agenda would distract Indians from the important task of social and economic advancement, hence "retard[ing] the process of integration."[35] His was a less coercive assimilationist agenda, but an assimilationist agenda nonetheless. However, Diefenbaker did advance the Indian policy file when he appointed the first Indian member of the Senate, James Gladstone, in 1958, and nominated him co-chair of a parliamentary joint committee to study, once again, Indian policy.

The joint committee met for two years, and served as a vehicle for churches, provinces, Indian rights organizations and non-native civil libertarians to make their positions known to Parliament and to the government. In terms of land rights, three issues are noteworthy. Firstly, non-native advocacy organizations and provinces came to support the idea that title to Indian reserves be vested in Indian individuals and held in trust by the federal government, rather than being owned directly by the Crown. This was seen as a way of encouraging Indian self-administration (not self-determination) and decreasing the arbitrary power of the Minister over reserve life. This shows the beginnings of a changing causal thought process among Indian policy watchers that links Indian control over land to furthering social advancement, rather than impeding it. This and the cautious acceptance by non-natives that Indian integration need not be achieved through Indian deculturation showed an acceptance not of native rights *per se,* but of the growing salience of cultural pluralism in the national post-war dialogue on Canadian citizenship.[36] The second development was the warning by the Nisga'a tribe of northwestern British Columbia, that if the federal government would not negotiate their aboriginal title claims, they would seek redress of their grievances in court. The third development was the surprising endorsement by the committee of a land claims commission to inquire into the British Columbia and Oka land questions.[37]

The Indian Affairs Branch's response to the joint committee recommendation was left to the Branch's director. In a reversal of the 1951 experience, there was support within the branch for the claims commission recommendation. The Director argued that the distrust and bad feeling of Indians toward the Branch was due in part to the failure of previous governments to address their land grievances. This distrust was getting in the Branch's way and making it difficult to administer social welfare policies. The director wrote: " . . . Such a barrier might be removed if we were in a position to say that we no longer had anything to do with such claims, that the Indians should take them to the Claims Commission, a body separate and distinct from the Branch."[38]

The support of the bureaucracy for the creation of an independent arbitrator was based on a self-interested analysis about what made its job easier, rather than a principled acceptance of the validity of Indian land rights. The independence of such an institution would allow the bureaucracy to smooth the policy environment by deflecting a key criticism of its target group. This need for independence overrode the finance department's concerns that the commission could make monetary awards outside of the government's expenditure management process.[39] With the support of a reformist Prime Minister, the Minister of Citizenship and Immigration and the Minister of Justice prepared a memorandum to cabinet, setting out the broad characteristics of an arbitration body, and sought approval from cabinet to draft the proposed legislation in February of 1962.

On the table was the proposal to create a three person commission to inquire into both title and treaty claims, as well as "other claims that might have no foundation in law . . . but which might merit consideration on grounds of honourable dealings and fairness and good conscience."[40] The proposed commission would make advisory judgments on monetary compensation for valid claims. There is no evidence that cabinet or government officials entertained the return of lands or any other forms of redress as part of a larger relationship building exercise. From February through March 1962, cabinet held four discussions on the creation of the commission. Three issues dominated the discussions. The first related to the mandate of a commission to hear Métis land claims. Cabinet directed the Ministers responsible to limit the scope of the commission to those native persons clearly within federal jurisdiction.[41] The second was the need for the government to have some control over the outcomes, or decisions, of a commission inquiry. Cabinet debated on whether or not the commission should be an arbitrator, since " . . . while it was difficult to resist any proposal put forward in the name of equity and justice, control of the inquiry would be important."[42] It is unclear from the record if cabinet was more concerned with maintaining fiscal control over the initiative, or if there were more principled concerns about reconciling the delegation of decision-making authority with notions of parliamentary supremacy. In the end, cabinet voted to give the commission only the power to make recommendations regarding the size of a cash settlement.

The third issue that drew cabinet interest was the timing of making a decision on the issue. The Diefenbaker government was facing an election call in 1962, and there was concern about whether raising interest in Indian land claims would be advantageous or not for the government in the upcoming campaign. While cabinet seemed committed to establishing a commission of some sort, it was not clear whether it would be better to make this position known prior to the campaign, when the government was far from being assured of victory. Voices around the table felt that " . . . on the contrary, many non-Indians felt that the government should give greater consideration to Indian claims and would approve the setting up of a Commission."[43] As the month of March ended, cabinet concluded that it would be to their advantage to make an announcement prior to the election call, indicating that the government, if it would win, would introduce legislation for a commission in the new session of Parliament.[44]

The Diefenbaker government was re-elected in June, but formed a hobbled minority government. The claims commission proposal came before cabinet in October, where the Minister of Justice and the Minister of Citizenship and Immigration both recommended the advisory option, with the Minister of Justice citing his reason why: "The Commission would not proceed on the basis of the ordinary rules of law but would be concerned with 'fair and honourable dealing' in considering the claims. Adjudication would have to be subject to appeal, presumably to the Supreme Court, and the issues themselves were not really legal."[45] Any voices to the contrary were silenced when the Prime Minister joined the discussion[46], and cabinet approved legislation for an advisory claims body.

The legislation, however, never passed through Parliament. It fell victim to the paroxysms of the Cuban Missile era, when the Diefenbaker government first lost its Minister of Defence over the government's nuclear weapons policy, and then lost two non-confidence motions in the House of Commons. Diefenbaker was forced to dissolve Parliament, and call another election. Canadians continued the era of government instability by electing a Liberal minority government under Prime Minister Lester Pearson in April of 1963.

Pearson's personal preoccupations were dominated by foreign policy and the more pressing domestic issues of the day. These were the establishment of the national pension scheme and managing federal-provincial relations with a Québec provincial government increasingly assertive of its powers and status within the Canadian federation. As a result, Indian policy did not garner the sustained attention of the Prime Minister. The portfolio also suffered from a lack of Ministerial attention, as the Prime Minister assigned the portfolio to five different Ministers in five years. This meant that the only stable element in the administration of Indian policy was the Indian Affairs Branch. Senior officials in the Branch recognized that government inaction on the land claims file was interfering, in their view, with the achievement of social welfare goals. In May, the Branch began to prepare a memorandum seeking the new cabinet's approval of claims commission legislation, this time squarely recommending adjudication, with the creation of a special court of Indian Claims to hear appeals of the Commission's monetary decisions. The Branch's interest in the Commission was self-serving:

The conviction in the mind of any Indian group that justice is being denied makes it extremely difficult to obtain the necessary co-operation between them and government that is so necessary in every field of endeavour that may be undertaken to improve their lot . . . If a claim is good, then it should be settled. Equally important, if a claim is bad, the Indians should know about it so they can put it aside.[47]

By December 1963, the Minister of Citizenship and Immigration presented the Branch's claims commission initiative to cabinet. The policy memorandum made the first mention of negotiation to cabinet in the context of institutional choices for resolving land claims, but only to dismiss it out of hand, and to assure cabinet that a claims commission would have no authority to enter into any negotiations. It states: " . . . It may be noted that the Commission has no jurisdiction to entertain claims directed towards amending or re-negotiating treaties. It is considered that these are contractual obligations which both the Crown and the Indians must honour."[48]

The memorandum does not set out the advisory option, nor does it provide the cabinet with any other policy alternatives. The memorandum also made it clear that the government knew very little about the fiscal risk to which the land claims file would expose the government. It remarked that, "indeed, this is a field without precedent in Canadian experience," but offered a very preliminary costing of at least $16,900,000. Cabinet approved the bill, but did so with the intention of only introducing it to the House for first reading, not intending to see it through the legislative process to the end. In effect, the government introduced the claims commission legislation as a trial balloon, allowing Indian bands and others to comment upon it and make their feelings known. Indian reactions were largely negative, given the proposed commission would not hear aboriginal title claims,[49] and given the proviso that Indians could not bring forth claims relating to provincial jurisdiction, which would have removed hunting and fishing claims from consideration.[50] The government allowed two years to pass before reconsidering the Indian claims commission proposal in March of 1965. No change in the principles of the bill was proposed, despite the representations of Indian groups and others during the two year hiatus from cabinet attention.[51] The government once more introduced the claims commission legislation into the House, but did not consider it a priority. The claims commission legislation was never passed.

The period from 1961 to 1966 is marked by instable minority governments that made it very difficult to move a legislative agenda through Parliament. The public salience of Indian land claims was very low and did not force the government to reassess its legislative priorities. Although

Indian national and regional organizations existed and had opportunities to make their policy agenda known to executive actors, these organizations had limited resource bases and had not publicly demonstrated the capacity to mobilize Indian communities. Such mobilization would have been an important reason for cabinet to prioritize Indian land rights legislation, and perhaps even to address title claims.

In this context of minimal external pressure and lack of any consistent ministerial direction, the only serious pressure to address land grievances came from within the Indian affairs bureaucracy. Driven by an internal admission of general policy failure, officials thought that addressing land grievances through an arbitration mechanism would garner Indian communities' cooperation to achieve what the bureaucracy felt was the important policy goal: improving social welfare outcomes and speeding up the process of integration. The bureaucracy's support for an adjudication mechanism was based on adjudication's ability to insulate the department from criticism in the event that the commission would deny the merit of a claim. In any event, the bureaucracy did not foresee serious political repercussions should a commission rule against an Indian grievance. Cabinet approved this blame avoidance strategy over its other preference to control policy outcomes, but no one at the table was prepared, in the end, to widen the scope of a commission's mandate to hear aboriginal title claims. While there was a growing acceptance that the government should address treaty violations, there was no clear acceptance that aboriginal title claims were legitimate grievances.

Trudeau's White Paper 1968–69: Equality versus Special Rights

Events not directly related to the land claims issue but nonetheless central to Indian policy in the mid-1960s would come to have important effects on the widening importance of Indian policy in the critical years to come. The 1960s civil rights movements and welfare state activism created a wider scope for public interest in Indian policy than ever before. This rising public awareness coincided with pressures within the Indian Affairs Branch to address the on-the-ground challenges to policy implementation. Native people were not "advancing," and it seems that few involved with the day-to-day implementation of Indian policy felt terribly enlightened by the experience. While upper level political attention to Indian policy waxed and waned during the 1960s era of minority governments, Indian Branch officials were looking for new ways to improve the delivery of services already in place, without necessarily challenging fundamental policy assumptions. Policy failure and growing public interest in the late 1960s brought Indian Branch officials to seek out new sources for policy ideas.

One outcome of this relatively new openness among senior Indian Branch officials was their ability to persuade the Minister to fund the Hawthorn Report, a national survey and the first large-scale attempt by social scientists across the country to evaluate the state of Indian communities. It was an accounting of Indians' socio-economic status and position within the labor force, the role of federal and provincial governments in the provision of welfare and education services to the native population, and the state of governance on Indian reserves. This comprehensive study, delivered from 1966 through 1967, illustrated to government officials and to a wider public the extent of Indian policy failure in the cold hard figures of poverty, social dislocation and economic marginalization.

The change of Indian welfare policy from obscurity to an issue of rising public salience is reflected in the government's decision, in 1966, to create the Department of Indian Affairs and Northern Development (DIAND), with its own minister at the cabinet table. When, in 1968, Pierre Trudeau led the Liberal Party to victory and the country's first majority government after six years of constant instability, the stage was set for yet another review of Indian affairs policy. Trudeau appointed the young and untested Jean Chrétien as Minister of Indian Affairs and Northern Development to oversee the development of an Indian policy white paper.[52]

The 1968–69 white paper exercise would be conducted on two fronts. The government went to great pains to organize a set of consultation meetings with Indian leaders across the country. This provided the first opportunity for Indian leaders to meet directly with senior government officials and the Minister. Indian leaders came to believe that they were finally being accorded a significant voice and role within the government's policy development process. These consultations were also held across the country for the first time, contributing again to Indian leaders' understanding that the policy development process was not strictly an Ottawa-centric exercise. What became clear, only at the conclusion of the policy development process, was that the Indian consultation exercise was totally secondary to the real policy development front. Battles between the following two axes in Ottawa determined the real policy development process: the first was the Prime Minister and the Privy Council Office (PCO),[53] and the second was Chrétien and DIAND. While Indian leaders were making it clear that treaty and aboriginal rights were, as they had always been, preconditions for a positive future between Indians and the Canadian state, the forces in Ottawa were coming to very different conclusions.

The policy review exercise of 1968–69[54] was again driven by government actors' definition of the Indian Problem as fundamentally a welfare and poverty issue, and actors within PCO quickly identified the source of Indian policy failure. Individuals within PCO viewed special legal status and rights as culprits that distracted Indians and kept them from progressing, tying them to a paternalistic and rigid Indian Affairs bureaucracy. The solution favored by PCO and the Prime Minister was to move away from a dialogue of special rights to embrace a global goal of non-discrimination and equal rights under the rubric of equal citizenship.

This fundamental rejection of Indian rights was heavily conditioned by Trudeau's condemnation of the special status claims brought forward by Québec's rising voices of ethnic nationalism. In the following quotation, Trudeau sets out his opposition to Québec nationalists' claims for collective rights:

> I have always opposed the notions of special status and distinct society. With the Quiet Revolution, Québec became an adult and its inhabitants have no need of favours or privileges to face life's challenges and to take their place within Canada and in the world at large. They should not look for their "identity" and their "distinctiveness" in the constitution, but rather in their confidence in themselves and in the full exercise of their rights as citizens equal to all other citizens in Canada.[55]

Indeed, it was to act as a strong voice against Québec's nationalist forces and special rights claims that brought Trudeau into federal politics. In this next quotation, Trudeau offers his rejection of Indians' special status claims using remarkably similar language:

> We can go on treating the Indians as having a special status . . . or we can say, "You're at a crossroads, the time is now to decide whether the Indians will be a race apart in Canada or whether they will be Canadians of full status." . . . They should eventually become Canadians as all other Canadians . . . and this is the only basis on which everyone in our society can develop as equals.[56]

Trudeau's liberalism and principled objections to ethnic rights meant that all policy initiatives under his Prime Ministership needed to be justified according to the central policy goals of equal citizenship and the non-recognition of special rights claims.

The first stage of the white paper process was for government actors to agree on the policy's fundamental principles. By February of 1969, the fundamental Indian policy objective of equal citizenship was the sole issue on which bureaucrats could agree,[57] and the parties sought cabinet approval on the global objectives of a new federal policy. In their minds, formal equality and citizenship conflicted fundamentally with special rights claims. Cabinet concurred that "steps should be taken to place Indians on the same basis as other Canadians, with full rights and responsibilities, thus permitting the Indian population to enter the main stream of social improvement." Chrétien proposed "the Indian Act and the Department of Indian Affairs be abolished, that the federal government retain responsibility for Indian lands through appropriate legislation, and that negotiations be initiated with the provinces with a view to having them assume responsibility for their resident Indians as full Canadian citizens." The Prime Minister said that "there appeared to be general agreement in the cabinet on the basis of the policy to be considered,"[58] and cabinet agreed that Chrétien would develop the policy's content and submit it for cabinet approval.

At that time, Trudeau and his cabinet clearly understood that an Indian white paper based on the elimination of Indian rights and status would provoke Indian dissatisfaction, but not, they thought, enough to sink the policy. Cabinet concluded that "in order to avoid problems of morale among the Indians as well as the federal public servants concerned, it was of the utmost importance that discussions of the proposed policy be limited for the time being to members of cabinet."[59] The government did not consider Indian opposition to be the greatest obstacle to its future policy, but rather the reaction of the provincial governments. Cabinet identified the most "serious obstacle" to policy implementation as provincial intransigence. Part of the policy package was to treat Indians like any other Canadian citizen, which would make the provinces responsible for providing social services to Indians.

While both the Trudeau/PCO and Chrétien/DIAND axes agreed on the fundamental policy principles, disagreements arose on how to implement them. One of the sticking points was what to do about land claims. Chrétien favored the introduction of an adjudicatory claims commission to address the treaty and aboriginal title grievances clearly expressed by Indian leaders in the consultation process. Chrétien, always the pragmatist, saw the claims commission mechanism as the carrot to secure Indian cooperation for a policy that would meet initial opposition.[60] However, the PCO axis saw this measure as contradicting the "non-discriminatory" ethos of the proposed new policy, since a claims commission recognized land grievances and the rights underpinning them as valid. The Prime Minister and PCO stymied the Department's proposal that the policy's implementation should include the claims commission. The result was "stalemate."[61]

In order to build a government-wide consensus on Indian policy and to force officials to thoroughly assess each policy implementation issue within the policy objective approved by cabinet, the Prime Minister's Office handed the policy development process over to a government-wide task force of officials, introducing new players into the dialogue. During the discussions from February to June, DIAND officials tried to persuade their colleagues on this task force, who had no experience in Indian policy and who were firmly wedded to liberal equality principles, of the pragmatic necessity to address land claims grievances as part of the overall policy. DIAND officials and Chrétien had at least attended the series of consultations with Indian leaders, and were fully aware of the importance of Indian treaty and aboriginal title rights to the wider Indian political agenda. The recognition of these rights was indeed one of the few policy implementation proposals on which Indians leaders across the country could agree, and served as the issue on which they could possibly act collectively. DIAND officials felt that the government had to respond to these grievances in order to sell the rest of the policy.

The claims recognition issue was one of the most contentious in these discussions.[62] Officials were not only concerned with principle, but also with the unknown outcomes such recognition would entail. Officials from Finance were concerned with possible fiscal exposure, and everyone struggled with the very idea of underlying aboriginal rights to land, particularly what that meant for other property holders. There were many reasons why a non-recognition policy made more sense to these government actors. However, the DIAND group was able to impress upon the other officials that pragmatic necessity needed to prevail over the fine application of principle. Claims should be settled.[63] The officials could not agree, however, on the institutional mechanism to put into place to settle claims. The options were: to adjudicate through a claims commission, to negotiate a monetary amount for the claims and have payment made through a wider social development package, or to embark on a further series of negotiations with Indians to determine a proper mechanism.[64] Importantly, these last two options are the first evidence in the story of land claims mechanisms, since 1948, that government actors proposed direct negotiations with Indian communities, although it was also clear that the negotiations alluded to here did not amount to the negotiation of new treaties, and it was not clear that only consultations were on offer. Nevertheless, the options were outlined for approval by a cabinet committee, the last step before going to the full cabinet.

Faced with dissension among officials on the mechanisms for claims settlement and equally mindful of the Prime Minister's personal philosophy regarding special rights, the cabinet committee came to recommend the least dangerous option: a claims commissioner mandated to investigate treaty-based claims with the power only to advise cabinet on conditions of settlement. The decision to exclude aboriginal title claims from the mandate of the commissioner was a victory of the Department of Justice over DIAND. More willing to see the aboriginal title issue as predominantly political, DIAND considered it necessary to include these claims within the commissioner's mandate in order to maintain the commission's legitimacy in the eyes of Indians. Justice was of the opinion that aboriginal title had no standing at law, and therefore should not be included within the commissioner's mandate.[65] The advisory claim commission model was a return to the Diefenbaker proposal of 1962. It was clearly the lowest common denominator that could make it through full cabinet. A stronger commission, with powers of adjudication, could not survive the internal policy development process mandated by Prime Minister Trudeau.

Chrétien brought the white paper to cabinet for approval on June 17th, 1969, and introduced the goal of the policy: " . . . to end Canada's apartheid policy on Indians, to eliminate the special relationship of the Indians with the federal government, to repeal the Indian Act and gradually work towards deletion of the constitutional reference on Indians."[66] The record of the cabinet discussion is short, but revealing. At the time of this cabinet meeting, the British Columbia Supreme Court, the first court of appeal in the province, was considering the first aboriginal title test case since 1879, brought by the Nisga'a of northwestern British Columbia, and the issue came up in a brief exchange. The Minister of Justice stated that " . . . it was essential for the new policy to focus on the future if it was to work . . ." and that the Commissioner would not hear aboriginal title claims " . . . otherwise there would be danger that . . . the government would be pressured into a political settlement on this issue." The Prime Minister indicated that "should the courts rule in favour of the Nishgas (sic) . . . the Commissioner would be automatically empowered to consider the case." This exchange reveals two things. First, it shows that a positive court decision on aboriginal title would increase the Indians' bargaining power via the government, forcing the government to address a long-standing set of grievances for which it had always been unprepared. Second, it shows that at this point in time, the government thought that positive court action would enlarge the scope of the commissioner's mandate, but would not actually force the government to negotiate these claims directly with Indians. Court action would open the government up to a recommendation by the Commissioner to negotiate, but in June 1969, that was the extent of how the government perceived its probable impact.

Jean Chrétien introduced the Indian policy into the House of Commons on June 25th, 1969. It represented a complete rejection of Indian aspirations and demonstrated how completely Indian voices had been side-lined from Ottawa's internal policy machine. It showed Indian leaders that the normal processes of consultation and discussion brought them no power, no benefits, and much disappointment. It was time to do business differently. It was time for the disparate regional Indian organizations that had formed over the course of the 1950s and 1960s to act cooperatively with a common agenda and to bring their case directly to the Canadian public.

Trudeau's white paper galvanized Indian political mobilization like no action had before. Within days, the National Indian Brotherhood, the Union of Ontario Indians, the Indian Association of Alberta, and other spokesmen rejected the policy. Muted approval of the policy from news-papers and other groups waned after it became clear that Indian opinion was against it. Press coverage became more critical of the policy in view of Indian opposition, and by the fall, academics joined the opposition ranks. The policy was in trouble. In November, cabinet was informed that the provinces would not easily fall into line behind the policy, given the Indian opposition: " . . . the provinces appeared to agree with the policy but wanted the federal government to get the approval of the Indians before their public concurrence was sought; some provinces were insisting that they would not meet with the federal government unless Indians were present at the negotiating table." At that point, the federal government decided that it needed to be "flexible" about the implementation of the policy, but felt that "the Commissioner of Indian Grievances should be appointed as early as possible provided . . . this would not be interpreted as a breach of the process of consultation on which all of the government proposals rested." [67] Trudeau appointed Mr. Lloyd Barber, Vice-President of the University of Saskatchewan, Canada's Indian Claims Commissioner on December 19th, 1969.

Harold Cardinal, President of the Indian Association of Alberta, wrote and published his blasting rejoinder to the policy titled *The Unjust Society.*[68] This publication and the official counter proposals put forward to the government in June 1970 amid press attention indicated that Indian policy had entered a new era of Indian political activism. The political mobilization of Indian associations across the country succeeded in put-ting the federal government on the defensive. By June 1970, Trudeau had hinted during a cabinet meeting with national Indian leaders that the gov-ernment would not force the policy, given such concerted opposition. While the government was forced to backtrack from its policy position, it did not so easily turn away from the policy's central ideological assumptions. The Trudeau government had spent a year developing an internal consensus on the policy, and was left to do public damage control while privately continuing to accept the central ideas of the policy. The appointment of the claims commissioner was the only part of the policy that was formally implemented before the government was forced to publicly abandon the white paper in June of 1970.

From the Vacuum Negotiation Prevails 1971–1973

The government's retreat from its white paper presented a critical juncture in Canadian Indian policy. Indians' concerted opposition had managed to sway general public and intergovernmental opinion away from the policy. The government's formal policy goals were soundly repudiated by its main client group, and Indian policy was left without a formal rudder. Government policy development after the 1970 defeat reverted to an ad hoc process, where the federal government adopted strategies in reaction to specific events. By the time the Supreme Court handed down its first decision on aboriginal title in January of 1973, the federal government was already down the negotiation road, with no internal actors seriously backing other alternatives. Support for the recognition of treaty and aboriginal rights as a means to achieve other policy ends had increased across the policy table, decreasing the isolation of DIAND on this issue.

Significantly, as voices around the cabinet table incrementally came to support a recognition policy, and recognition by way of direct negotiation with Canada's Indian and Inuit peoples, critical voices outside of the government policy deliberation process joined in support of the negotiation option. Key among these voices was that of the Indian Claims Commissioner. The Commissioner's call to the federal government to negotiate claims directly with Indian people could not be brushed aside because the federal government came to view the Commissioner as fulfilling an important policy niche during this time of increased tension, that of Indian-federal government mediator. In order to diminish the escalating social and welfare costs of reserve communities, the federal government needed to maintain a dialogue with Indian leaders, but the white paper had so angered Indian communities that the federal government could not take this dialogue for granted in the immediate future. The government could not afford to undercut the legitimacy of the Commissioner's office once it became clear that he provided one of the only credible mechanisms to affect this dialogue.

This next section traces the development of government thinking on the recognition of Indian's special rights, and how government actors came to accept negotiation as the basis of Canada's land claims policy. This development is incremental, and belies the common hypothesis in the literature that the government executed a *volte-face* in August 1973, instituting a negotiation policy solely as a result of the Supreme Court of Canada's *Calder* decision. It shows how the government's non-recognition policy ran counter to its immediate economic interests in two main instances: the James Bay power project in northern Québec, and the need to readdress the terms of Treaties 8 and 11 in the Northwest Territories.

The Indian Claims Commissioner: Promoting a Dialogue vs. Non-Recognition

One of the first orders of business in the summer of 1970 was for the government to respond to the Indian community's demand for a meaningful and formal role in the policy development process. As Jean Chrétien submitted to cabinet: " . . . the public appear to feel that the Government has advanced its position, the Indians have responded, and it is now incumbent on the Government to accept the Indian's requests for a forum in which differences can be reconciled."[69] Indian leaders were determined not to be shut out from the centre of power in the Canadian policy process. That goal could not be achieved without developing the mechanisms that would put Indian leaders in the same rooms with the key departmental officials and cabinet sub-committee members where policy battles are ultimately decided. Chrétien recommended the creation of a joint committee of senior departmental officials and Indian representatives, reporting directly to a small committee of cabinet ministers. For Indian leaders, these consultative mechanisms would necessarily address "differences about treaties, aboriginal rights, and land tenure," and Chrétien did recommend that "rights questions" be within the purview of the officials' committee, but not of the cabinet sub-committee. He also added that the federal government would find the mechanisms useful for other reasons. Chrétien submitted to his cabinet colleagues that creating Indian policy mechanisms that broke down departmental divisions furthered the goals of white paper: " . . . Widening [Indians'] horizons through an Indian-interdepartmental committee would bring the Indians into closer touch with other Departments, thus preparing the way for their eventual acceptance of the concept of services flowing from a variety of agencies rather than from one Department.[70] Cabinet agreed with these proposals, but noted that should Indian representatives " . . . refuse to participate because of the issue of aboriginal rights, the Minister of Indian Affairs and Northern Development would not pursue this initiative but seek further guidance from cabinet on this issue."[71]

While it was fairly easy for cabinet to approve Chrétien's mandate to enter discussions with the National Indian Brotherhood about the shape of these consultative mechanisms, it was not so easy for the National Indian

Brotherhood to garner the approval of the regional Indian associations. While the white paper and the issue of special rights had "provided a rallying point . . . for bringing together the disparate views of the old and the young,"[72] Indian regional organizations were contesting the appropriate role of the National Indian Brotherhood as a national umbrella organization. Jean Chrétien attributed difficulties in establishing Indian-cabinet consultative mechanisms to the power struggles which unfolded into the spring of 1971 between these Indian organizations. While progress on the establishment of these consultative mechanisms was frustrated, Indian insistence on the centrality of their rights to any progress in any area of Indian policy continued unabated. Again, Chrétien reiterated to the Prime Minister that " . . . it would be a mistake to assume that the rights issue will fade away if left to itself," and that any attempts by the government to address the larger policy agenda " . . . such as Indian lands, amendment of the Indian Act, and the participation of provincial governments" would not go forward until the government "provided for the discussion of all grievances based on both claims and supposed rights."[73]

Chrétien's interim solution was to strengthen the role of the Indian Claims Commissioner, Lloyd Barber, who had decided very early on in his tenure that his first task was to work on building positive relationships with Indian leaders across the country before addressing specific grievances.[74] Barber was particularly taxed in his effort to do so because Indian leaders had refused to deal with him since his position was identified with the hated white paper. Barber made the strategic decision to maintain his neutrality from Ottawa by maintaining his offices at the University of Saskatchewan, and by actively promoting government support for the funding of Indian claims research. He also lobbied Trudeau, the PCO, and Chrétien to increase his mandate to hear aboriginal title claims.[75] By 1971, Barber had built a positive personal reputation among Indian community leaders. It became clear that the critical obstacle between greater dialogue between Indian leaders and the Commissioner rested in his restricted mandate. Since Barber had garnered the personal confidence of Indian leaders, Chrétien saw Barber as a solution to the impasse which had arisen among Indian organizations over the form and content of the consultative mechanisms. Chrétien put to Trudeau that widening the Commissioner's mandate could be done "without changing our basic position on aboriginal rights."[76]

Chrétien's proposal placed Trudeau's aversion to the recognition of Indian's special rights claims directly in opposition to the Prime Minister's wish to accomplish other Indian policy goals. The Prime Minister and cabinet were placed in a position to choose between the ideological goal of non-recognition and the social-economic goal of Indian "advancement." The

Prime Minister was very clearly aware of the trade-off, as he "recalled that the question of aboriginal claims had been discussed at length . . . in 1969; he saw no reason to change that position now, although he recognized that, having the Commissioner listen to Indian representatives on the subject appeared to be the only way in which to get a meaningful dialogue going on the other issues to be considered by the government and the Indian community."[77] In this relatively small battle between principle and pragmatism, Trudeau chose pragmatism. In August of 1971, the Prime Minister authorized the Commissioner to investigate and make recommendations to the government on aboriginal title claims.

The Commissioner became an instrumental advocate for Indian groups, prompting the federal government to increase funding of Indian rights and treaties research in July of 1972. The government disbursed research funding to regional Indian organizations because to refuse such funding would be construed as a "breach of faith" and would "largely nullify the work of the Commissioner on Indian Claims."[78] The Commissioner became a vocal proponent for negotiated versus arbitrated or litigated solutions to specific Indian grievances during this period, indicating his preference to both Indians and government actors alike.[79]

Treaties 8 and 11:
Economic Development vs. Non-Recognition in the North

The Trudeau government's ideological commitment to the non-recognition of Indian special rights continued to be challenged in the light of Indian political mobilization, not only in the south, but also north of the 60th parallel. Since the 1950s, the Canadian north had seen an important increase in resource exploration and development, with the development of petroleum and mining resources forming the backbone of the region's economic future. With oil and natural gas exploration going on in the Mackenzie River delta, northern Indian and Inuit communities addressed renewed concerns about the impact of economic development on their social systems and traditional land use practices. Indian and Inuit communities in the north demanded that the federal government directly negotiate their land claims prior to the debut of large scale economic development projects. In February of 1970, the Yukon Native Brotherhood formed to prepare a land claims proposal based on their unextinguished aboriginal rights. By December of 1971, the newly formed Inuit Tapirisat of Canada had contacted Lloyd Barber to seek his assistance in developing their aboriginal title claim.[80]

While the Trudeau government in 1970 knew that these aboriginal title claims were being developed in northern communities, they were not yet formally presented to the federal government for action. The item which was directly in front of cabinet at that time was the unfulfilled reserve land provisions under Treaties 8 and 11 which had been signed with Indian communities in 1899 and 1921 respectively. Under these agreements, the federal government had promised that lands were to be reserved for exclusive Indian use. These reserves were never established, partly because there was no pressure from settlers to restrict Indian communities to designated reserves, and partly because Indian communities were concerned that once reserves were created, that their movements would be restricted. However, the increasing pressures of northern economic development, in conjunction with renewed Indian interest in the land rights guaranteed to them in these treaties, landed the question of how to respond to these treaty provisions squarely in front of the Trudeau cabinet.

The unfulfilled land provisions of Treaties 8 and 11 were known to the federal government for some time. In 1959, the Diefenbaker government had established a commission of inquiry to seek recommendations of what response should be appropriate. The commissioner recommended against the creation of northern reserves, seeing these as inimical to future economic development. Instead, the commissioner recommended that in lieu of reserves, Indian bands be given a cash settlement and guaranteed a percentage of future mineral revenues in perpetuity. In November of 1968, Chrétien adopted these recommendations and proposed that the federal government negotiate such a settlement with Indian bands, and so address the issue once and for all. This proposal was shelved as part of the white paper review process demanded by Trudeau, but the Prime Minister handed the issue to a special sub-committee of senior officials. In May of 1970, a month before the Prime Minister was to publicly back away from the white paper, cabinet reviewed this sub-committee's report of Treaties 8 and 11.

The white paper placed the Trudeau cabinet in a quandary. The officials thought that the economically preferred course of action was for the government to negotiate a cash settlement rather than create new reserves. To create new reserves would have the federal government perpetuate key provisions of the very Indian Act that, according to the white paper, the government intended to abolish. However, officials pointed out a key difficulty with the cash settlement in lieu of reserves proposal. The officials argued that to offer a cash settlement would in effect be seen as re-negotiating a treaty as opposed to strictly fulfilling the government's existing treaty obligations. To re-negotiate a treaty would have huge implications for the non-recognition goal of the Trudeau government:

> It could be implied from the [cash settlement] proposal that the Government of Canada acknowledges that the aboriginal inhabitants of

Canada have continued to maintain an interest in the lands that requires
to be satisfied . . . the Government is not prepared today to enter into
new proceedings to acquire the proprietorship in Canada . . . The Sub-
Committee was of the view that the proposal amounted to entering
into a new proceeding and as such could open up the whole question
of aboriginal rights. In this event the Government might be required, in
order to be consistent, to undertake similar proceedings to extinguish
the Indian interest in British Columbia, the Yukon, Québec and the
Maritimes, and the Eskimo interest in the north.[81]

In effect, any government response would contravene some important aspect of the Indian white paper; but most importantly, the pro-
development option could force the government to recognize aboriginal
title not just in the north, but across the country. This alone was inimical
to Trudeau's rights ideology, but it also raised the specter of complicat-
ing intergovernmental relations. The cabinet, not yet forced by Indian
mobilization to back away from the policy proposals, opted to delay. It
could do so by forwarding the issue to the Indian Claims Commissioner
for further study.[82]

By the spring of 1972, government response to Treaties 8 and 11
could no longer be delayed. Chrétien identified the reasons why. Firstly, the
northern treaty claims had become totally entwined with the larger aboriginal title claim of the Inuit, which had been submitted to the federal government that February. This had led to a great deal of publicity, and "the
claims and grievances are finding echo and support in the pronouncements
of native people's associations in the South, particularly those of Indian
leaders, and of white supporters in various parts of Canada." Significantly,
resource developers were persuaded by this mobilization of Indian and general public opinion that the federal government needed to take definitive
action. The question remained how the government would respond.

Chrétien laid out the options to his cabinet colleagues. He clearly
considered the non-recognition assumptions of the 1969 Indian policy proposals to be no longer feasible. "Related questions concerning aboriginal
rights, the 'renegotiation problem,' Indian reserves in principle, and antici-
pated high costs for native peoples' land settlement, should be seen today
in the light of current problems of northern development and of the negative reaction by many Indians against Indian Policy, 1969."[83] The time had
come for the government to concede that it would in some way need to recognize Indian land rights: " . . . It must be accepted, as a fact of life that
any initiative by the Government on the land entitlement issue under the
Treaties will probably lead to claims involving aboriginal rights." He laid

out two broad choices for the government: wait for a legal determination on the validity of Indian rights, or reach a negotiated settlement.

He pointed out to his colleagues that there was no established jurisprudence on the issue, and thus, the government had no way of reasonably determining how " . . . the courts would react if the Northwest Territories Indians were to seek legal remedies." In any case, he argued that waiting for a judicial determination would not solve the government's underlying issues in the presence of Indian political mobilization and their increasing ability to impact Canadian public opinion:

> But legal proceedings take a very long time and time would not be on the Government's side if the Indians, pending court decisions, resorted to political and public relations campaigns, with favourable response from Canadians at large and possibly with unpleasant disturbances in the Territories that could be very upsetting not only for development but to northern communities generally.[84]

Chrétien proposed a negotiation strategy that would allow the government to put land, cash and future resource revenues on the table. He felt that a cash-only solution, which he had favored in 1968, was no longer feasible, given the political awakening of northern Indian communities. He pointed out that "the Government stands to gain much from showing political generosity," and that by negotiating with Indians in the north, "a real breakthrough might be made in the Government's relations with native peoples . . . elsewhere in Canada."

Cabinet agreed.[85] There is no record of the give and take of the discussions themselves, so it is unknown how many voices joined Chrétien's, or whether it was difficult to convince the Prime Minister. However, by the spring of 1972, the Trudeau government had committed itself to a negotiation of Indian treaty rights in the north, months prior to the Supreme Court's Calder decision in January of 1973. The government had taken a significant step away from the non-recognition policy of 1969, and had begun down the path of negotiation versus litigation.

Negotiation versus Federalism: The James Bay Hydro-Electric Project

The Treaties 8 and 11 issue could well have marked both the beginning and the end of cabinet's flirtation with a negotiation response. Instead, events in northern Québec tested the Trudeau cabinet's commitment to negotiation south of the 60th parallel. South of 60, the federal government does not have a free hand, and is ever mindful of the possible impact of federal policy choices on intergovernmental relations.

In October of 1971, the federal cabinet was apprised of Québec's intention to begin construction of the huge hydro-electric project in the province's north. The James Bay project was to provide primarily for Québec's growing domestic power needs, but any surplus power generated through the project could be exported to the lucrative American market. In the fall of 1971, the full ecological impact of the proposed project was as yet unknown, but there would clearly be an adverse impact on the traditional occupations of the approximately 5000 native people, both Cree and Inuit, of the area. The territorial rights of Québec's northern native people had never been extinguished by a treaty, and the province had a legal obligation to obtain the surrender of existing native rights under the terms of the 1912 Québec Boundaries Extension Act, which transferred these northern lands under provincial jurisdiction. The federal government could legitimately intervene in the project in order to protect Indian interests since Indian affairs was its constitutional jurisdiction. The Indians of Québec Association had demanded that the province negotiate a settlement of their territorial rights before construction on the James Bay project began, and it demanded that " . . . in the absence of a settlement or negotiations towards that end beginning immediately, it would seem that the Crown in right of Canada as a guardian of the Indian interest would be obliged to exercise all legal recourses available to it, including Court proceedings, to force the resolution of this problem . . .."[86]

Unlike the issue of native claims in the Yukon and Northwest Territories, the land claims of Indians and Inuit in the James Bay area would test the willingness of the federal government to act in its Indian affairs jurisdiction in Québec at the potential cost of disturbing the very delicate federal-provincial relationship.[87] Chrétien apprised cabinet of " . . . a real prospect of a difficult confrontation [with Québec] on the matter of Indian rights."[88] With no pressure to act immediately, the need to be sensitive to the federal-provincial dynamic, the unclear ecological impact, and disputes regarding the economic viability of the project, cabinet chose to do nothing for the moment. In January, the Prime Minister ordered his Ministers take "great care" to maintain a position of neutrality on the project.[89]

By February 1972, a federal-provincial task force reported that while there were environmental concerns about the project, the impact of the project on the region's native population was "the most pressing and serious item to be resolved."[90] The federal response to this public finding was slow, with DIAND, Justice, and PCO unresolved on how to proceed. Chrétien had already espoused the negotiation option on the Treaties 8 and 11 issue, and sought a consistent approach with James Bay. Stalled by provincial intransigence and unwillingness to negotiate with them, the James Bay

Cree officially asked Chrétien to intervene on their behalf. In May, the Cree had held a press conference, and spoke favorably of federal involvement. Chrétien felt that it had become ". . . . essential that a positive position be taken by the Federal Government to bring about negotiations between the Indians and the Government of the Province of Québec."[91] The Clerk of the Privy Council, however, cautioned that the federal government should not seek a place at the negotiation table without the express request of the native groups.[92] Cabinet concurred, and Chrétien was allowed to approach the Québec government. In these discussions, the provincial government advised its federal counterparts that they would not be allowed to be a party to the negotiations.

The federal government then faced the decision of whether it would demand a space at the negotiation table, despite provincial objections. In June the government had publicly announced its intention to negotiate the Treaty 8 and 11 claims, and by July, the government had received representations from native rights advocates and environmental organizations questioning the lack of apparent federal activity in James Bay. As a result, the federal Minister of Energy, Mines and Resources recommended to cabinet that the government seek a place at the table.[93] This was a critical development because it indicated that support for a negotiation option was brought to the table by a minister other than Chrétien, widening the coalition for negotiation with native peoples to include a minister responsible for a key sector of the Canadian economy. On July 14th, 1972, cabinet accepted the recommendation to take a stronger line with the Québec provincial government.[94]

The permission for the Indian Claims Commissioner to review aboriginal title claims, the decision of the government to seek a negotiated solution to treaty claims in the Northwest Territories, and its decision to extend its role in the James Bay negotiations amounted to a significant series of steps by the Trudeau cabinet away from the non-recognition of native special rights it so strongly adopted in 1969. The 1970–1972 period challenged the government to weigh its ideological goals against the achievement of other important government objectives: normalizing the relationship between it and Indian associations after the white paper fiasco; allowing for the development of northern economic resources; and managing federal-provincial tensions, always a premier issue in Canadian politics. These decisions were most notably brought on by the political mobilization of Canadian Indian organizations and the effect on Canadian public opinion of their concerted opposition to the white paper.

These incremental, yet important, changes in government policy happened during the time the first aboriginal title test case was wending its way through the court system. By May 1970, the Nisga'a had lost their case in two courts, and in 1971 the Supreme Court granted the Nisga'a leave to appeal. Although the government was aware that the Supreme Court was deliberating on the legal merits of aboriginal title, cabinet documents show that it was not the prospect that the Nisga'a may win their case that drove the decisions of the Trudeau cabinet. Key to the situation was that Indians' political mobilization and the wider politicization of land claims made it possible for native people to capitalize on a situation of judicial uncertainty. This is not to say that Trudeau or his cabinet had embraced the concept of aboriginal property rights without reservation. However, in the two years preceding the Supreme Court's *Calder* decision, the cabinet had struggled with the concept of aboriginal rights, compromised previous principled objections to those rights, and already weighed the value of negotiation versus litigation. By the end of 1972, the pragmatic Jean Chrétien was no longer isolated in cabinet on the issue, and the pro-negotiation position of Lloyd Barber added a credible external voice that Trudeau could not ignore.

The Supreme Court Rules: The Calder Decision and Cabinet's Response

On January 31st, 1973, the Supreme Court finally ruled on the issue of aboriginal title. The case was heard by seven of the nine justices. Of the six justices who directly addressed the issue of aboriginal title, all agreed with the basic principle that "the Aboriginal Indian title does not depend on treaty, executive order or legislative enactment."[95] Rather, aboriginal title was a legal right which arose from native people's historic occupation and use of their lands. This conclusion was a huge win for native people, but its potential impact was tempered by the justices' indecision as to whether aboriginal title had indeed been extinguished through the assertion of provincial sovereignty. Other questions were left unanswered as well: the criteria which would establish in a court of law that native title existed; the conditions under which this title could be lawfully extinguished; and the scope or content of this new property right. Thus, the *Calder* decision told the nation that aboriginal title was a legal property right, but not whether this property right continued to exist in British Columbia. The justices were devoted to the interpretation of a judicial doctrine, and made no pretense of entering the realm of public policy by exhorting the government one way or the other on how to proceed.

What could the government do? The Trudeau cabinet had a number of options. First, with no entrenched bill of rights, the Canadian government could have responded by passing legislation, explicitly extinguishing these rights with some measures for compensation in line with government appropriation of other property rights. While technically possible, this very hostile response was unlikely given the government's general position that it would respect natives' legal rights.[96] This course of action was also highly unlikely (indeed, there is no evidence that it was considered), given the general public support of opposition parties for aboriginal rights.[97] Second, with legislative unilateralism unrealistic, the government could send a reference to the Supreme Court to clarify its reasoning on the outstanding aboriginal title issues. Third, the government could do nothing and wait for Indian groups to litigate the question further. Fourth, the government could negotiate with the plaintiffs in the *Calder* case, the Nisga'a, but not create any institutional mechanisms or take any policy position to deal with future claims. Or fifth, it could once again review its policies for future action, and create institutions to deal with any claims that would come before it.

In the first week after the *Calder* decision, the Trudeau cabinet began to address the impact of the decision and its options. On February 6th, a strategic committee of cabinet concluded that the Minister of Justice would consider sending a reference to the Supreme Court, while Chrétien would prepare a general policy document on native peoples for cabinet's consideration. The next day, however, Chrétien and Trudeau met with Nisga'a leaders in a historic face-to-face closed door meeting. The Nisga'a informed the Prime Minister that "the Nishga [sic] Nation did not wish to have the matter referred back to the Supreme Court of Canada . . . they wished that the government would commence negotiations on their behalf with the government of British Columbia, with respect to their land claims." Cabinet agreed to not pursue the matter in the Supreme Court as a result of the Nisga'a meeting, and it also agreed that Chrétien would begin exploratory discussions with British Columbia while he prepared an overall policy paper.

While DIAND would consult with Justice on the development of the policy paper to cabinet, external events kept the pressure on and the negotiation option in the forefront. On February 14th, the Yukon Native Brotherhood presented its land claims brief to the government proposing a negotiation framework. In April, Chrétien established a negotiating team within DIAND to review the Yukon proposal. The Indian Claims Commissioner was busy publicly and privately touting the value of negotiation over adjudicatory methods,[98] and he sat in on meetings with DIAND officials tasked with evaluating the department's existing settlement machinery as part of the larger policy development process.[99]

After four months of internal bargaining, Justice and DIAND came to submit separate memoranda to cabinet, signalling an inability to reach consensus on key issues of policy, the degree of divergence at this point not possible for me to determine.[100] However, the *Calder* decision had robbed Justice of its previous objections to recognizing aboriginal title's potential existence in Canadian law, and the likely divergences from the DIAND proposals would rest on the relative values of litigation strategies. The DIAND paper is a much fuller development of the thinking which had impacted government decision-making during the prior two years. The core message of the DIAND position was that the land claims issue was not strictly a legal issue, and the government's approach needed to address the evolving political relationship between Canada and native peoples. Delay was no longer an option, because unresolved grievances threatened to "create fanaticism" and "growing militancy." Both natives and non-natives had come to share the view that the government had "a legal and moral obligation to deal with the question," and as a result, a strictly legal response to land claims would be inappropriate. It is worth quoting at some length:

> Although various Indian groups appear to have valid legal claims to some form of rights, the matter of settling Native claims is not a purely legal one . . . If it were a purely legal problem, it could be referred to the courts and the Government would abide by the judicial decision . . . A court decision could not resolve the practical problems effectively . . . The Indians would not easily accept an adverse judgment; the grievance would still remain. In any event, the problem is more social and political than legal . . . this course of action limits the possibility of dealing effectively with important aspects of a comprehensive settlement.[101]

Chrétien was highly aware that the process of settlement was as politically relevant and important as the eventual conclusion of settlements. The alternative to legislate a framework without prior negotiation was rejected because " . . . a decision by Parliament which appeared to be arbitrary would be bitterly opposed in Native communities." The preferred alternative of the 1960s, the special arbitrator in the form of a claims commission, was rejected as well, since decisions on claims " . . . require mutual consent and are not suitable for delegation to an appointed body" and since " . . . provincial participation, which will be necessary, could not be achieved by a commission." Since matters other than strictly monetary compensation were now on the table, neither federal nor provincial governments were willing to delegate decision-making to another party.

The only remaining alternative was to engage in a process of direct negotiation, despite the fact that "no firm estimate of cost can be made in advance of negotiations." Cabinet required further clarifications on key strategic issues and at the end of June, Chrétien and Justice presented recommendations on who would negotiate on the Indian side of the table, and who would be eligible to benefit from land claims settlements.[102] They recommended that should the provinces be unwilling to join in the negotiations, the federal government should be prepared "to assist [Indians] in the courts in asserting their title."[103]

Thus, in July 1973, Trudeau's cabinet agreed to adopt a negotiation policy to address Indian grievances in Canada. It was announced publicly on August 8th, 1973: "The Government is now ready to negotiate with authorized representatives of these native peoples on the basis that where their traditional interest in the land concerned can be established, an agreed form of compensation or benefit will be provided to native people in return for their interest."[104] The government would also negotiate claims arising from unfulfilled lawful obligations under existing treaties.

REFLECTIONS ON THE CANADIAN CASE

The Canadian case suggests why political mobilization greatly increases the probability that governments will introduce negotiation strategies. It does so in a number of key ways. First, in a climate of mobilized opinion, a government cannot reasonably be assured that they will be able to avoid future blame by delegating policy-making authority to courts or an arbitrator. Governments find a future course of litigation less attractive because winning a legal case would not necessarily deflect political consequences. In this respect, political mobilization makes negotiation more likely because other options lose their long-run attractiveness.

Political mobilization was also critical because it eventually forced the federal government to make tradeoffs between various goals. Prior to the mobilization of native groups in the late 1960s, actors in the Canadian government were unchallenged in the causal belief that recognition of native rights would impede the achievement of its global policy goal: the assimilation of Indian people into the body politic. Indeed, no one of any importance inside the government questioned the wisdom of assimilation writ large. The organizational and political weakness of native rights associations during this period meant that native groups could not reach or sway other opinion on the merit of their collective rights. Only those parts of an Indian reform agenda which sat well within a civil libertarian program received government attention. Native peoples' political mobilization after 1969 meant that the Trudeau government was confronted with policy decisions where a strict stance against Indian land rights would be costly. These clashes between pragmatic versus principled politics eroded

Trudeau's non-recognition policy, and broadened the support around the cabinet table for strategies to address Indian land claims. Chief among these strategies was negotiation.

The importance of the *Calder* decision as an explanation for the August 1973 announcement of a negotiation policy needs to be evaluated in light of two factors: the growing political strength of indigenous peoples and the consensus-building process so necessary to cabinet government. When the *Calder* decision came down, it did so in a context of cabinet support already shifting in favor of negotiation. *Calder* did not so much create proponents for the negotiation option as it further weakened the opposition of Trudeau and officials within the Department of Justice. The court decision also made it impossible for the Trudeau cabinet to drag out its subsequent policy deliberation process. Cabinet needed to reach a consensus quickly, and in 1973, negotiation was the policy that had already taken the lead. It did so because no other option allowed the government to reach a comprehensive political settlement between the Canadian state and indigenous peoples.

Chapter Four

Cabinet Decision-Making and Maori Land Rights in New Zealand (1944–1989)

INTRODUCTION

In 1970, Harold Cardinal and other representatives of Canada's status Indians stood together before Prime Minister Trudeau and his cabinet in a then unprecedented display of political unity and resolve. Archival documents show that continuing political agitation among Canada's indigenous communities and the landmark *Calder* decision would prod, and finally persuade the Canadian federal government to implement a land rights negotiation strategy. Indigenous political mobilization would force Canadian policy-makers to reevaluate the political costs of not recognizing indigenous collective rights and decrease policy-makers' utility for a long-run litigation strategy. Political mobilization would build allies for policy change within the executive branch and around the cabinet table. Judicial change would persuade some that these rights were legitimate. More importantly, judicial change would persuade all that inertia was impossible. In New Zealand, a similar story emerges. The contentious politics of public protest would emerge in the 1960s and bring Maori land rights politics squarely into the public eye. This protest would culminate in Dame Whina Cooper's dramatic land march of 1975. But the Maori, almost four times the relative size of Canada's indigenous population, would wait 14 more years until the Court of Appeal stirred the judicial waters with the Lands Case, and the New Zealand government would respond with a negotiation policy.

On the basis of historical and contemporary government documents, interviews with government policy-makers, and secondary sources, this chapter lays out the development of New Zealand's policy responses to Maori land grievances since the Second World War. I examine how New Zealand policy-makers evaluated the legitimacy and seriousness of Maori demands for the recognition of their collective property rights. I show how the set of feasible policy alternatives changed over time, the reasoning policy-makers found persuasive when opportunities to make policy changes arose, and finally which factors proved critical in shifting the balance of cabinet opinion toward a negotiation policy.

As in the Canadian case, sequencing is important. The recognition and protection of Maori land rights depend fundamentally on the support and political will of cabinet. Cabinet allies do not appear overnight, and cabinet opinion is rarely a reflection of judicial thinking alone. Without allies in place, pushing for the protection of Maori rights within the executive itself, the consolidation of judicial victories into positive legislative outcomes remains ephemeral. Without such allies, the erosion of existing indigenous rights in the face of judicial indifference or even hostility remains likely. This chapter shows that Maori political mobilization and the increase of protest outside of the traditional mechanisms of racial conflict resolution (such as the legislature and the political party system) built allies for policy change within. Also, like the Canadian case, the 1989 decision of the New Zealand government to establish a negotiations policy came after a critical judicial decision. This decision provided the pressure for senior officials and cabinet ministers to re-evaluate their collective response to Maori land grievances in a context where all understood that inaction was impossible. Maori political mobilization *prior* to judicial change meant that the necessary response to the court ruling was a *political* response. The government approved the negotiation policy option only after accepting the political need to redefine the relationship between Maori and the New Zealand state. Maori collective property rights, especially land rights, are at the heart of this relationship.

The New Zealand case also offers noteworthy differences to the Canadian and Australian land rights stories. The first key difference relates to the risks of recognizing Maori collective rights. The Treaty of Waitangi (1840) established a legal and political precedent recognizing Maori land rights across the whole colony. The historical recognition of Maori collective rights decreased the contemporary risk of a land rights recognition strategy. Contemporary policy-makers faced a decision to recognize continuing obligations rooted in a historical contract, rather than a more normatively challenging decision to recognize unspecified indigenous property rights flowing from unknown systems of law. Where some conservative politicians would never agree with the recognition of race-based property rights on their merits and sign a treaty themselves, they may reason that, despite the shortsightedness of their forefathers in striking a treaty bargain, a deal is a nevertheless a deal. To not recognize the Treaty and deny the obligations flowing from it would be to besmirch the honor of the Crown.

Maori land claims politics therefore revolve around the Treaty of Waitangi's moral and legal force. The Treaty changed the nature of the debate around the recognition of Maori rights. The Treaty did not, however, lessen the importance of executive policy-makers' other key decision. Would they delegate power to regulate Maori land grievances to a third party? The choice to delegate or not to delegate illustrates a second noteworthy difference to the Canadian and Australian cases. This difference is the norm of parliamentary sovereignty and how the strength of this norm ordered policy-makers' underlying preferences for negotiation over other outcomes, such as litigation and arbitration. This is a particularly concrete example of how political culture affects actors' preferences over policy outcomes.

The norm of parliamentary sovereignty affects the relative size of the set of feasible policy alternatives. It does so by decreasing the political legitimacy of policy solutions that delegate policy-making power to others at the perceived expense of Parliament. This norm holds that the power to govern, the power to make policy, is the preserve for the democratically accountable branches of government. In New Zealand, this norm is particularly strong. This has meant that generations of New Zealand politicians have operated within the confines of and subsequently reinforced the idea that the policy-making role of the judiciary or special arbitrators *should* be minimal. This is not to say that delegation of policy-making power has never occurred in New Zealand, but rather that a government's decision to delegate decision-making power in this specific normative context is a remarkable outcome and likely to be a product of unusual circumstances.

How did this relatively truncated set of policy alternatives affect the likelihood that the New Zealand government would initiate a negotiation policy at each choice opportunity? With arbitration and delegation to the courts considered relatively suspicious options, New Zealand governments historically privileged inaction or non-delegated policy alternatives, including advisory commissions and negotiation. This did not mean, however, that negotiation was automatic. The challenge of building a coalition within cabinet for a negotiation policy, distinct from *ad hoc* negotiation, remained difficult. As in Canada, developing a cabinet consensus for a negotiation policy was a function of personality and ideological balance on the inside and the mobilization of Maori behind a land rights agenda on the outside.

Unlike the Canadian case, partisan politics and the balance of cabinet opinion on Maori land rights became highly intertwined. Until recently, policy advance or policy retrenchment on Maori rights depended significantly on which political party was in power. With the formal inclusion of Maori in the franchise regime at the outset of representative government and the subsequent creation of designated Maori seats in Parliament, Maori have a long history of building alliances within the established political party system. Maori, unlike their indigenous counterparts in Canada or Australia, have a long tradition of institutionalized political action to complement (or compete with) newer forms of political contestation. Since the 1930s, the Maori political elite has built linkages with the Labour Party. When the Labour Party has been in power, cabinet opinion has been more favorable to Maori rights claims. The flip side of this partisan differentiation has been that when Labour's competitor, the National Party, assumes power, fewer members around the cabinet table have had linkages with Maori political communities, and therefore little to gain in pushing the Maori rights file forward. This chapter will follow how Maori participation within the political party system helped or hindered the development of land rights negotiation policies.

This chapter proceeds as follows. I provide a quick survey of Maori rights politics prior to the Second World War. This includes an examination of the Treaty's political and legal status; patterns of Maori land tenure; and the place of Maori interests within the political party system. I then examine the first incidence of Maori land rights negotiation during the close of the war era, and then examine policy developments after the rise of Maori protest politics in the 1960s. I conclude with reflections on the New Zealand case.

SETTING THE SCENE:
THE TREATY OF WAITANGI, MAORI LAND TENURE,
AND MAORI PARTISAN POLITICS PRIOR TO WWII

The Treaty and Maori Land

Like Canada and the United States, a treaty of cession established the early legal and political relationship between the Crown and indigenous peoples. Whereas in North America, numerous treaties were signed, in New Zealand, there is just the one, the Treaty of Waitangi, signed in 1840. The Crown and over 500 Maori chiefs were signatories to this one treaty.[1] Two versions of the document exist, the Maori and the English texts, and there continues to be debate on the Maori and non-Maori interpretations of its terms. The Treaty consists of three articles. The classic non-Maori understanding of the Treaty was that Maori ceded their sovereignty (article one) in return for being guaranteed undisturbed possession of their *taonga*, or treasures, including their lands (article two). What is not in dispute is that the Treaty established that Maori lands were alienable only to the Crown, and that all rights and responsibilities of British citizenship were extended to the Maori (article three) at the colony's inception. Therefore, Maori land rights stem from this basic compact, and the status of Maori land rights depends on the legal and political status of the Treaty.

The pressures of settlement and the need to finance the new colony led to what are now accepted as questionable land acquisition practices by the Crown. There were various mechanisms by which Maori lands (held under customary Maori title) were passed on to the Crown, and then were sold or leased to other parties under the regular land title system. The most damning was the government's wholesale appropriation of Maori lands in the 1860s after the Maori rebellions in the agriculturally rich regions of the North Island. Other than outright confiscation, Maori lands were also passed to the Crown through pre-emptive deeds, and through the government waiving its right of pre-emption, and allowing Maori to sell lands directly to settlers.

A series of legislative acts dating from 1862 were designed to regulate Maori land issues and disputes. The Maori Land Court, with jurisdiction over Maori lands, was established. While these land acts and the Maori Land Court system recognized and incorporated Maori landholding practices within New Zealand's judicial apparatus, they also facilitated the rapid transfer of Maori lands to settlers. One mechanism was the individualization of collective tenures, where the Court would enumerate the interest in a block of Maori-held land across a number of owners, and then allow individual Maori to sell or lease their "part" of the land.[2] The individualization of Maori title not only broke down the power of Maori tribal authorities to resist land alienation. Individualization also fragmented given plots of land across increasing numbers of owners as land interests were handed down from generation to generation. This fragmentation of Maori land ownership rendered it increasingly difficult for any one person to develop his land interest in an economically feasible way.[3] Even by the 1930s, most of the lands that remained in Maori hands were not suitable for commercial farming.[4] In these myriad ways, approximately 63 million acres passed through Maori hands, leaving approximately 3 million acres in Maori ownership by the early 1970s.[5]

Of the lands which are held under Maori ownership, virtually none of it is held under customary (i.e. aboriginal) title.[6] Under provisions in the various Native land acts, Maori could "trade in" customary title for a Crown-created freehold grant, thereby extinguishing the customary interest in land. Therefore, unlike Canada, there is a widespread assumption that aboriginal title no longer exists with respect to land (although arguments for the continuing existence of aboriginal title to riverbeds, seabed, foreshore, and bodies of water are contested in the courts).[7] Maori land claims are largely claims for the government to restore the honor of the Crown by acknowledging its role in the historic dispossession of Maori in contravention of the principles of partnership underlying the Treaty of Waitangi. Lands claims are predominantly demands for reparative justice based in a language of contract, where the colonizer did not live up to its part of a sacred bargain.

The courts were not persuaded that the Treaty was indeed "a sacred bargain," and instead dismissed the legal status of the Treaty fairly early. In 1877, an important judicial decision concluded that the Treaty of Waitangi did not have the weight of law.[8] The Treaty was termed "a simple nullity," and its provisions could not be enforced at law unless Parliament ratified it. By the early 1900s, the principle that the Treaty's provisions were justiciable only insofar as they are recognized by statute was thoroughly entrenched in New Zealand jurisprudence. Thus, a consistent call among some Maori was for the government to respond to the rights guaranteed through the Treaty by ratifying it, and making its terms enforceable in the courts.

The unwillingness of policy-makers to ratify the Treaty was linked to a strong normative view of the proper role of the judiciary in this parliamentary system. The pressure to make Maori customary rights enforceable in the courts was resisted in 1909 by the Solicitor-General and now famous jurist, Sir John Salmond. In a letter to Maori parliamentarian Sir Apirana Ngata, Salmond argued, as the Crown's legal officer in charge of legislative drafting, that native land legislation would not foreclose Maori efforts to seek a declaratory judgment that aboriginal title still existed. Rather, Salmond argued that it would properly ensure that " . . . when a dispute arises between Natives and the Crown as to the right to customary land, the dispute shall be settled by Parliament and not otherwise . . . to allow the matter to be fought out in the Law Courts would not, I think, be either in the public interest or in the interest of the Natives themselves . . .."[9] This identified Maori land grievances to be properly conceived as political, not legal questions, and the mechanisms for their resolution should rest within the political sphere.

Maori Political Development and Partisan Alignments

Prior to the Second World War, the Treaty had little if any resonance for non-Maori New Zealanders. What limited importance it did have was its confirmation that both Maori and non-Maori operated within one sovereign nation (article one), all sharing the same position as equal citizens within a common political enterprise (article three). The importance of article two in guaranteeing special Maori rights fell away in the New Zealander consciousness.

Article three, guaranteeing Maori full citizenship in the new colony, meant that Maori politics has been channeled through mainstream governance institutions much more than in Canada or Australia. With the beginning of representative government in 1854, male property holders had the suffrage. Although the suffrage did not exclude Maori *per se*, the slow individualization of Maori land tenure made the male Maori property owner a rare person. Through the franchise's property restrictions, Maori were de facto excluded from institutionalized political participation. The place of Maori within the colony's governance structures was an acute issue in the decade to follow. The 1860s brought the Land Wars and the Crown's confiscation of Maori lands. With tensions high between Maori and the European settlers, some argued for Parliament to include specific Maori representation in Parliament, in an attempt to amalgamate Maori into New Zealand's system of law. This position represented a midpoint of sorts between two extremes, the Crown's recognition of distinct Maori governing institutions (and sovereignty) outside of the state on the one side, and the complete denial of Maori distinctiveness inside the state on the other. James Fitzgerald, the Native Minister, espoused the moderate position to a colleague in 1865:

> You may mock me as to Maoris sitting in Parliament. My dear Friend, I am not a fool nor attribute to political forms mysterious virtues, but I know all that the sitting in parliament brings in its train and I say that ignore tenure to land and ignore the sitting in parliament and all that belongs thereto and the alternative is war, extermination to the weaker race and financial disaster to the stronger.[10]

In 1867, the government passed Fitzgerald's Maori Representation Act, designating four seats in Parliament to be held by Maori representatives. In 1893, two important events occurred. First, women got the vote. Second, Maori (male and female) were prohibited from casting votes in the general, or non-Maori, electorates. This cemented a racial division of the electorate into two separate electoral rolls which would continue until 1975.[11] This essentially meant that there were no Maori swing voters in the general electorate. Easily outnumbered in the House of Representatives, the only time that Maori voters and Maori parliamentary representatives have had a pivotal role to play in partisan politics was when the parties relied on the Maori seats to form a majority government. While the Northern Maori,

Eastern Maori, Southern Maori, and Western Maori seats guaranteed some degree of Maori representation in Parliament, these seats "in no way provided an adequate avenue for the expression of Maori opinion, nor were they an effective vehicle for Maori development."[12] Originally an interim measure, the seats continue to exist, and since their inception, New Zealanders have debated their abolition from time to time. In 1993, the number of Maori seats was allowed to increase in accordance with the size of the Maori electorate. In 2003, there were six Maori seats in Parliament.

The Maori seats, however, have had their uses. New Zealand's system of ethnic representation has guaranteed at least partial inclusion of Maori voices within Parliament. With the failure of the Maori Parliament movement of the 1890s, the Maori seats provided a way for a new Maori leadership to protect, in whatever way possible, Maori interests by working inside party and parliamentary politics. At the turn of the century, a new Maori cohort took their place in Parliament. Called the Young Maori Party (though not an official political party), the new Maori parliamentary leadership was often biracial, educated in European institutions, and partisan. Apirana Ngata, Te Rangihiroa (Peter Buck) and Maui Pomare came to the House and aligned themselves with the Liberal Party. These Maori leaders were instrumental in achieving some legislative gains, particularly in the establishment of Maori land councils that served as building blocks for Maori involvement in the management of reserve lands.[13] However, even with strong Maori leaders in cabinet such as Ngata, the ability of Maori to stem the tide of land loss was marginal and subject to their ability to gain the support of other parliamentarians. In a period where the greater electoral pressure was to provide land for white settlement versus the protection of Maori land interests, support of other parliamentarians was weak.

While the new generation of Maori parliamentarians would protect land issues as much as they could, they saw the future of Maori within the state and not separate from it. They advocated the One Nation concept of undivided sovereignty and saw Maori economic and social advancement linked to Maori acceptance of that national construct. This was particularly represented by the Native Minister in the Liberal Party governments of the 1920s, Apirana Ngata. Yet, these conservative Maori politicians had to compete electorally with other Maori who represented other streams of Maori thought. Maori also called for the ratification of the Treaty into domestic law, asserted a separate political autonomy through both tribal and pan-tribal structures, and demanded that the government address historic land grievances, especially those arising from government confiscations and shady purchases.

In the late 1920s and early 1930s, a Maori religious movement emerged, challenging the Young Maori Party, and eventually forging the now longstanding partisan linkage between Maori and the Labour Party. Firm in the belief that the Maori were God's chosen people, Tahupotiki Wiremu Ratana began a spiritual movement in 1918 that relied on faith healing, called for the unity of the Maori and the ratification of the Treaty. He founded the Ratana Church, and as time progressed, the movement became more and more political. In the early 1930s, supported by the many Maori unemployed battered by the Depression, Ratana turned his attention to winning the Maori seats in Parliament. In 1932, Ratana Party member Eruera Tirikatene took the Southern Maori seat. In 1935, Tokoura Ratana won the Western Maori seat, and in 1938, Tiaka Omana took the Eastern Maori seat.

The rise of the Ratana movement coincided with the emergence of the New Zealand Labour Party. Founded in 1916, Labour courted Maori representatives during the 1920s, and would consolidate its initial voter base during the Depression. In 1925, Labour made a promise: In return for Maori support, Labour would investigate Maori land grievances should it form the government.[14] When Ratana member Tirikatene came to the House, he supported Labour and was part of the political alliance bringing Labour to power for the first time in 1935. During the last term (1946–1949) of this first Labour government, the Maori seats gave Labour the majority in the House.

After the Depression, the New Zealand party system consolidated itself into a two party system, with Labour and National the two major parties competing to form the government. The National Party formed in 1936 out of the remnants of the Reform and United parties. National brought together a socially conservative, anti-socialist, and free-enterprise coalition of farmers and business-oriented urban voters. The Labour Party has historically enjoyed far greater electoral support among Maori than does the National Party. The story of Maori land claim politics during and after the Second World War is therefore entangled in the web of partisan politics.

To summarize, the pre-war Maori land rights context was as follows. Though the Treaty of Waitangi guaranteed Maori rights over their lands, the Treaty itself had never been ratified by Parliament, and therefore had no legal force. The courts, in effect, did not have the power to recognize a Treaty-based land claim. The other legal basis for a land claim, the existence of customary aboriginal title, had not been tested. However, the history of land legislation and land loss effectively removed the possibility that the Court of Appeal would find aboriginal customary title to still exist. This meant that unlike the Nisga'a case in British Columbia, a Maori threat to ask the Court of Appeal to make an aboriginal title determination was not a particularly credible one, especially without a cue from the Court that it was willing to reconsider established law. No such cue was forthcoming.

Pressure for change needed to come from the political arena. The possibilities for policy change to negotiate land grievances would depend on Maori ability to build support around the cabinet table. The alignment between Maori and the Labour Party during the Depression meant that the ability for Maori to effect policy change in the recognition of their rights and aspirations was more likely when Labour was in power, but such a policy was never guaranteed.

CABINET AND ITS POLICY CHOICES (1943–1989)

Ad-Hoc Negotiation of Maori Land Claims in the WWII and Post-War Eras

There had always been demands from Maori for the government to address their land grievances and the Crown's role in their dispossession. In 1927, after years of lobbying from the Tainui tribe, the Liberal government established a commission of inquiry (the Sim Commission) to investigate the Crown's role during the late 19th century in the confiscation of Maori lands. The commission was only mandated to recommend whether some confiscation claims merited monetary compensation, not whether the confiscation policy was itself just or unjust.[15] The Labour government under Prime Minister Savage was involved in sporadic discussions with the Tainui tribal authorities in the late 1930s on the size of any monetary settlement, but the issue remained unresolved at the outbreak of the Second World War.

The willingness of Labour to address the land claims issue was always constrained by a party platform that stressed "equality with racial individuality,"[16] and this hesitation was even more strongly felt in the National Party, which had little in the way of linkages with the Maori political community. The Labour government addressed Maori issues primarily as class issues, and made progress in furthering social welfare reforms such as housing which would benefit Maori as equal, yet economically marginalized, citizens. The decision of the Labour government to focus its attention on confiscation claims, and not just class issues during the end of the war was a result of two factors.

The first factor was that Maori mobilization originally encouraged to support the war effort. In 1942, the Labour cabinet supported the creation of the Maori War Effort Organization, which was chaired by the four Maori Members of Parliament. The organization worked through tribal councils and sub-tribal structures to encourage voluntary recruitment among other things.[17] By the end of the war, Maori involved in the Maori War Effort Organization had begun using its auspices to encourage wider Maori political unity.[18]

The second was the growing importance of the Maori seats to Labour's majority in the House of Representatives. For the Labour government's first term (1935–1938), the party held 55 out of 80 seats, including the two Maori seats held by Ratana. By 1943, Labour's support in New Zealand's farming sector had softened considerably,[19] and Labour's majority whittled down to five seats. The support of the Maori representatives became the wedge on which the Labour government would rest. In 1946, Labour won a squeaker majority of 42 seats in the House, and the Maori seats made all the difference.

It was this conjuncture of Maori importance in the House and new Maori mobilization with the Maori War Effort Organization that got the Labour government negotiating a series of Maori land grievances in 1943.[20] The Labour government, with Maori Member of Parliament Eruera Tirikatene acting as the principal liaison between tribal authorities and the government, negotiated with the Tainui, Ngai Tahu, and Taranaki tribes on the size of monetary settlements which would constitute "full and final" settlements of these claims. In some ways, these claims were uncontroversial in that the Crown's confiscations and purchases of the lands at issue were clear breaches of its honor. The method of compensation, money in lieu of land or the return of sacred sites, proved controversial in the long run by maintaining a sense of continued injustice among Maori that would eventually reopen these settlements in the 1980s.

Although the Labour Party lost in the elections of 1949, the arrival of the conservative National Party to the front benches did not signal the immediate end of these negotiations. National "cleaned up" the series of negotiations which Labour had already begun and also negotiated with claimants whose claims were accepted as valid by the Surplus Lands Commission (established in 1946 under Labour's tenure). However, once the National government dispatched these last claims, it signaled the end of New Zealand's pro-negotiation stance. If there was any optimism about the National government's intention to build on Labour's policy legacy, and consider further Maori land claims, such optimism was firmly dashed in 1953. With no Maori Members of Parliament in its caucus, National did not have an Eruera Tirikatene to push for the further resolution of claims at the cabinet table. In 1953, the National government passed the Maori Affairs Act, section 155 of which held that "Maori customary title to land shall not be available or enforceable by proceedings in any court or in any other manner."[21]

This post-war attempt at negotiations is interesting for a number of reasons. Firstly, the period is relatively unaddressed in the New Zealand literature on the history of land claims.[22] What little consideration there is of this policy action questions whether these negotiations were indeed meaningful, arguing that the Maori had insufficient bargaining power to affect the nature or monetary size of any settlement.[23] Although the Minister of Maori Affairs was the lead minister bringing the issue of compensation to cabinet, the process was apparently driven by the Treasury department whose preoccupation was to limit the consideration of claims to those which had been investigated by an appointed commission of inquiry or the Maori Land Court, and to limit the size of any monetary compensation to the smallest amount that the Maori claimant would accept.[24]

The few accessible cabinet documents on file are not as informative of the cabinet debates as similar Canadian documentation during this period,[25] but a few characteristics of the spare evidence on how the National Party cabinet viewed the land claims issue are noteworthy.[26] There is absolutely no mention of the Treaty of Waitangi, and therefore no explicit linkage of these claims to the broader political agenda of Maori autonomy and rights. There is also no language placing these claims within a framework of formal equality or rights of citizenship, to which the National Party would have been more prone. There is no ideological treatment of the issue of Maori grievances and how these claims fit within the larger framework of Maori policy. These claims are addressed as compensation issues, with limited discussion on whether cabinet should seek further clarification on matters of law. The approach of cabinet seems very ad hoc and unconcerned with these claims as anything other than financial transactions of very little political consequence.

The apparent lack of political consequence of Maori land claims for the National government is also reflected in National's lack of interest in the Treaty as a national symbol. The only Treaty discussions held by the National cabinet during the 1950s was on whether to designate February 6th, the day the Treaty of Waitangi was signed, a national holiday. The Minister of Internal Affairs recommended in August 1950 that cabinet accept the New Zealand Founders Society's request that such action be taken.[27] The decision of cabinet to this suggestion was that since "there did not appear to be any general public desire for a special observance of the anniversary of the signing of the Treaty of Waitangi as a New Zealand day," cabinet would postpone further consideration. The record of the discussion indicated that " . . . The observance of [February 6] might tend to emphasize unduly the Maori aspects, whereas a New Zealand Day should be one recording all aspects of New Zealand development," particularly "the attainment and enjoyment by New Zealand of full constitutional and political capacity."[28]

Cabinet consideration of the Treaty was postponed for seven years, despite continued representation by the New Zealand Founders Society. In 1957, cabinet heard that new voices were added to this call for Waitangi Day, in the form of the Associated Chambers of Commerce, the Maori Women's Welfare League, and municipal councils.[29] Apparently the new evidence of widening public support for the idea six months before an election did the trick, and cabinet agreed to declare Waitangi Day a holiday. The National Party government fell in the 1957 election. The transition to Labour did not ensure quick action, as it took the second Labour government (1957–1960) three more years to introduce the required legislation. The legislation was forthcoming only after the Maori member of the Labour cabinet, Eruera Tirikatene, reportedly threatened to embarrass his own government by introducing a private member's bill should the government not act.[30]

The immediate post-war period in New Zealand demonstrates that policy initiatives on Maori issues which were explicitly linked to a special rights or treaty agenda were halting even under Labour governments (1935–1949, 1957–1960). The lack of widespread non-Maori interest in these rights meant there was insufficient pressure for Maori cabinet ministers (who were sidelined from the Maori Affairs portfolio) to build wider cabinet support for any meaningful pro-Maori policy action. When the National Party assumed power in 1949, it concluded Labour's negotiations, but National backed away from expanding Labour's initiative. The lack of wide public profile of land grievances and the lack of Maori voices within the National Party[31] made it easy for the National government to ensure that the land claims problem could be dispatched in 1953 by removing even mild judicial pressure on governments to act.

Maori Mobilization in the Public Eye: The 1960s

As land claims faded from Parliamentary debate and the public eye in the 1950s, demographic changes were underway that would usher in a new era of extra-parliamentary Maori politics in the late 1960s. In the post-war era, Maori joined the urbanization of the New Zealand population with a vengeance. As New Zealand's urban poor and working class increasingly took on a Maori face, two phenomena occurred. First, the Maori electorate entrenched itself further in the Labour Party. Second, urbanization led to the formation of new centers of pan-Maori political activism to complement, or compete with, the more legislative and partisan strategies of the established Maori political class. While the 1950s was a quiet decade for Maori protest on land grievances as far as the general public was concerned, this would change by the end of the 1960s. By 1970, a new generation of Maori political activists would emerge to embrace a wider repertoire of political activity, such as demonstrations, public petitions, and tent embassies.

It is difficult to overstate the demographic and political importance of Maori urbanization during and after World War Two. While urban drift was a national (indeed, global) phenomenon, rates of Maori urbanization far eclipsed those of the non-Maori population over the same time period. To illustrate, in 1926 only 8% of the Maori population was resident in urban areas, compared to 58% of the non-Maori population.[32] Maori and non-Maori were effectively segregated, and the rural Maori population was largely landless. Only two decades later, the 1945 census showed that the Maori urban population had doubled to 16% as landless Maori left the Depression-ravaged rural economy. The non-Maori urban population had only increased by 5% over the same period, to reach 63%. By 1956, one in four Maori lived in an urban area. By 1971, the Maori and non-Maori urbanization rates began to converge, with 70% of the Maori population and 81% of New Zealand's total population in urban centers.[33] Importantly, Auckland dominates New Zealand's urbanization story. From 1936 to 1956, Auckland's total population grew by 69%. The growth of Auckland's Maori population over these twenty years is astounding. In 1936, just under 2000 Maori lived in Auckland. By 1956, the Maori population grew to just over 11,000, a 500% increase. Auckland's *tangata whenua*,[34] the Ngati Whatua, soon found themselves the minority among Auckland's Maori. Not only were Maori drifting into cities at increasing rates, but the Maori population was growing quickly overall. With an average annual increase of 3.5%, the Maori population was growing one and half times quicker than New Zealand's non-Maori population.[35]

New political organizations arose based on the Maori's new urban reality and increasingly crossed tribal lines. The 1950s saw the establishment of new urban *marae* that brought together Maori who were separated from their traditional tribal networks. In 1951, the Maori Women's Welfare League organized to address the growing issues of Maori urban politics, inadequate housing and disappointing health statistics. The Maori Women's Welfare League, led by Whina Cooper, would pressure governments the traditional way, through linkages with the Labour Party and New Zealand's social service bureaucracy. While the Labour Party maintained deep linkages with the Maori political community, the sheer growth of the Maori population presented policy challenges that the National Party government could not ignore. With the four designated Maori seats held by Labour, no Maori in the National Party caucus and the Maori Women's

Welfare League identified with Labour as well, the National Party government thought to secure non-partisan policy advice from the Maori community through new mechanisms.[36] In 1962, the National Party government amended the Maori Welfare Act to establish the New Zealand Maori Council (NZMC), designed to be an elective institution representing "the Maori" voice and advising the government on Maori issues. The NZMC was based on the existing Maori council system, and was not accountable to tribal authorities. Some argued that the NZMC was possible only because none foresaw that it would have much real political power: " . . . the creation of such a body . . . could be conceded in 1961 because, with the land settled and Maori tribal structure greatly weakened, the Maoris would have neither reason nor inclination to use it for obstruction."[37] The circumstances of the NZMC's birth, a construction of the state whose raison-d'être was to meet the National Party's policy needs, meant that for its first decade at least, the NZMC represented a fairly conservative slice of Maori opinion.

The 1960s Maori political mosaic would be a swirl, a mix of new Maori voices and older tribal authorities. By 1970, these voices would converge behind a demand for meaningful recognition of the Treaty and the role of land dispossession underlying Maori poverty. The land issue would provide a basis for Maori cooperation much in the same way that it had united disparate indigenous voices in 1960s Canada. In New Zealand, Canada and Australia, events in the 1960s would challenge the equal citizenship and formal equality agenda, and put in its place a dialogue of indigenous special rights based on their status as the New World's oldest occupants. The initial politicization of Maori as a separate people carrying special rights would manifest itself through that particular New Zealand obsession: rugby.[38]

New Zealand's view of itself as constituting "one people" with equal rights for all was not without foundation. Maori had, after all, enjoyed universal male suffrage since 1879. New Zealand's women, Maori and non-Maori alike, were the world's first women to join a national electorate. The Maori did not share the history of official state-sponsored racism of the American South. Also, unlike Canada's and Australia's indigenous people, Maori have had a long history of formal inclusion within the apparatus of the state. Beginning in 1960, Maori activists used New Zealand's rugby experience to challenge New Zealand's "one-ness" and highlight the reality of growing racial economic inequality. New Zealand's national men's rugby team, the All Blacks, enjoyed a longstanding reputation as among the world's best. However, in keeping with apartheid, South Africa's policy of barring non-white athletes from sporting events held on South African soil, the New Zealand Rugby Union dropped Maori players from the All Blacks' roster when on tour in South Africa. Ironically, when in South Africa, the All Blacks were all white.

In 1960, the All Blacks were scheduled to play in South Africa without their Maori players. This time, however, the Rugby Union's accommodation of South Africa's apartheid regime became an opportunity to illustrate the fragility of New Zealand's "one nation" construct, since to divide the All Blacks would be to divide the nation. Maori and their supporters called upon the New Zealand government to intervene. The government's subsequent refusal to get involved in the Rugby Union's decision provided a basis for pro-Maori recruitment during the next decades. In 1973, the Labour government would cancel the tour amidst fear of protest violence, and in 1981, the Springboks would come to New Zealand and spark the largest bout of civil disobedience the country has since seen.

The 1960s rugby tour was the first inkling that many New Zealanders had "that Maori would be prepared to resort to new methods of organized protest,"[39] instead of channeling political demands through political parties or Parliament. The rugby tour issue also showed the potential for Maori activism to build linkages to non-Maori social activism. By the end of the 1960s, this new Maori activism extended the basis for unified Maori political action by joining older Maori voices for ratification of the Treaty into domestic law. The relative economic deprivation of Maori communities, disproportionate representation of Maori in prisons, and a wide array of social pathology was linked by Maori activism to the failure of New Zealand to stand by the bargain that the Treaty represented. In effect, Maori activism came into the 1970s drawing a causal chain from New Zealand's historic refusal to view the Treaty as a meaningful political compact to contemporary social welfare outcomes.

The inclusion of land dispossession within the causal story of Maori disadvantage had always been present, but it was explicitly politicized anew during this era of incubating protest. In 1967, the National Party government threw Maori land dispossession into a potent rhetorical brew already spiced up by rugby and racism, when it passed the Maori Affairs Amendment Act 1967. The legislation addressed the fragmentation of Maori land tenure across increasing numbers of owners. Both Maori and non-Maori agreed that fragmentation of tenure made it very difficult for Maori to make economically efficient use of the lands remaining in Maori control. The government's preferred solution to the fragmentation problem was based on two reports from the Department of Maori Affairs.[40] Both of these reports identified collective land tenure as an important source of Maori economic marginalization, and recommended various means of converting land from Maori freehold tenure to normal freehold title. Although the recommendations varied on how coercive the Crown could be in acquiring Maori lands,[41] the message to the National cabinet was one they were ideologically predisposed to hear. The solution to Maori economic development was not to address the Treaty and the rights it guaranteed, but to diminish further the role of Maori collective ownership within the land tenure system. Considering no Maori person was in cabinet and the Maori Affairs bureaucracy was uninterested in exploring solutions that respected the principle of Maori collective land tenure, it is little surprise that the 1967 legislation was passed.

Scholars and Maori activists identify the 1967 legislation as an important catalyst that brought urban and, increasingly, college-educated activist Maori to cooperate with the remaining rural and tribal Maori leadership.[42] The legislation served as a mechanism to bring different Maori groups together. It was a " . . . turning point whereby Maori opinion began to form a more articulate position on issues that directly affect Maoridom."[43] Just as Trudeau's white paper kick-started a new wave of indigenous protest in Canada, so too did the 1967 Maori legislation in New Zealand. Soon, Maori land dispossession, the ratification of the Treaty, Maori social outcomes, racism and Maori separateness were linked in the rhetoric used across groups. The NZMC, the Labour Maori Members of Parliament, and newer Maori voices joined in opposition to the legislation. "It is doubtful if any other piece of legislation concerning the Maori has been attended by so much publicity and heated debate."[44]

Although the old and the new sectors of Maori activism came to share policy demands, they did differ on the question of tactics. The younger, university educated, and more militant sectors of urban Maori activism would question the political strategies of their elders. Instead of working through partisan politics, they preferred direct and visible action. In 1970, two organizations formed to change the face of Maori politics. In Auckland, Maori youth activists based in university student politics formed Nga Tamatoa, The Young Warriors. Nga Tamatoa would soon have chapters in Christchurch and Wellington. Nga Tamatoa would be recognized as " . . . the first urban Maori protest group to employ 'Pakeha'[45] tactics such as demonstrations, petitions, and press releases."[46] The rhetoric of Nga Tamatoa borrowed heavily from the Black Power movement of the United States, and the issues of racism and land dispossession became increasingly intertwined in the public eye. Nga Tamatoa called publicly for the repeal of the Maori Amendment Act 1967, meaningful Maori control of Maori land, the cancellation of all sport contacts with apartheid South Africa, and the cancellation of Waitangi Day celebrations until the Treaty was truly honored.[47]

With Nga Tamatoa, Maori protest politics hit the streets, and from the perspective of your average white New Zealander, seemingly out of nowhere.

The National Party Considers Treaty Ratification, 1971

It was in this context of new protest politics that the issue of the Treaty of Waitangi finally made it to the National cabinet agenda. In March 1971, cabinet instructed the Ministers of Justice and Maori Affairs to prepare a paper on why previous governments had not ratified the Treaty. Cabinet instructed the Ministers to recommend whether the time was ripe to proceed with ratification.[48] After consultations with the Foreign Affairs department, the Ministers presented their joint policy paper.

The paper noted that ratification of the Treaty by Parliament is unnecessary if the Treaty is recognized as a Treaty under international law. If so, the government would be bound by its provisions regardless, and ratification would be unnecessary. The Ministers then noted that whether the Treaty is in fact a treaty under international law "cannot be answered in certainty." The paper's authors made no mention of the possibility of seeking a judicial determination of the Treaty's legal status. The Ministers concluded by recommending against the Treaty's ratification. The most pressing reason for this recommendation was the uncertainty of both the legal and political outcomes of ratification:

> The most important objection to giving the Treaty the force of law . . .
> is the uncertainty to which the incorporation of the very general language of Article II into New Zealand would give rise. However, what is sought by some Maori may well go further . . . What they really want is a Maori Bill of Rights following or based on the text of the Treaty, which would presumably have a status superior to that of an ordinary Act of Parliament.[49]

In this excerpt, the ministers linked the statutory recognition of the Treaty with a larger project of constitutional reform that compromised the hallowed principle of parliamentary sovereignty. The Ministers later asserted that such a constitutional reform would be nothing less than undemocratic and " . . . alien to New Zealand traditions and practice." The paper recognized, however, that government may well have to respond to Treaty grievances, because in the political climate of escalating protest, the document " . . . has a moral force that Governments will be less and less able to put aside." However, the Ministers did not find this moral force as yet adequate to spur government action, and recommended that cabinet decline to ratify the Treaty.

The National government offered symbolic appeasement in lieu of substantive action: "We think it possible that if some significant step were taken to increase the status of Waitangi Day for New Zealanders generally it would considerably diminish the concern and resentment that many Maori undoubtedly feel over the Treaty." This suggestion illustrates that the National Party cabinet had a limited appreciation of the depth of Maori feeling on the Treaty issue. They did, however, feel it was politically important to consult with the NZMC on which existing legislation the Council felt most contravened the spirit of the Treaty. However, cabinet demonstrated a lack of commitment to undertake a full review of the legislation when the Minister of Maori Affairs raised the idea a year later to establish a Standing Committee of Parliament to do precisely that, as "[his] colleagues did not support this proposal."[50]

In the absence of detailed survey analysis, there is no conclusive evidence that Maori issues were among those issues that drove the National Party from office in 1972.[51] The National Party had formed the government for twelve years. At the time, observers felt that the winds of change need not blow too hard to topple the over-tired and somewhat atrophied party from the government benches. "The National Government had virtually run out of ideas and energy, and the electorate seemed bored."[52] It was clear that the National Party's electoral position had been eroding in the years leading up to the 1972 election. Whether Maori protests since 1967 had a cumulative and discernable affect on New Zealanders' 1972 voting habits is hard to say.

The Third Labour Government and the Waitangi Tribunal, 1972–1975

The climate of protest may not have had a persuasive effect on the National government, but it provided both the pressure and the opportunity for the Labour Party to differentiate itself further from its competitor on the Maori issue after the November 1972 election. The engine behind Maori policy change in the third Labour government was Matiu Rata. A member of the Te Aupouri tribe of the country's far north, Rata's personal and political history encapsulated the larger changes affecting Maori in post-war New Zealand. Matiu Rata's family left rural New Zealand during the war years, and Rata spent his formative years in Auckland. By times a merchant seaman, laborer, and spray painter, Rata joined the two major networks that brought Maori into political leadership at the time: the Ratana church and trade unionism. He entered politics as an organizer for T.P. Paikea, the man who held the Northern Maori parliamentary seat for Labour. When Paikea died, Rata won the Northern Maori seat in 1963, and took on the mantle of parliamentary leadership.[53]

Rata distinguished himself on the Opposition benches, and in 1967, he was the Opposition's lead spokesman in the House against the Maori Welfare Amendment Act. He was a strong and vocal opponent of sporting contacts with apartheid South Africa, and had a key role in bringing Maori issues to the Labour Party by chairing its Maori Policy Committee. Matiu Rata led Labour to incorporate the Treaty's ratification as part of the official party program. When Labour won the 1972 election in a landslide, the Labour caucus chose Rata as New Zealand's first Maori Minister of Maori Affairs.[54]

Once installed in government, Rata identified the Treaty ratification issue as an important government priority, and cabinet quickly approved his request to submit a policy paper on ratification.[55] Two months later, Rata submitted draft legislation on the legal acknowledgement of the Treaty. Instead of approving the legislation immediately, cabinet chose to submit Rata's draft legislation to a caucus committee for intra-party consideration.[56] The momentum for the quick passage of legislation was evidently lost while Rata tried to build a coalition in caucus (as well as the cabinet) for his ratification legislation.[57] The Treaty of Waitangi legislation disappeared from cabinet's 1974 list of legislative priorities,[58] and did not resurface for discussion within the cabinet committee system until October of 1974.[59]

The draft legislation that Rata prepared after caucus consultation no longer proposed the ratification of the Treaty. The ratification proposal, which would implicitly change the balance of power in favor of the courts, did not have the support of caucus. The momentum for policy change was not totally lost, however. Rata proposed the establishment of a non-binding tribunal of inquiry, the Waitangi Tribunal, and empowered it to investigate "any act done or omitted or proposed to be done or omitted by or on behalf of the Crown or of any local authority."[60] Significantly, Rata's draft would allow a tribunal to investigate any government action, including all historical and current land grievances. The Tribunal alone would have the jurisdiction to interpret Treaty principles, with no appeal of that interpretation to the courts.

Despite these concessions, the proposed legislation met the resistance of cabinet members, for a number of reasons. Firstly, they were concerned about the scope of the bill to investigate historical grievances, and expressed " . . . that the Bill should be amended to make it explicit that it will refer only to acts done after the passing of this Bill. To re-open past legislation to the scrutiny of the tribunal would create an impossible situation."[61] Cabinet also insisted that the legislation restrict the Tribunal's mandate to investigate only the national government's actions. These were significant restrictions, and evidently battles Rata felt he could not win. He made the amendments, and in November 1974, introduced the legislation, named the Treaty of Waitangi Act, to Parliament.

From its introduction to Parliament until the following winter, the Tribunal legislation underwent public scrutiny. Early on, public submissions of the legislation were chiefly concerned with the Tribunal's inability to impose its recommendations on the government, and its inability to investigate historical grievances. Internally, Rata and the Maori caucus lobbied for the Tribunal to hear grievances arising after 1900 (rather than after 1975), but encountered roadblocks from senior officials within the conservative government departments like Justice, Finance, and Treasury.[62] Unlike the Canadian case at this time, the role of the Prime Minister seems quite marginal. Formerly the Minister of Finance and a relatively conservative voice in the party, Prime Minister Rowling emerges from cabinet pages as neither a strong ally nor a deterrent to the Waitangi Tribunal. Rata was left to build a consensus across the Labour cabinet and party on this controversial legislation during August and September of 1975, just months before the next election.

While Rata fought for the Tribunal legislation within caucus and cabinet, significant Maori political action was occurring outside of institutional politics. Frustrated with the continuing ability of the Crown to appropriate Maori lands,[63] a perceived lack of significant progress on Maori land issues, even under a Labour government, and the non-legal status of the Treaty, key Maori activists convened a meeting early in 1975. They formed a new group called Te Roopu Ote Matakite ("those with foresight"). Matakite's main goal was to fight for Maori land rights. By the end of April, Matakite had the support and personal involvement of representatives from Nga Tamatoa, the Auckland Maori District Council, the Maori Women's Welfare League, and the New Zealand Maori Council. Dame Whina Cooper accepted Matakite's request that she come out of retirement and lead the organization. Matakite also decided on its inaugural strategy: " . . . an arresting gesture that would unite Maoris under their banner and focus Pakeha attention on their concerns."[64] Their bold gesture was to hold a land march from the northern tip of the North Island to the national capital, Wellington, for a distance of 700 miles. The marchers would travel from *marae* to *marae*,[65] collecting New Zealand signatures on a land rights petition and the signatures of Maoridom's traditional leadership on a separate "memorial of right." For Whina Cooper, the march would accomplish the following:

> I wanted to draw attention to the plight of Maoris who were landless.
> I wanted to point out that people who were landless would eventually

be without culture. I wanted to stop any further land passing out of Maori ownership, and I wanted the Crown to give back to Maoris land it owned that was of traditional significance to Maoris. The march itself was to dramatise these things, to mobilize Maori opinion, to awaken the Pakeha conscience. And I agreed to lead it because the great leaders of the past were dead—Caroll, Ngata, Buck, Te Puea, Tau Henare, Paraire Paikea. I was the last one that had known all those people.[66]

As a recognized leader in her own right, Whina Cooper bridged generations of Maori leaders. She would invoke her role in symbolically linking Maori across time in the fight against land dispossession at the very beginning of the March. On September 14th, 1975, the octogenarian Whina Cooper, with one hand grasping her cane and the other her five year old granddaughter's hand, walked down a gravel track in New Zealand's north country, and the Land March was on. Nine days later, the marchers and "thousands of supporters" walked across the Auckland harbor bridge.[67] With the slogan "not one more acre," up to 30,000 people joined the Land March from September 14th to October 13th, collecting signatures from 60,000 supporters for the land rights petition. The Land March clearly identified land rights as the heart of Maori policies in a hugely public way. It was a particular challenge to the Labour Party, since it threatened to delegitimize Rata's leadership position should no adequate response be forthcoming. The Land March must have galvanized action within the Labour caucus, because the government passed Rata's legislation on October 10th, three days before 5000 marchers arrived on Parliament's front lawn in the rain.

One month later, Labour was tossed from power, and under Robert Muldoon, "a conservative man with fixed ideas,"[68] the National Party would hold the reins for another nine years. A land-rights backlash is not a likely source of Labour's downfall in the 1975 election. Firstly, opinion polling show a long-run favorable trend in voters' intention to vote National over the 1972–1975 period,[69] with the National Party gaining significant support in July 1975, two months before the marchers had left for Wellington.[70] Secondly, the National Party was able to turn the election into an indictment of Labour's stewardship of the economy. Robert Muldoon hammered the Labour government with the country's worsening economic situation. Rampant inflation, a trade deficit and the perceived weakness of Labour leader Rowling compromised Labour's electoral position.

This period in the early 1970s illustrates that the strength of the New Zealand norms of parliamentary sovereignty and consensual decision-making necessitated collective cabinet responsibility. These norms structured the thinking of both elected and unelected decision-makers in both political parties. Even with the concerted efforts of Matiu Rata, the Labour Party, which had publicly committed itself to ratification and therefore to giving the courts a much greater role in the question of land rights disputes, could not build an internal coalition, once in government, to effect this radical change. The Labour caucus also would not back the delegation of decision-making power to the Tribunal, an option which was never even considered by the National Party when in power. Thus, the feasible set of policy alternatives, meaning those which could achieve the necessary support across cabinet and caucus, were limited to either continual delay, establishing consultative mechanisms (commissions of inquiry or the Waitangi Tribunal), or negotiation. Interestingly, the spate of negotiations which ended in the early 1950s did not build a constituency of interest within the bureaucracy for a wider implementation of a negotiation policy, which by then the Trudeau government had established in Canada.

This period also shows that the polarization of Maori politics across the two competitive political parties meant that, in the absence of bureaucratic actors with a perceived self-interest in addressing Maori land claims, pressure for change from within the circles of power occurred only when Labour was in power. The historic Ratana-Labour alliance, forged in the depths of the Depression, delivered Maori votes, Maori political talent, and Maori electoral seats to the Labour Party. Since 1943, the Maori seats were " . . . the safest seats in the country."[71] However, the Maori political alliance with Labour did not guarantee success. It ensured the minimum condition that some Maori voices would be heard around the cabinet table and in caucus meetings. In the infrequent periods of Labour's tenure (1943–1949, 1957–1960, 1972–1975), the difficulties of building an internal consensus on a Treaty and Maori land policy were still serious enough that political contestation provided the external pressure necessary for even a Labour government to act.

With the Maori seats in the House of Representatives locked in the Labour firmament, and with Maori voters limited to the Maori electoral roll, the National Party had little electoral incentive to build meaningful linkages with the Maori community. The National Party could afford to be conservative in their Treaty policies. In its dying days, the third Labour government passed legislation that had the potential to make the National Party more responsive to Maori interests in the future. The Electoral Amendment Act 1975 gave a Maori person the option of enrolling on either the Maori or the general electoral roll. At each census, a Maori voter can choose where he thinks his vote would do the most good. This meant that since the 1978 election, Maori voters could cast their vote for their local parliamentary candidate.

1975–1984: The Muldoon Era

Highly combative, socially conservative, pugnacious and dictatorial, Prime Minister Robert Muldoon dominated his cabinet like perhaps no other Prime Minister in New Zealand's history.[72] One of his cabinet colleagues writes,

> Muldoon sat in his . . . office, surrounded by the instruments of power. There his ice-blue stare impelled subservient action from his staff . . . he acted as a general in total control, while his cabinet ministers remained tied to their more inflexible departmental systems . . . Even with this ministerial colleagues, Muldoon was ruthless. He dominated cabinet and made sure at every reshuffle that we all knew where the real power lay. That was perhaps natural enough: he was our leader. But his dictatorial sway reached to caucus, Parliament, the party and the media."

Muldoon allowed his ministers very little discretion in how to run their portfolios, and did not reciprocate the expectation of loyalty with a willingness to consult.[73] He also chose men for cabinet, many of them farmers and reflective of the National voting base, who shared his social conservatism. Maori grievances had landed on punishing soil.

As both the Prime Minister and the Minister of Finance, Muldoon's attention was dominated by the financial crises brought on by the oil shocks, rampant inflation, and careening balance of payments situation which devastated the New Zealand economy by the end of his tenure. Worsening economic conditions contributed to increasing Maori protest activity throughout this period, but the arguments of protesters linking Maori economic outcomes, land dispossession, historical land grievances, and rights to Maori self-determination found no sympathy with this Prime Minister. Philosophically, Muldoon embraced the value of cultural pluralism within a One Nation construct, and viewed the Land March as " . . . a symbol of discontent. No more than that."[74] He rejected historical land claims as "a nonsense." [75] Opportunities to change his thinking from inside government were difficult given the tone he set in cabinet.

The pressure to respond to Maori land grievances continued to mount from the outside, with protests and demonstrations increasing. Two demonstrations were extensively covered in the media. First, a Matakite splinter group established a tent embassy on Parliament's front lawn, demanding immediate action to the Land March. However, once he learned that the splinter group did not enjoy Whina Cooper's support, Muldoon had the police forcibly remove the tenters. Second, a group from the Ngati Whatua tribe occupied Bastion Point to protest the government's intention to allow a high-cost housing development in central Auckland. A valuable piece of Auckland real estate, the protesters argued that the government had acquired the land in a morally questionable (though legal) chain of events, and that the land should be returned to the Ngati Whatua, now basically landless.[76] The Bastion Point protest lasted 506 days. The protest ended in April 1978, when Muldoon had the police arrest 218 occupiers for trespassing.

With the tent embassy dispersed, but the Bastion Point protest keeping Maori land rights in the public eye, the Muldoon cabinet grudgingly implemented the Waitangi Tribunal in 1977. The cabinet had deferred a decision to implement Rata's Tribunal in 1976, but evidently, in 1977, the Tribunal's potential uses became more attractive. The value to the government of the Tribunal was mainly as a race relations pressure-valve, giving Maori a place to file their grievances rather than taking them to the streets. However, the Tribunal received minimal financial support during its early years. While unsympathetic to historical land grievances, the Muldoon government did make moves to address concerns over present-day Maori land loss in the face of a petition to Parliament by Dame Whina Cooper.[77] Cabinet approved the principle that Maori land compulsorily taken or alienated to the Crown for public purposes would be offered back to its Maori owners once that public purpose had ended, and the Crown would discuss reasonable terms with the Maori claimants.[78]

The prospects for a review of Maori land policy may have looked better after the 1978 election, when Muldoon appointed Ben Couch to the Maori Affairs portfolio. Couch was among three Maori who were elected to general seats for the National Party. Muldoon considered Couch a man of integrity, with "no time for radical views and the stirrers."[79] A former member of the All Blacks, Couch himself had been one of the Maori players barred from touring South Africa in 1949. Despite this experience, Couch toed the National Party position on sporting contacts with South Africa. Couch's more mainstream views on Maori political relations, his junior position within cabinet,[80] and the ethos of cabinet meant that a fundamental re-evaluation of the Treaty would not occur until the Muldoon era came to an end.

The Fourth Labour Government—Arbitration and Negotiation Emerge, 1984–1989

The fall of the Muldoon government in a snap election in June 1984 brought the Labour Party back to the Beehive.[81] The transition to Labour paved the way for new expertise and ideas on the status of the Treaty, and forced a new conversation at the cabinet table on the status of Maori as *tangata whenua* or "first peoples" within the constitutional structure of the New Zealand state.

Labour's renewed interest in Maori grievances was not solely a result of new energy and faces around the cabinet table. The once unquestioned alliance between Maori and Labour had undergone a serious schism in 1979. From 1975 to 1979, the Maori star of the third Labour government, Matiu Rata, suffered a series of demotions and was stripped of his Maori affairs portfolio in Labour's shadow cabinet. Rata reportedly did not enjoy the personal confidence of Labour Leader Rowling.[82] Politically isolated and personally diminished, Rata perceived that Labour was taking its Maori constituency for granted. He also felt that the Labour-Maori alliance had forced him to constantly compromise his political loyalties, as demonstrated by the concessions he had to make to pass the Waitangi Tribunal legislation through cabinet.[83] In a move which surprised the political world, Rata resigned from the Labour Party in November 1979. The move was highly controversial, drawing the ire of Maori who thought Labour remained the real vehicle for change, as well as the support of Maori who thought Maori politics had come of age and needed its own voice. Then, Rata founded Mana Motuhake, a new Maori political party to contest both general and Maori seats. In a 1980 by-election for the Northern Maori seat, Rata did not win, but managed to poll 37.9% of the vote. In 1981 and 1984, Mana Motuhake eroded the Labour vote,[84] but in both elections, Maori voters still cast their lot with the Labour Party. If voting for Labour was the most important expression of the Maori choice, non-voting was not far behind. With a 27% non-voting rate (compared with 11% for the general electorate),[85] Mana Motuhake had a large pool of Maori voters that it could potentially mobilize. While Maori voters still turned to the Labour Party, the fourth Labour government was aware that it could not take its traditional Maori electorate for granted.[86]

With Rata sitting on the other side of the House, new faces in the Labour Party drove its Maori policies. One of the Labour Party's driving forces in the reconsideration of Maori and the New Zealand state was Geoffrey Palmer, law professor and constitutional scholar. Palmer was a force to be reckoned with, and his workload in cabinet reflected his importance. Palmer assumed the portfolios of Deputy Prime Minister, Minister of Justice, Attorney-General, and Leader of the House in Prime Minister David Lange's first cabinet.

Palmer writes that his approach to Maori issues was significantly affected by his experiences at the University of Chicago Law School, at the height of the civil rights movement. In his studies of American constitutional law, he became impressed with the role of the judiciary in protecting minority rights, as established by the *Brown v. Board of Education* decision.[87] This experience was the foundation of Palmer's long-running scholarly concern with the lack of effective checks to executive power in New Zealand. As an expert on the New Zealand executive branch writes, New Zealand has " . . . a political executive untroubled by challenges to its hegemony by an interfering and retarding upper house, by federal components to the political system with their own sources of power and authority, by judicial review of its decisions, or . . . by troublesome, multiparty parliaments."[88] The only significant check to executive power is a maximum electoral term of three years. Palmer sought to rectify this fundamental imbalance of power once in office.

The second source of Palmer's intellectual development was the growing reputation of the Waitangi Tribunal. As a new and untried institution, the Muldoon government largely ignored it. However, under the stewardship of the Tribunal's Maori Chairman, Judge Eddie Taihakurei Durie, the Tribunal began to incorporate Maori practices into its meetings, and became generally more sensitive to the political and cultural context of its Maori claimants. The Tribunal began to develop a positive reputation among Maori. Starting in the early 1980s, the Tribunal released reports on contemporary environmental management issues that put up front and centre the principles of Treaty as guiding its own recommendations for government action. The Tribunal, a commission of inquiry, was effectively developing a Treaty-based Maori rights jurisprudence that emphasized the principle of political partnership between Maori and non-Maori. The Tribunal offered pragmatic solutions that gave practical effect to the partnership principle. Palmer writes that the sound approach and growing credibility of the Tribunal provided "an intellectual and legal framework which could be relied upon with confidence and adopted by the courts."[89]

Palmer had also drawn a different causal link between the evidence of a Maori social underclass and the government's recognition of the Treaty. Unlike his predecessors in cabinets past, he identified negative social outcomes of the larger Maori community as the consequence of New Zealand's historic refusal to honor the partnership principle at the heart of the Treaty: " . . . Social deprivation which threatened the fabric of the New Zealand community was caused, at least in part, by serious injustice which the Crown resolutely refused to address. Measures were required to address both the social deprivation and the injustice—to deal with one and not the other would not be enough."[90] Palmer's view was both to limit the power of the executive in the arbitrary use of power, and to provide Maori with leverage to force future governments to the bargaining table, since ultimately, it was through negotiation with Maori that grievances would be resolved.

Palmer's interest in the judicial limitation on executive power and his views on the Treaty led him to pursue a multi-pronged approach to reform in cabinet and in caucus. This reform approach consisted of three policy proposals. The first sought to strike a new balance of power between the judicial and executive branches of the New Zealand state. He proposed an entrenched Bill of Rights that would incorporate the Treaty of Waitangi among its articles. Palmer thought that " . . . no supreme law for New Zealand can be contemplated unless it contains appropriate recognition of the Maori as *tangata whenua*." Through an entrenched Bill of Rights, Palmer would give the courts the power to trump Parliament by disallowing legislation according to Treaty principles.[91] This proposal was a huge challenge to New Zealand's political culture. The second policy proposal was to expand the role of the Waitangi Tribunal to hear grievances dating to 1840. This proposal was at once a reward to the Tribunal for its pragmatism and also an attempt to mainstream protest politics. The third policy proposal was to incorporate mention of the principles of the Treaty into government legislation as a matter of standard practice. This was an interim measure the government would pursue while discussions on the Bill of Rights developed.

Palmer and the Minister of Maori Affairs, Koro Wetere, worked jointly in spearheading the process of building consensus within cabinet on these three policy initiatives. Even though these initiatives had been part of policy discussions within the Labour Party prior to the election of 1984, Palmer indicates that support for them around the cabinet table or across officialdom was neither assured nor universal.[92] Palmer's suggestion of ideological qualms around the cabinet table does not include an exploration of who exactly represented the counterforce, but Palmer does indicate that part of the problem in undertaking this process of consensus-building lay in the lack of expertise and intellectual vibrancy on Treaty issues within the senior bureaucracy itself. Uninterested and in the past not called upon by Ministers to consider the Treaty during the policy development stage, the senior public service was largely incapable of advising Ministers on the impact of the Treaty principles across the policy spectrum. Palmer singled out the Maori Affairs bureaucracy for its stellar lack of policy development capacity. Consequently, the task of preparing papers outlining the policy implications for his three proposals came to rest within the Justice and Treasury departments.[93] The initial task of building bureaucratic expertise within the Justice department to support Palmer and Wetere's reform proposals also needed to extend to other departments as the Waitangi Tribunal's on-going investigations reached out to cross all sectors of public policy, including fisheries, agriculture, pollution management, language, and of course, land. By June of 1986, officials had canvassed their departments and identified difficulties in applying Treaty principles to current areas of policy. They agreed to incorporate a mandatory reference to the Treaty during the policy approval stage of all future legislation.[94]

While the building of Treaty expertise was a long term challenge for Palmer and Wetere, they were successful in getting cabinet approval to develop the Bill of Rights proposal for parliamentary consideration as well as pushing through the amendments to the Waitangi Tribunal. Palmer introduced the Bill of Rights policy paper to Parliament in 1985, and the parliamentary hearing process began Palmer's attempt to build a public coalition of support behind the proposal. Despite work with the Maori caucus and in the Maori community, the submissions to Parliament by Maori voices were mixed and underwhelming.[95] Palmer identifies the "suspicious, uneasy, doubtful, or undecided" attitude among Maori as the factor which eventually "sank" the possibility of moving forward with a Bill of Rights that included the Treaty.[96] Palmer thus suggests that in the face of divided Maori opinion, he could not have swayed uncertain members of cabinet to support the inclusion of the Treaty in a Bill of Rights.

On the issue of expanding the Tribunal's investigative mandate and capacities, Maori opinion was solid, and cabinet moved quickly. Within five months of assuming office, Koro Wetere sought and received cabinet approval to move the legislation amending the Tribunal to the top of the government's legislative priorities, and by December 1984, cabinet approved the draft legislation.[97] The value of the Tribunal to the Labour Government lay in its growing reputation and legitimation among Maori as well as in its role in interpreting the terms of the Treaty. The Tribunal had made itself useful. It could viably act as a pressure valve for Maori dissension, which would otherwise find its way to the streets, and it provided an independent source of ideas on which public officials could draw in their new task of incorporating analysis of the Treaty in the policy development process.

The growing reputation and usefulness of the Waitangi Tribunal to the Labour government is reminiscent of the Trudeau government's acceptance of the Indian Claims Commissioner within the Canadian context. A direct comparison as well is the emphasis of both commissions on the appropriateness of political solutions to indigenous grievances. The Tribunal consistently advocated the development of consultation and negotiation mechanisms between government departments and appropriate Maori tribal and sub-tribal groups as the appropriate means of establishing the partnership principle at the heart of the Treaty. It is within this context of growing ideological commitment to a partnership between Maori and non-Maori that Palmer and Wetere revived ad hoc negotiations on the key claims which languished under Muldoon's tenure.

The Court Speaks: The Lands Case, Arbitration, then Negotiation

The 1989 decision of the Labour government to establish a formal negotiations policy, thereby moving from an ad hoc and reactive to a consistent and proactive approach to the negotiation of Maori grievances, is a result of the series of political events unleashed by the Court of Appeal's 1987 decision in what has become known as the Lands Case.[98] Like the Supreme Court's *Calder* decision in Canada, the Lands Case provided a huge catalyst to focus cabinet's attention on Maori grievances and on how these grievances related to the government's wider policy goals. The court decision allowed Maori negotiators to wield new leverage because the achievement of the government's economic restructuring policies depended on how well the government responded to Maori land claims. The court decision placed the cabinet under un-ignorable pressure. Like in Canada, delay and an ad hoc approach to Maori land grievances around the cabinet table were no longer feasible. This pressure allowed Palmer to override the dissent of his colleagues. Key to the story of how New Zealand came to adopt a negotiations policy are the support from a senior cabinet minister for far-reaching initiatives supporting Maori self-determination, the political acumen of the New Zealand Maori Council to push Palmer from outside cabinet, and the political pressure which had been the product of years of Maori political protest. This meant that cabinet simply could not legislate Maori rights away, as it had in 1953.

The linking of Maori land claims with Labour's neo-liberal program of economic restructuring occurred during the drafting of the government's key economic legislation, the State-Owned Enterprises Act (hereafter SOE Act). Following the devaluation of the New Zealand dollar in July 1984, the Labour government undertook radical liberalization of the economy. The restructuring of the state sector was part and parcel of New Zealand's radical economic refurbishment. Under the government's program, the government created corporations to manage state assets free from ministerial control. Managers of the SOEs were charged with running these corporations as profitable enterprises subject to the pressures of the free market. These state assets included land, forests, electricity, and coal. The transfer of these assets to SOEs, Maori feared, would make it difficult for the government " . . . [to return] transferred lands to Maori were there to be successful claims to the Tribunal in the future,"[99] especially if the SOEs were to create new property interests in these lands. Therefore, the SOE Act included two sections. Section 27 prevented a SOE to sell lands subject to a Maori claim registered with the Waitangi Tribunal before the enactment of the legislation. Section 9 would become its critical section: "Nothing in this Act shall permit the Crown to act in a manner inconsistent with the Treaty of Waitangi."

The account of why the government included these sections in the legislation is somewhat mixed. One scholar attributes it to the recommendation of the Waitangi Tribunal to protect Maori interests.[100] Geoffrey Palmer, the Minister responsible for drafting all government legislation, writes that its inclusion was deliberate and part of his policy initiative of incorporating references to the Treaty into government legislation.[101] Interviews I conducted with Treasury officials in Wellington indicated that the section was a throw-away, or "window-dressing" clause inserted in the eleventh hour of late-night legislative drafting, with little understanding of its future consequences. The truth is probably a mix of all three accounts. Whatever the reasoning, the legislation was enacted on December 18th, 1986.

Despite the assurance sections 27 and 9 were meant to provide, the New Zealand Maori Council started legal proceedings in the Court of Appeal. The Council sought greater protection of Maori interests with respect to claims filed into the future before the SOE policy was implemented. By seeking a judicial determination, the Chairman of the Council, Sir Graham Latimer, took a strategic risk that the Court would not rule in the Council's favor. Although a lower court ruled in favor of Maori customary fishing rights in a recent case,[102] the Crown had not yet pursued the case to test the thinking of the Court of Appeal. Although the Lands Case did not put the question of customary land rights before the court, it was the first case relating to Maori rights in land where the Court of Appeal had the opportunity to interpret section 9 of the SOE Act. To explain his thinking behind pursuing the case, Sir Latimer indicated that 10 years previously, he would not have tested the Court's thinking, fully expecting the Court's rejection of Maori rights at that time.[103] However, the Waitangi Tribunal had been actively developing its thinking on the Treaty principles since the early 1980s, and the judicial context was ripe for change.

Latimer's gamble paid off. The Court of Appeal delivered five separate judgments on June 29th, 1987. The Court was very close to according the Treaty of Waitangi constitutional status, ruling that the Treaty conferred a moral and political (but not a legal) obligation upon the government to enact legislation which did not contravene the terms of the Treaty.[104] The finding of the court was to order the government and the Maori Council to develop a system of safeguards: " . . . as regard claims made on or after 18 December 1986 the system should aim to ensure, if there is any likelihood that the Waitangi Tribunal will recommend return to Maori ownership, that such a recommendation could be acted upon."[105]

In early July, cabinet sat down to review its options in light of the Lands Case. Cabinet overruled the option of further litigating the issue by seeking an appeal of the Court's decision to the Privy Council.[106] To do so would undermine New Zealand's national independence by inviting outsiders to interpret the meaning of the Treaty within New Zealand's constitutional structure.[107] The system of safeguards had to protect Maori interests in lands as well as allow the government to continue with its economic restructuring program. The Labour government, Geoffrey Palmer specifically, was left to design such a response: " . . . In effect what the court said was the Crown had to come up with a scheme and there was not much guidance in the judgments about what its elements should be. Hammering out those details was one of the most challenging tasks I ever faced as a minister."[108]

Like the Trudeau government thirteen years before, the government of New Zealand faced a court decision that forced the government to do something, but the discretion about what that something would be rested with cabinet. The Minister of Justice and his team of officials derived a set of conditions which any institutional mechanism for the protection of future land claims needed to meet. The central quandary for the Minister was how to protect future claims from the actions of future governments in a parliamentary system with few formal checks on executive power in a political culture which considered parliamentary sovereignty a virtue and a politicized judiciary a vice. The government could only credibly provide such protection by allowing itself to be bound into the future by the decision of an independent actor that was somehow democratically accountable. Palmer and his advisors needed to execute a tricky tap dance.

Part of a solution was to delegate some authority to the institution which proved to have the capacity to interpret the Treaty and had earned the confidence of Maori and non-Maori alike, the Waitangi Tribunal. Palmer proposed a system where lands would be transferred to SOEs and only sold to other interests with a caveat that assets may be under claim. The role of the Waitangi Tribunal would be to investigate a Maori claim to those assets, and make a binding determination on whether they should be returned to the Maori claimant. If the Tribunal made such a determination, the Crown would be liable to the SOE and any third party for compensation.

The weakness of this solution is that the Tribunal exists as a result of the Treaty of Waitangi Act. A simple parliamentary statute, it requires a simple majority in the House to change its terms. The Waitangi Tribunal can be abolished or changed by a majority government as long as the government maintains the confidence of the House. The Tribunal's survival, in other words, rests primarily on its own political legitimacy.[109]

Talks between Palmer and Latimer halted during the 1987 election campaign, but continued after the electorate returned Labour to power. Latimer sought not only the strengthening of the Waitangi Tribunal, but also sought reasonable assurances that the powers of the Tribunal would not be weakened by statute at a later date. The answer lay not in placing further legal constraints in the government's path, but in formalizing the consideration of Treaty issues within the machinery of cabinet government. Cabinet agreed to establish a standing cabinet committee on Treaty of Waitangi issues, and to develop procedures and expertise for the direct negotiation of Maori grievances.

The Labour government's private decision in November 1987 to pursue a negotiations policy is therefore the companion piece to giving the Waitangi Tribunal the power to adjudicate some of the claims which would come before it. Adjudication would present future cabinets with significant fiscal risk should they not address Maori grievances, while direct negotiation of claims with the Crown would in theory decrease the likelihood that aggrieved Maori would seek an arbitrated solution. A direct negotiation policy would also signal to Maori and others that cabinet was not prepared to cede the tasks of governing to either the Tribunal or the courts.

From late 1987 to 1989, the Labour government began developing the mechanisms which would be necessary for a negotiations approach to Maori land grievances. The Treaty of Waitangi Policy Unit was established within the Justice department in 1988. Work began on developing the principles which would form the substantive parameters of the Crown's negotiation policy and would coordinate the Crown's position on claims coming before the Tribunal. The cabinet did so under continuing pressure, since the successful Lands Case sparked further litigation on Maori rights to coal, fisheries, and later on, broadcasting. Geoffrey Palmer became Prime Minister in August of 1989, and he reports that by that time, cabinet members were raising their increasing concern with losing the momentum on Treaty matters to the courts. The time came to "take the initiative."[110] Cabinet needed to signal to the courts and the wider public that the executive, not the judiciary, would drive Treaty policy. In December of 1989, the government publicly announced its commitment to enter into direct negotiations with Maori claimants.

In October 1990, the fourth Labour government fell, and was reduced to a mere 29 out of 97 seats in the House. Labour paid for its huge neo-conservative economic restructuring efforts. However, the National Party continued to implement Labour's negotiation policy. Sir Douglas Graham, a conservative business man from Auckland, had Prime Minister Jim Bolger's confidence. Sir Graham assumed the Minister of Justice and the new Minister in Charge of Treaty of Waitangi Negotiations portfolios. The National government remained committed to Labour's negotiation policy.[111] The negotiations, above all else, would recognize the Crown's historical wrongs, lead to a modern reconciliation, and allow Maori and the state to restore their relationship. In an April 2001 interview, a senior National Party member argued that a negotiation response would have occurred given the cumulative pressure of Maori protests, but he speculated that the Lands Case brought about a negotiation response "ten years sooner." The political calculation, he argued, was not electoral, as National did not think it would gain Maori votes and expected to lose non-Maori votes. The National cabinet believed negotiation to be "in the right," and so the negotiation policy continued under its stewardship.

REFLECTIONS ON THE NEW ZEALAND CASE

This study explores the emergence of indigenous land claim negotiation policies in a comparative perspective. I have established the two basic decisions an executive must make in order to choose a negotiation response. This first is to recognize indigenous rights as special rights, flowing from indigenous people's status as pre-existing political communities and their own systems of law. This recognition dimension requires policy-makers to accept, if grudgingly, that indigenous politics goes beyond the politics of equal rights and equal citizenship. The second basic decision an executive must make to arrive at a negotiation outcome is not to delegate decision-making power to a third party. To negotiate is to resolve a dispute face to face, rather than calling upon a judge or arbitrator to rule in one party's favor over another.

In the New Zealand context, the recognition dimension has been less contentious than in Canada or Australia. The existence of one treaty covering both the North and South Islands, as well as the history of land alienation from Maori to the Crown and on to the settler population, have decreased the potential cost of recognition. They did so by making it very unlikely that customary land rights continue to burden land titles, thereby decreasing the political uncertainty surrounding a recognition decision. This does not mean, however, that a decision to recognize Maori land rights and special rights was costless. To negotiate with Maori over historical land grievances still departed from an assimilationist or equal citizenship agenda. To negotiate claims was to strengthen the Maori claim that the predominant or most important relationship between Maori and the state was as *tangata whenua*, not as undifferentiated citizens of a unified nation. To negotiate was to give symbolic credence to the Maori claim that the Crown and Maori tribes were equal parties in the foundation of the colony.

This chapter shows that a strong norm of parliamentary sovereignty colored policy-makers' views on the appropriateness or the cost of delegation in the New Zealand context. The strength of this norm differentiates New Zealand from both Canada and Australia. At each choice opportunity, policy-makers resisted measures that would give courts a greater role in resolving Maori grievances with the Crown. Sir Apirana Ngata, Matiu Rata, and Geoffrey Palmer each pushed proposals to give Maori more political leverage through the courts, and each failed to some degree. Ngata met the resistance of key legislative drafters; Matiu Rata could not bring cabinet and caucus on side with his initial vision for the Waitangi Tribunal; and Geoffrey Palmer would back away in the end from his entrenched Bill of Rights. Only Geoffrey Palmer would partially succeed in his agenda, but only in the extraordinary circumstances unleashed by the Lands Case. And yet, while Palmer was forced to delegate some power to the Waitangi Tribunal, he also deemed it absolutely necessary to rebuild the state-Maori relationship through direct negotiation.

The New Zealand case therefore shows the limits of the blame avoidance hypothesis which would predict that as issues become increasingly contentious, governments should be more willing to delegate decision-making capacities to the courts or other actors. The blame avoidance hypothesis predicts delegation in the presence of political contention, but it does not factor in the importance of political norms that condition governments' view of how judicial and executive power is properly balanced. In this parliamentary system, cabinet has always jealously guarded its power to govern, and viewed the judicial option as inherently compromising that power.

It was Maori protests, such as rugby demonstrations, the Land March, tent demonstrations, and annual demonstrations on Waitangi Day that convinced policy-makers the long-term relationship between Maori and the Crown required fixing. The protests put land rights and the vehicle for those rights, the Treaty, up front and center. Land rights and the Treaty became issues on which a significant cross-section of Maori voices could agree. So long as protests continued, the political costs of inaction or delegation mounted, since a government could hardly enjoy victories in the courts if Maori could continue the struggle in the press and on the street. Maori protest led policy-makers and others outside government to question the costs of previous policies and future strategies. The New Zealand case shows that like the Canadian, the introduction of a negotiation policy was preceded by 1) the ad hoc negotiation of particular claims, 2) the political mobilization of Maori outside of the mainstream parliamentary institutions, and 3) the growing credibility of an independent commission of inquiry which recommended negotiation as the appropriate mechanism for addressing Maori land grievances.

The Lands Case, like the *Calder* decision in Canada, removed cabinet's do nothing or "wait it out" option, and so provided the pressure for cabinet to reach a consensus on significant policy change. The Court of Appeal decision gave Maori important leverage by legitimating the principle of partnership inherent in the Treaty of Waitangi compact, but just as importantly, the court made its historic decision when the New Zealand Maori Council had allies around the cabinet table, a credible outside ally in the Waitangi Tribunal, and the political wherewithal to make the most of the opportunity. In 1987, Maori leaders were able to work with their cabinet allies to prevent the erosion at the cabinet table of the momentum gained in court, in contrast to their inability to stop the National government from eroding their rights in 1953. With the National Party in power, no allies around the cabinet table, and no protest demonstrations to make a long-run negotiation strategy attractive, it is difficult to see how a judicial decision in the early 1950s affirming Maori rights would not have simply been overturned and negated through cabinet fiat. Therefore, cabinet's decision to negotiate in 1989 must be seen as the outcome of the important sequencing between prior Maori political mobilization and subsequent judicial change, rather than judicial change alone.

Chapter Five
Cabinet Decision-Making and Indigenous Land Rights in Australia (1945–1998)

INTRODUCTION

On August 16th, 1975, Labor Party Prime Minister Gough Whitlam made an important political pilgrimage to Wattie Creek, a remote area on a large pastoral property in Australia's Northern Territory. There, the Prime Minister poured a handful of soil into the awaiting hand of Vincent Lingiari, a stooped and aged cattle stockman and elder of the Gurindji people. Though the photo of the event would become the iconic image of Australia's first recognition of aboriginal land rights, the Prime Minister did not let the picture say it all. Lest he be misunderstood, the Prime Minister added:

> I want . . . to promise you that this act of restitution which we perform today will not stand alone—your fight was not for yourselves alone and we are determined that Aboriginal Australians will be helped by it . . . Vincent Lingiari, I solemnly hand to you these deeds of proof, in Australian law, that these lands belong to the Gurindji people and I put into your hands this piece of earth itself as a sign that we restore them to you and your children forever.[1]

The Prime Minister clearly signaled that the Commonwealth's response to the Gurindji land claim would form the basis of future government policy toward aboriginal land claims. The trip to Wattie Creek was not just an effort to bring good tidings to one old aboriginal man. The trip was also supposed to build public support for the Prime Minister's new land rights legislation introduced in the House of Representatives earlier in June. Did the Commonwealth legislation institute a negotiation policy? The answer is yes, kind of. Gough Whitlam's land rights legislation was a radical turning point in Australia's aboriginal policy, but it was limited.

Though a policy of the national government, the legislation did not implement a nation-wide land rights policy. The legislation established a negotiation policy where aboriginal people in the Northern Territory would join
miners, the government and pastoralists in the wider land management bargaining table. Unlike the 1973 Canadian and the 1989 New Zealand policies, Gough Whitlam's 1975 initiative was geographically limited to land
claims arising in the Northern Territory, and invited only 15% of Australia's indigenous community to a land rights bargaining table.[2] It would take
18 more years of fits and starts before the Commonwealth would enact the
Native Title Act in 1993, and force the States to negotiate land rights under
the Commonwealth's statutory land rights regime.

Like the Canadian and New Zealand cases, the Australian case illustrates the importance of aboriginal political mobilization to redefining the
place of land and land rights within the Australian Commonwealth government's aboriginal policy goals. From 1945 to the mid 1960s, aboriginal
policy reform was driven by an equal rights and civil libertarian agenda
where aboriginal land rights did not gain the support of mainstream social
welfare reformers. Prior to the 1960s, policy-makers and others generally
believed that the recognition of collective indigenous rights would circumvent the basic goal of aboriginal policy—assimilation. Australia's aboriginal people would win support for the extension of individual rights and
civil liberties, voting rights for instance, but not land rights. The issue of
aboriginal land rights did not clearly emerge on the public scene as the
primary ingredient in aboriginal demands for policy reform until the Gurindji began their protest at Wattie Creek. Land rights would become an
unavoidable issue in the cabinet deliberations on aboriginal policy, when
the Gurindji claim was quickly followed by the Gove land rights decision
in 1971, and the tent embassy protest in Canberra in 1972. Aboriginal
political mobilization and public protest in Australia, from 1967 to 1972,
marked the arrival of aboriginal people as a political force in Australian
politics. Though less developed organizationally than their counterparts
in Canada and New Zealand at the time, by 1972 Australian aboriginal
activists demonstrated that land rights *could* unify and mobilize the wider
aboriginal community across rural and cultural divides. The aboriginal
community showed its ability to influence mainstream public opinion and
garner limited support for the recognition of their customary rights. Not
coincidentally, Gough Whitlam first promised that the Labor Party would
recognize customary land rights when he visited aboriginal activists at the
tent embassy protest in 1972.

Gough Whitlam made his promise while in Opposition. His promise
marked the endpoint in a process of differentiation that led the Labor Party

to support aboriginal rights, while the Country and Liberal Parties spurned them. As in New Zealand, the cleavages structuring the party system would have important implications for how political parties would approach the aboriginal land rights issue. The Country and Liberal Parties represented rural and socially conservative interests that would resist aboriginal collective rights for both material and ideological reasons. The Labor Party, by contrast, would find its support among those voters more willing to accommodate indigenous collective rights claims—the urban professionals of the New Left, students, and social welfare activists who increasingly allowed that aboriginal control of land and its resources could further, not hinder, aboriginal integration and advancement.

Once the Labor Party committed itself to recognizing aboriginal land claims, the question of how it would do so was perhaps less structured than in the other parliamentary cases. Once the Labor Party chose to recognize land rights, the decision of whether or not to resolve land grievances by delegating decision-making power to the courts or an arbitrator was wide open. With no historical precedent of bargaining between the Crown and aboriginal people, policy-makers were not wedded to a particular bargaining model. There was no clearly defined policy alternative that the Commonwealth's bureaucracy historically favored, as in Canada, and there was no innate suspicion against delegation that so affected New Zealand's policy-makers. In this Australian context of relatively undefined policy alternatives, an independent actor commissioned by the Labor government would have enormous influence in designing the institutions to resolve land claims disputes. Ted Woodward, the Australian Land Rights Commissioner, would be an important champion for a non-delegation response. Avoiding blame through a delegation strategy would not solve the political problem that aboriginal political mobilization had created. Woodward was convinced that a political rather than a legal solution would build an on-going relationship between aboriginal peoples and the Australian state. Woodward's solution was to reject the Canadian model of negotiating one-time regional agreements, but to accept a negotiation model whereby aboriginal people would have a seat at an on-going bargaining table with the government and mining companies. Woodward's vision would be the underpinning of Gough Whitlam's land rights legislation.

The Australian case shows both the importance and the limitations of judicial change in explaining the emergence of land claim negotiation policies. Like the *Calder* case in Canada, the 1971 Gove land rights case was the first test of aboriginal title in Australia's courts.[3] The final judgment in the Gove land rights case, however, denied the existence of aboriginal land rights within Australia's common law. The denial of aboriginal rights by the court did not, however, mean that the government of the day did not have to make a policy response. Though the Country-Liberal government chose not to recognize aboriginal rights as a result of the court decision, the court decision itself served to further outrage aboriginal activists. The judicial decision did not prevent the Labor party from making its bold step to recognize what the court would not. In the presence of a politically mobilized aboriginal constituency, the Gove land rights decision was a blow to aboriginal hopes, surely, but it was not a death knell for further policy reform.

The partial implementation and fitful diffusion of Australia's land rights negotiation policies also stands as a useful contrast to the Canadian and New Zealand experiences. The Australian case still shows how the sequencing of indigenous political mobilization and judicial change led the Commonwealth government to recognize land rights and to provide a negotiated process as an alternative to grievances' resolution through litigation alone. The Australian case also shows how the sequencing of political mobilization and judicial change can be a necessary, but insufficient condition for the emergence of a national land rights negotiation policy. The Australian case illustrates perhaps even more strongly than the Canadian the influence of federalism on constraining the implementation of negotiation policies to those areas where governments do not risk intergovernmental conflict. The constraint of intergovernmental peace is particularly acute in the Australian case, for it was only under the extraordinary political pressures brought on by the High Court's *Mabo* decision in 1992 that the Commonwealth would find the political will to impose a land rights regime on resistant State governments.

This chapter proceeds as follows. First, I establish the historical context in the World War Two period. I then examine how demographic and economic changes in the 1950s and early 1960s led the aboriginal policy community to demand a constitutional amendment in 1967. The 1967 constitutional referendum gave the Commonwealth government the right to legislate in aboriginal affairs across the entire country. The 1967 referendum therefore marks the beginning of the Commonwealth's role in making truly national aboriginal policies. The next section of the chapter examines each opportunity the Commonwealth cabinet had to consider and reconsider its approach to aboriginal rights. The main choice opportunities are the following: a 1968 response to the Gurindji claim; a 1971 response to the Gove land rights decision; a post-1972 response to the tent embassy and the Woodward Commission reports; the attempt during the 1980s by the Labor government to extend the Northern Territories land rights scheme across the Australian polity; the catalyst of the 1992 *Mabo* decision and the struggle that yielded the Native Title Act of 1993. The national advocacy of aboriginal groups and organizations was a critical component in the drive to the Native Title Act. The final section of the chapter outlines, however, how fragmentation across and within aboriginal claimant groups at the local level has challenged States' negotiation strategies on the ground. I examine the impact of this fragmentation in a case study of Western Australia.

SETTING THE SCENE

Aboriginal Policies Prior to World War Two

Although the initial colonies that came to form Canada and New Zealand negotiated treaties with indigenous people, the Australian colonies never negotiated land cession agreements. The British asserted their sovereignty and assumed ownership of the Australian continent on the legal basis of *terra nullius*. The legal doctrine of *terra nullius* or "vacant land" held that if lands were uninhabited at time of discovery, the act of discovery vested in the colonial Crown both sovereignty over and unencumbered ownership of the land. The Crown held its title to the land with no encumbrances, and was free to dispose of its lands as it wished (e.g. through lease or sale). In the Australian case, the legal system got around the plain fact that the continent was inhabited by concluding that the aboriginal peoples were uncivilized, could not have a system of laws, and therefore, the continent was deemed legally uninhabited and up for grabs. The constitutional classification of the colony as *terra nullius* effectively voided aboriginal title as a matter of common law.

Partly because of the lack of a historical bargaining relationship between the British and aboriginal peoples, the six Australian States[4] retained exclusive jurisdiction over aboriginal affairs at the formation of the Australian federation in 1900. The State governments also retained exclusive jurisdiction over land use and management issues, including subsurface mineral and petroleum rights. Only in the Northern Territory did the Commonwealth government have the constitutional authority to legislate with respect to both aboriginal affairs and land management. This apportionment of jurisdiction meant that unlike in Canada, the State governments were the key government actors in the field of aboriginal affairs outside of the Northern Territory.

Neither the States nor the Commonwealth were interested in recognizing or protecting aboriginal land rights. The logic of the day asserted that aboriginal people were a weak and inferior race that would die out in Darwinian fashion. Until they reached their end, however, the role of the state was to protect this dying race from settler violence. Australian governments created reserves onto which aboriginal people were forcibly segregated, particularly where settler demand for land was high. These reserves were not lands over which its aboriginal occupants exercised some management authority or had ownership rights.[5] Rather, the reserves were strictly State-owned lands designated for "indigenous use," over which the State Protector exercised complete authority. This authority included the ability to regulate almost every facet of aboriginal individuals' lives, including their ability to leave the reserves and to move unimpeded through the countryside.

Within the Northern Territory, settlement pressures were low. The remoteness of the area and the unsuitability of the non-arid land for intensive agriculture meant that aboriginal groups maintained contact with traditional lands to a far greater extent than in the southern states. With the development of the pastoral industry, aboriginal peoples and pastoralists lived in a type of conflicted symbiotic relationship. While aboriginal people were subject to protective legislation, and were a cheap or even unpaid source of labor in the Territory's sheep and cattle stations, their incorporation within the pastoral economy as domestics, stockmen and shearers gave some the ability to maintain a physical connection with their traditional country.[6] In sum, the Commonwealth government was responsible for aboriginal policy in an area of the country where the legal dispossession of aboriginal people was certainly complete, but where the day-to-day connections between aboriginal people and land were relatively unbroken. Therefore, the settler competition for land, which lies at the root of aboriginal land grievances, was the least marked precisely in the area where the Commonwealth government had constitutional authority.[7]

What statutory recognition of aboriginal connection to country existed was limited to pastoral leases in the least settled areas of the country.[8] In Western Australia, South Australia, and the Northern Territory, pastoral leases contained a clause allowing aboriginal peoples access to pastoral lease lands for the minimal purposes of hunting, subsistence or engaging in ceremonial activities. The pastoral lease clauses represented the sum of legal aboriginal land rights in Australia.

The issue of land rights, most pressing for aboriginal people in more settled areas, did not motivate calls by non-aboriginal social activists prior to the war. As in Canada, support within the non-aboriginal community for aboriginal policy reform focused on social welfare policy and the gradual formal inclusion of aboriginal individuals within the citizenship regime. Since aboriginal policy was a State jurisdiction, there were significant differences across the continent on how "aboriginal natives" were defined, the degree to which their lives were regulated by the State, and the conditions under which aboriginal persons could receive social assistance. A major demand by aboriginal activists and social welfare reformers during the war years was to change the constitution via intergovernmental agreement or national referendum, allowing the Commonwealth to legislate in aboriginal affairs.[9] Social reformers' interest in expanding the Commonwealth's role in aboriginal policy was conditioned by the framing of aboriginal policy as a primarily social welfare and citizenship issue, and was part of a larger process of "civilizing" the aboriginal population. To illustrate, in a fairly typical letter to Prime Minister Curtin in 1945, the Native Welfare Council lobbied for Commonwealth intervention on these grounds:

> On humanitarian grounds, as well as in our self interests, it is due to these men of the stone-age to ease them into our twentieth century civilization and turn them into useful members of society . . . it is evident that the State finances and planning are totally inadequate for the task of bringing our Aborigines the benefits of our civilization which is their undoubted right and destiny . . . [10]

Aboriginal political and organizational mobilization, hampered by fragmentation across State boundaries and the remoteness of aboriginal communities, was embryonic during this period. Thus, it is difficult to imagine how they could have put forth a land rights agenda, given the climate of the time. A few under-resourced organizations existed; the Australian Aborigines League was the most established.[11] What aboriginal activists did articulate in a piecemeal fashion was the need for aboriginal peoples living on reserves to have some security of residence, as aboriginal individuals could be summarily removed from reserves by State officials. While the land issue largely fell on deaf ears, aboriginal activism on the formal equality front found greater favor. The League lobbied the Commonwealth government to act in the field of aboriginal affairs to support the extension of equal citizenship rights to aboriginal people: " . . . Cannot our legislators evolve a scheme for Australia and cannot that scheme be that every civilized man and woman, full blood or half-caste shall have full equality in law . . . Is there no time that we can look forward to when we shall be fully human in the eyes of white legislation?"[12] Therefore, at the end of World War Two, the political mobilization of aboriginal groups was less developed and more fragmented in Australia than in Canada or New Zealand. There was no regional or national aboriginal land rights lobby or forum capable of inserting land rights within Australia's assimilationist social policy agenda of the time.

The question of extending the Commonwealth's powers in aboriginal affairs was put to Australian voters in a national referendum in 1944. The aboriginal question was not the only one facing voters however; the referendum included fourteen items spanning social and economic policy areas where the Commonwealth was seeking to extend its reach to facilitate the larger agenda of post-war economic reconstruction. The electorate rejected the proposals, although Commonwealth officials did not attribute the loss to voters' dissatisfaction with the aboriginal policy item. After the failure of the constitutional reform referendum, the Commonwealth government resisted persistent calls to assert itself in aboriginal policy. It did so on the grounds that the Commonwealth's financial burdens arising from the war were already considerable.[13]

One of the legacies of the Commonwealth's decision not to involve itself in aboriginal affairs outside of the Northern Territory was the resultant lack of a federal bureaucratic structure that linked the Commonwealth government with aboriginal communities in the States, and through which aboriginal policy demands could be channeled. Consequently, there were no senior bureaucratic actors within the Commonwealth administration who had to confront the systemic failure of assimilationist aboriginal policies and who could press upon cabinet the importance of addressing indigenous land issues on a national basis, as the Canadian Indian administration had begun to do in the post-war period. The Commonwealth government, removed from the administration of aboriginal affairs in the settled regions of the country where aboriginal dispossession was the most acute, had no internal incentive to re-examine the implementation of aboriginal policy, or to begin internal questioning on the underlying goals of assimilation.

The lack of internal questioning within the federal bureaucracy was also mirrored in the widespread ideological agreement across Australia's political elite on the fundamental goals of aboriginal assimilation. Most importantly, there was no discernable difference across political parties on aboriginal or race policy. Furthermore, the parties did not need to politicize race in order to differentiate themselves. The major and persistent cleavages that divided parties were the class and rural/urban divides. Therefore, the trade-union based Labor Party was pitted against the principal non-Labor parties. By the end of the war, the two non-Labor parties, Country and Liberal, would present an anti-socialist coalition, with the Country Party representing rural pastoralist interests within the coalition.[14] This lack of partisan differentiation on the aboriginal policy dimension meant that while aboriginal policy reform had few allies within the political elite, policy reform which was premised on equal citizenship was just as likely (or unlikely), regardless of which party formed the government. The partisan differentiation on the rural cleavage, however, would mean that aboriginal land grievances which would threaten rural leaseholders would receive a much less sympathetic hearing when the Liberal-Country coalition was in power.

To summarize, by the end of the war, the Commonwealth government faced no serious pressure, neither internal nor external, to address aboriginal land grievances. The very concept of aboriginal land rights was foreign, as the Australian courts had long ago established that the aboriginal title did not exist in the law. Aboriginal political mobilization at regional and national levels was nascent, highly fragmented, and basically unable to put land rights on the national political agenda. Even if it had, the Commonwealth was constitutionally constrained from acting in the aboriginal policy field, except in the Northern Territory, exactly where aboriginal land dispossession was the least acute. Lastly, Commonwealth bureaucratic actors had no incentive, based on administrative self-interest, to re-examine the land dimension within a failing assimilationist agenda.

The Incubus for Land Rights Politics: 1945–1965

The 1950s and early 1960s were marked by the drive of Australian social reformers and civil libertarians to dismantle the discriminatory and coercive aboriginal protection regime, and to extend full citizenship rights to all adult aboriginal people across Australia. Just like their counterparts in Diefenbaker's Canada during this time, social reformers began to reject the coercive elements in Australian governments' policies for aboriginal 'advancement,' and opted for a milder version of the same by accepting that aboriginal people should have some say over the pace of their integration. By the close of the decade, these social reformers began to link land issues within their reformist agenda. As part of this new emphasis, the Federal Council for Aboriginal Advancement (FCAA), formed in 1958, began to advocate that reserves should be transferred to the control and ownership of their aboriginal occupants.[15] White social reformers began to voice these demands during the time when State and Commonwealth interest in aboriginal reserves was increasing due to the mining boom.

The 1950s was a continuation of past inertia of government action on aboriginal land grievances, but the placidness of government policy belied fundamental economic and social changes that would set up the emergence of Australian land rights politics in the 1960s.[16] The first major development was the expansion of the Australian mining sector. Spawned by war-time demand for minerals, the Commonwealth government began a geological surveying program which, when combined with scientific advances in mineral exploration, led to the discovery, starting in the late

1940s, of significant and economic deposits of key minerals,[17] particularly in Western Australia, the Northern Territory, and Queensland. The world-wide post-war economic expansion ensured a significant export market for these minerals, and by the early 1960s, international mining companies came knocking on Australia's door. Since minerals were held by the Crown, the Commonwealth had a direct interest in ensuring the development of its mining resources in the Northern Territory, whether these resources were found on pastoral lease or aboriginal reserve lands. Aboriginal attempts to gain control over mining on aboriginal reserves would help spark the land claims era.

The second economic development was slower to develop, but no less important. It would begin in the early 1950s, and would come to fruition in the mid 1960s—the modernization of the pastoral economy. The economic viability of the pastoral sector was conditioned on reasonable livestock prices and low input costs, particularly human labor. With increasing wage awards, the expansion of the cash economy in the Australian hinterland, drought, tight credit and decreasing livestock prices, the terms sustaining the ambivalent yet symbiotic relationship between pastoralists and aborigi-nal people progressively fell apart.[18] Pastoralists would gradually, and then increasingly, shed their aboriginal labor force in order to mechanize their operations, leading to social and economic dislocation, as aboriginal popu-lations drifted to towns and cities. The drift of aboriginal people to towns and cities as fringe-dwellers strengthened the framing of the "aboriginal problem" as a predominantly social welfare and racial discrimination issue in the eyes of mainstream Australia. As aboriginal welfare became a vis-ible issue, social welfare reformers and civil libertarians (both aboriginal and non-aboriginal) pressured the Commonwealth to take over where the States had clearly failed. By the mid-1960s, aboriginal and non-aboriginal activism had created a solid constituency of Australian public opinion, call-ing for an amendment of the constitution to expand Commonwealth power into aboriginal policy across the Australian continent.

The overall urbanization of Australia's indigenous people was rapid in the late 1960s; however, the distribution of aboriginal people across cit-ies and States deserves mention because it has implications for the political parties' voting bases. Australia's aboriginal community grew in major cen-ters, while still maintaining a greater demographic presence in rural Aus-tralia than, for instance, the Maori maintained in rural New Zealand. To contrast, 70% of the Maori population but only 44% of Australia's indige-nous population were urbanized in 1971. In Australia, there were also huge disparities in urbanization rates across States that persist today. In Victoria, half of the State's aboriginal population lives in Melbourne. In Queensland

and Western Australia, only between 20% and 25% of the State's aboriginal populations live in their respective capital cities.[19] Given the statistic that the proportion of the total aboriginal population living in Australia's capital cities increased from 10% in 1966 to 31% in 1996,[20] aboriginal urbanization is concentrated in three places—smaller urban centers (with populations less than 1000), Sydney, and Melbourne.

This urban migration led to a growing social pathology in urban aboriginal communities, but it would also have the effect seen in New Zealand. Urban migration would create new centers for young aboriginal activism that would be inspired by the repertoires of the American civil rights movement. At the same time when mainstream Australia came to support a role for the Commonwealth in aboriginal social welfare policy, the issue of land rights was emerging in the public demands of aboriginal activists to a place of greater prominence from behind the civil libertarian agenda.[21] These new centers of aboriginal protest activism would gradually gain allies among the middle class New Left—particularly students and young lawyers. Like Canada and New Zealand, these new activists located aboriginal poverty within a specific history of land dispossession, making a causal link between marginalization and lost lands. However, aside from some remarkable protests like the February 1965 Freedom Ride from Sydney through rural New South Wales, aboriginal political mobilization was limited to local event-based public protest, and increasingly tied land rights to gaining control over reserves.

1966–67: The Commonwealth and the Constitutional Referendum

While an aboriginal land rights dialogue was beginning to emerge, the Country-Liberal coalition government did not seem to link land rights to its consideration of a constitutional referendum. In 1965, retiring Prime Minister Menzies publicly disagreed with the need for constitutional change given the repeal, by that point, of most discriminatory State legislation, and the government did not return to the issue until after the 1966 federal election, when the Country-Liberal coalition was returned to power. Internally, the Prime Minister's Department felt that the Commonwealth could exert policy influence in the States through its constitutional spending power[22] without having to seek formal legislative jurisdiction.[23] However, given external pressure to amend the constitution, the Attorney-General and the Minister of Territories disagreed on appropriate Commonwealth tactics. The Attorney-General thought that Commonwealth action was necessary, citing that " . . . the Government would be wrongly criticized for lacking sympathy for the aboriginals" should it do nothing.[24] He advised cabinet that should a referendum be successful, that the Commonwealth make it clear that it would not act without the co-operation of the States. The Minister of Territories disagreed. He felt that whatever public benefit the Commonwealth might gain in the short term did not outweigh the future disadvantages:

> The Aboriginal problem is largely a social one. Irrespective of the benevolent intentions of governments, there are severe limits to what governmental action can achieve. Thus the removal of constitutional limitation would have the effect of attracting pressure on the Commonwealth Government to take action in a field in which it would, in the nature of things, be unable to satisfy the critics, who do not see the difficulties but only the lack of immediate results. One of the major difficulties is that the more that special efforts are made for Aborigines the more they are being sheltered from the competitive influences that have made the rest of the community self-reliant.[25]

By early 1967, cabinet concluded that a referendum on the aboriginal item would carry by a wide margin. The Prime Minister's Department suggested that the disadvantages of seeking constitutional amendment on aboriginal policy alone could be mitigated by expanding the scope of the referendum, in the hope that wide popular support for the aboriginal item would carry other constitutional measures. If the government would add its preferred question, relating to the increase of seats in the House of Representatives without changing the number of seats in the Senate, then "[Ministers] may also feel that little would be lost, and perhaps something gained."[26] Cabinet agreed.[27] On May 27th, 1967, 91% of the Australian electorate voted in favor of granting the Commonwealth concurrent jurisdiction in aboriginal affairs. Cabinet's gamble didn't pay off, however, as only 40% of Australians found in favor of the parliamentary seat question.

While this new constitutional power was in many ways inflicted on an unwilling coalition government, the very strong referendum result was a significant symbolic statement of Australia's growing popular commitment to a non-discriminatory national response to aboriginal issues, and therefore an important victory for civil rights and social welfare activists.[28] The referendum was a victory, though the intra-state distribution of voter support for the measure cooled in rural areas.[29] The referendum gave aboriginal policy national salience, particularly in urban areas, and the Commonwealth needed to signal that it took its new responsibilities seriously. The referendum thrust the Commonwealth into a challenging field in which it had relatively little policy expertise and an underdeveloped policy coordination apparatus. Prime Minister Holt created a policy advisory group, the Council of Aboriginal Affairs (CAA), which would report to the

Prime Minister, and be housed within the Prime Minister's Department. The Prime Minister tapped on the shoulder of H.C. Coombs, central banker, power broker, and man of great personal prestige, to head the CAA. Holt would assemble a small group of intellectuals in the CAA, which between them had bureaucratic experience, anthropological knowledge of aboriginal peoples, and solid reputations inside and outside of government. The CAA would be supported administratively by the newly created Office of Aboriginal Affairs (OAA). The impact of the CAA, however, would be contingent on its access to the Prime Minister.

What none could have foreseen was Prime Minister Holt's accidental death in December 1967. In January 1968, John Gorton became Prime Minister. He did not share Holt's vision for the CAA. Gorton "sidelined" the CAA from the Prime Minister's Department, and had the CAA report to cabinet through a new Minister in charge of aboriginal affairs.[30] The Minister, Liberal Party member Bill Wentworth, was an advocate for increasing aboriginal control on reserves. On the down side, Wentworth was new to the table, had little credit among his established colleagues,[31] and would prove to be a cabinet lightweight. Despite these administrative handicaps, the CAA had the potential to make policy innovation a reality, and would come to be an important ally in the internal struggle over land rights to come.

The referendum was not a national endorsement of aboriginal land rights, but the land rights issue was forced onto the Commonwealth's agenda soon after. The Commonwealth government would finally be confronted with the land rights dimension of aboriginal protest as two challenges to the Commonwealth's aboriginal policies in the Northern Territory emerged in the late 1960s: the Gurindji strike, and the Gove land rights case. The first would ensue from the economic changes in pastoralism, and the second would arise from mining on aboriginal reserves. For the first time, cabinet would confront the implications of recognizing land rights, and examine its policy options. The Country-Liberal government's handling of these two issues would accelerate partisan differentiation on the land rights issue, eventually leading the Labor Party to position itself as the champion of aboriginal land rights, as it sought to regain power for the first time since 1949.

CABINET CONSIDERATION OF ABORIGINAL LAND RIGHTS

The Gurindji at Wave Hill Station

In August 1966, 170 Gurindji stockmen went on strike at the Wave Hill cattle station in the Northern Territory. The initial motivation of the strike was to protest wages and working conditions on the huge pastoral property leased by a British pastoral group and owned by a British lord. The framing of the dispute began to change from an aboriginal David vs. British Goliath labor show-down to a land rights protest when the Gurindji moved their camp from the station's main encampment to Wattie Creek. Wattie Creek was still included in the Wave Hill pastoral lease, but was of particular religious significance to the Gurindji. In April 1967, a month before the referendum, the Gurindji petitioned the Governor-General, asking the government to excise 550 square miles from the 6000 square mile Wave Hill lease. The Gurindji would use the land to develop their own pastoral enterprise and conduct some mineral exploration. Significantly, the Gurindji wanted not just any 550 square miles, but land of their own choosing. This demand transformed the Gurindji labor strike into a claim based on traditional connection to country. It also extended the parameters of the aboriginal land issue to involve lands and property interests outside of reserves. On the advice of the Minister of Territories, the Governor-General rejected the Gurindji petition.[32] The Commonwealth informed the Gurindji that they could discuss the use of other lands, including reserve lands or unoccupied Crown lands, in the general area.[33]

The Gurindji strike would steadily attract more interest in the popular press, and support for a positive response by the Commonwealth to the Gurindji demand for land emerged by March of 1968. Public support in the metropolitan southeast was a reflection of many motivations, from anti-monarchists seeing the Gurindji issue as an effort to establish aboriginal self-sufficiency in opposition to the British aristocracy,[34] to voters who were looking to see the Commonwealth do something positive for aboriginal people in the post-referendum era. The growing public discussion of the Gurindji strike in places like Sydney and Melbourne led Minister Wentworth to publicly comment, in March, that while he was sympathetic to the Gurindji's demand for land ownership in order to be economically self-sufficient, it could not come at the cost of pastoralists.[35] Wentworth's public statement must have drawn the ire of cabinet, because a few days later, cabinet effectively told Wentworth that until he brought an aboriginal policy proposal to the cabinet table, he was not to conduct a policy debate in public.[36]

Had Wentworth's comment merely stated the obvious tradeoff of protecting pastoral property rights at the expense of furthering aboriginal economic advancement, cabinet's move to shut down Wentworth's public comments may not have happened. By giving credence to the Gurindji's ownership claims, Wentworth not only bypassed cabinet, but he also signaled a potential split on aboriginal land issues within the Country-Liberal coalition cabinet. Wentworth, a Liberal, was of the opinion that the coalition government should not lose the public momentum on aboriginal issues to the Labor Party in the vote-rich southeast, as Sydney and Melbourne accounted for approximately 40% of the voting power in the House of Representatives.[37] By early April, Wentworth publicly advocated that the government excise eight square miles of the Wave Hill lease, and hand it over to the Gurindji.[38] Wentworth's comments and the growing editorial sympathy for aboriginal land rights in the *Sydney Morning Herald* and the *Melbourne Age*[39] galvanized the pastoral industry to lobby the key senior cabinet members from the Country Party, particularly the Minister of the Interior, Peter Nixon.[40]

The jostling and maneuvering that followed between the Liberal, Wentworth, and the Country man, Nixon, on the aboriginal land rights file is rooted in their different bases of partisan support. Although the fortunes of both parties were linked in that each needed the other to form a non-Labor government, the fortunes of the Liberal Party began to erode in 1966 to a degree not shared by its coalition partner. The Liberal Party was the vehicle of its founder, Robert Menzies, and with Menzies' retirement in January 1966, the party would convulse into leadership squabbles.[41] The Liberals' leadership difficulties arose during a time when Labor would increasingly target the Liberal electoral base. The Liberal Party was traditionally the "principal vehicle of the business community and of the urban and suburban middle class," though it also drew support among conservatives in rural areas.[42] In 1967, Gough Whitlam assumed the leadership of the Australian Labor Party, and with his strong guidance, he sought to expand the Party's membership and electoral appeal from its trade union base to include the urban and sub-urban white collar voter.[43] When the coalition lost the Senate majority in the 1967 Senate elections, Labor exerted the ability to defeat government proposals for the first time. Wentworth, as a Liberal, had good reason to think that the coalition government should not lose further ground to Labor in the large cities, especially on a relatively unimportant issue as aboriginal land rights.

The Country Party had no such worries. Since the 1920s, the party was the "main parliamentary representative of farmers, country towns, and the embattled non-metropolitan way of life."[44] The Country Party drew its support solely from rural Australia, and did not compete, as did the Liberal and Labor Parties, for urban votes.[45] Despite the declining economic fortunes of the pastoral sector in the 1950s and 1960s, the Australian farmer and grazier remained among the most politically interested and conservative members of the Australian electorate. They also kept their faith with the Country Party.[46] The Country Party also benefited directly from the drawing of federal district boundaries, as district size (in terms of voter enrollment) could vary by a maximum of 20% from the State average.[47] This rule ensured the over-representation of rural interests in Parliament at a time when the rural population was decreasing. The Country Party strongly protected the over-weighting of rural interests as part of the coalition, " . . . even when the alliance with the Liberals was strained by the vehemence of that insistence."[48] Country Party ministers reportedly had no qualms in pushing the rural agenda at the coalition cabinet table. As one scholar writes: " . . . within the government the presence of Country party ministers, who were often both embarrassingly specific in their demands and obdurate in seeing that they were met, was a frequent source of irritation."[49] Country Party intransigence on the aboriginal rights issue, among others, would eventually prove too much for aboriginal peoples' lukewarm Liberal allies.[50]

The Gurindji strike also mobilized the Country Party's traditional voting base. In mid-April, the Northern Territory Cattle Producers Council[51] made its case to its obdurate champion in cabinet, Peter Nixon. The graziers called the legitimacy of the Gurindji claim into question. Firstly, the Gurindji claim was "conceived and inspired by communists," and interpreted Wentworth's public support for the Gurindji claim reflecting "a desire to forestall further communist activity by a fait accompli." Secondly, the Council disputed whether the Gurindji were indeed the traditional owners of the Wattie Creek area. The Council was concerned about the dangerous precedent that interfering with pastoralists' property rights would set, and strongly advised the government against precipitously granting the Gurindji some land without developing a wider policy on aboriginal land claims: "Sooner or later the government must express its attitude to these claims. Its ability to do so will be prejudiced if it makes a part-concession now without a policy."

Although the pastoralists supported a government policy that did not recognize aboriginal land rights, their concern that the coalition government not act in a piecemeal and reactive fashion was echoed by Coombs and the OAA. They were worried that Wentworth, now branded internally as a loose cannon, and too eager to capitalize on publicity, would squander the opportunity created by the Gurindji to develop a Commonwealth land rights policy. The OAA was concerned by the pastoralists' charge that the Gurindji were not the true traditional owners, and were aware that should the Commonwealth make a land concession, and later the Gurindji claim be proven questionable, the future legitimacy of a broader land claims policy would be compromised.[52] Coombs and the OAA advised Wentworth to push cabinet for the implementation of investigative institutions to independently assure the merit of aboriginal claims before they were negotiated:

> The Council of Aboriginal Affairs advised the Minister against his mode of approach and any attempt to precipitate settlement. It recommended him as a prior step to set up a regular procedure of an administrative, or quasi-judicial or, if necessary, judicial character to investigate and recommend concerning all such claims, and to promulgate knowledge that such a procedure was available . . . He may be unready for a full-face encounter with the situation, but it is not going to go away or die. His best course now seems to be to set up, though a little late, the regular processes of inquiry we have already recommended.[53]

Ignoring the OAA's advice to think in terms of long-term policy change, Wentworth chose to follow Nixon's lead in cabinet, although the public still saw Wentworth as the lead minister on the land rights file. Unlike the OAA, Nixon was of the opinion that once the Wattie Creek controversy died down in the press, the land claims issue would indeed go away and die.[54] This was not an unreasonable conclusion, since there was no nationally recognized aboriginal leadership that could act collectively and keep land rights on the public agenda in a sustained way. Nixon may have preferred to ignore the Gurindji claim altogether, but he had come to the conclusion that " . . . irrespective of general policy attitudes, it may be found necessary to go ahead with some provision of land in the particular situation of Wattie Creek."[55] For Nixon, the main and delicate task at hand was to manage the Wattie Creek issue without inflaming pastoral interests. His agenda did not include recognizing aboriginal land rights and encouraging other such claims to surface in the future.

From May through July of 1968, the Department of the Interior took the lead in developing the Commonwealth's policy response to the Gurindji land rights claim.[56] The first, and most difficult question, was whether cabinet was prepared to recognize aboriginal land rights by granting the Gurindji land at the place of their choosing:

> If occupation of the land at Wattie Creek is confirmed, either by excision, sub-lease or permissive occupancy . . . this will encourage pressures to confirm and extend that recognition. It is not possible to say how many other groups would be encouraged to occupy land in the same way, but a series of attempts would almost certainly be made . . . Acceptance of the principle of land rights for Aboriginals would however open up other substantial issues such as whether some set

procedure should be adopted for the investigation of claims; this raises
the further question whether Wattie Creek should be dealt with ad hoc
or under such a procedure. If Ministers favored the establishment of a
set procedure a further paper could be prepared covering the principles
and procedures which might apply . . . [57]

Nixon's preferred solution, reached with Wentworth's support, was
not to recognize such rights and therefore " . . . not breaching its existing
policy on Northern Territory land rights." His position was that the government " . . . not grant land title to Aborigines or other persons except in
ways consistent with land policy generally and so far as Aborigines are concerned in ways consistent with its policies of Aboriginal advancement."[58]
Nixon's proposed solution was to create a township on the Wave Hill lease,
and establish a residential centre that could support the Gurindji population. The township would not be at Wattie Creek, recognize no land rights,
and would leave pastoral lease rights undisturbed. Cabinet endorsed the
plan on July 2nd without any discussion with the Gurindji, and proceeded
to reaffirm the assimilation goals that any Commonwealth response to land
rights would have to support:

> [Cabinet] declared firmly that the ultimate objective would continue to
> be assimilation . . . While recognizing that it will take generations for
> Aboriginals to become fully assimilated into the Australian community,
> the Cabinet's position it that it will hold patiently and purposefully to
> this aim. It will measure any policy proposals against it and would want
> to avoid proposals which, by identifying Aborigines as such and setting
> them permanently apart from other Australians, are likely to have the
> effect of acknowledging and establishing a policy of continuing sepa-
> rate development leading to an eventual racial problem.[59]

The reaction to the government's announcement was negative on all
sides. Cabinet's decision brought the ire of the cattle industry which was
opposed to any response whatsoever to the Gurindji claim,[60] while spark-
ing condemnation in the southeast press. The Country-Liberal coalition
government's non-recognition policy galvanized more student protests in
favor of aboriginal land rights, and aboriginal activists admonished the
Gurindji to stay at Wattie Creek. However, the publicity did eventually die
down, partly due to a series of government announcements that indicated
the government's willingness to provide capital funding for aboriginal enterprises,[61] and partly due to Nixon's strategy of not engaging the press on
the aboriginal land rights question. In a remarkable letter from the senior

cabinet member to his clearly junior colleague (and copied to the Prime Minister), Peter Nixon effectively demanded that Bill Wentworth stay silent on aboriginal land rights, now that "active publicity has died away":

> I would urge you to let the matter lie . . . I acknowledge that there is room for genuine difference of opinion about what is best for the Aboriginal people concerned but the Government having made a decision which it believed to be the best in all circumstances I would suggest that it is of no benefit to the Aboriginals concerned or to the Government if in fact you have made a reference to the matter in a public statement which allows you to be reported as apparently in disagreement with the decision.[62]

By committing this demand to paper in lieu of a carefully placed word in a quiet corner, Nixon took off his gloves, threw down the gauntlet, and informed Wentworth of their respective places in the pecking order of cabinet power.

The Country-Liberal coalition government's response to the Gurindji claim highlighted the power of rural interests around the cabinet table who were stalwart in their denial of aboriginal land rights. The Country Party outmaneuvered Wentworth, who was the most promising ally for aboriginal land rights in cabinet at the time. Outgunned at the cabinet table, Wentworth repeatedly chose to ignore the advice of the only pro-aboriginal sector of the federal bureaucracy, the OAA. During this time cabinet chose a non-recognition strategy, and refused to go further to consider the institutional mechanisms it could have established to regulate aboriginal land grievances in the future. What suggestions there were to establish such institutions came from Coombs and the CAA. Although the CAA did not have the opportunity to fully develop a cabinet paper exploring and weighting the relative advantages of such institutional mechanisms, it did initially value quasi-judicial institutions which could independently investigate and establish the merit of aboriginal land claims.

The coalition government's handling of the Gurindji claim would have important political effects. The Gurindji claim and the subsequent publicity brought new supporters, students and white-collar liberal professionals, to the aboriginal rights dialogue, and these supporters would find a home within the Labor Party at a time when it was beginning to expand beyond its traditional trade union base. The growing support in urban Australia for the general concept of land rights would encourage the Labor Party to identify itself as the political party willing to recognize aboriginal land rights, although Labor did not yet flesh out how it would go about doing so, or the institutions it would establish to resolve aboriginal land grievances.

The lack of a larger policy program, in 1968, reflects the reality that Australia had enough mental work to do in asking the "to recognize or not to recognize" question. This lack is also partly a result of the absence of an indigenous organization that Australians could consider a nationally representative indigenous voice which could challenge Australians with an alternative policy vision. The national body representing regional aboriginal advancement organizations included both aboriginal and non-aboriginal voices in support of land rights, but aboriginal land rights activists were increasingly constrained by the assimilationist goals to which non-aboriginal reformers still held. While political protest was quickening, the organizational development of a distinct indigenous representative body at the national level was still in its infancy.

The Gove Land Rights Case

Just after the publicity waned on the Gurindji claim, another aboriginal group in the Northern Territory moved for the Commonwealth to recognize aboriginal land rights, this time challenging mining interests. From 1965 to 1968, the Commonwealth had negotiated with Nabalco, a subsidiary of Swiss Aluminum, on the mining of bauxite and the construction of an alumina plant in one of the most remote regions of northern Australia, the Gove Peninsula. The bauxite lay within the boundaries of the Arnhem Land Reserve, the traditional territory of the Yolngu people. The agreement reached between the Commonwealth and Nabalco allowed the mining project to proceed, with the condition that Nabalco pay a percentage of mining royalties into an aboriginal development fund. The Yolngu were not involved in the negotiations for the mining lease, and grew more and more aware of their inability to mitigate the consequences of the mining project.[63] In December 1968, the Yolngu people of the Gove Peninsula filed an injunction with the Northern Territory Supreme Court to stop the mining project until the court made a judicial determination of aboriginal title to the Arnhem reserve lands. This was the first judicial test of aboriginal title in Australia's history.

As they had in the Gurindji claim, the OAA and the Department of the Interior were diametrically opposed on how the government should respond to the Gove land rights case. The OAA advised Wentworth to persuade his cabinet colleagues to pursue an out-of-court settlement, and use the opportunity to negotiate with other aboriginal groups on the economic development of reserve lands.[64] One of the members of the CAA who had attended initial *in camera* hearings of the Gove land case advised

Wentworth that the political argument that aboriginal land rights continued to exist in Australia would " . . . turn out to have a heavy resonance in our future public life." He advised the Minister that "even if [the aboriginal plaintiff's] submission finally fails for reasons of law, [their] reading of Australian history will be widely disseminated, and will have an appeal to public sentiment that your Government would be unwise to ignore."[65] Clearly, the CAA felt that in light of the Gurindji claim and growing public support for land rights in the southeast, the government's decision to pursue a strong non-recognition argument in policy and in court was unwise and short-sighted.

The pro-recognition and pro-settlement voices represented by the CAA were challenged by the Attorney-General and the Minister of the Interior. Peter Nixon was opposed to a settlement strategy for a number of reasons. Firstly, the Attorney-General had advised that the Yolngu were not likely to win their court case, and Nixon felt that "if Aborigines have no legal rights to the land, then they should be told so (by the courts)." Nixon would push the Attorney-General to make sure that the Northern Territory Supreme Court would rule on the issue of aboriginal title.[66] An out-of-court settlement would, Nixon argued, encourage other land claims by exaggerating the real judicial value of aboriginal rights. This logic suggests that Nixon felt a clear ruling against aboriginal title would discourage further land claims activity. He felt that the costs of defending the aboriginal title claim vigorously in court were low, since "real international damage" was "doubtful," and "apart from a vocal minority," it was also "doubtful if Australian public greatly concerned (*sic*)."[67] Nixon not only had a very different reading of the future public mood on land rights, but he also felt that public opposition to Commonwealth intransigence on land rights could be deflected by drawing attention to its welfare initiatives:

> Any criticism can, however, in my view be met by pointing to the extensive programmes of educational, social and economic assistance to Aborigines as both offsetting any claims they may have for past dispossession of land and as being of more value to them by encouraging and assisting them to enter the main stream of Australian life.[68]

Despite being saddled with an ineffective Minister in Wentworth, the CAA would continue to jostle internally throughout 1970 for the Interior Department and the Attorney General to accept some sort of land tenure, freehold or leasehold, in the Northern Territory, that would use traditional relationships to land as part of the tenure process. The CAA would also promote the cautious idea of establishing an Aboriginal Land Fund, which would serve as the Commonwealth's aboriginal land policy outside of the Northern Territory. The Land Fund would purchase properties on the free market and place them in trust, then delivering the land to aboriginal groups capable of exploiting the land economically.

In March 1971, William McMahon took over the job of Prime Minister in the Country-Liberal government, and over the next months, proceeded to shuffle cabinet. Nixon was moved from the Interior portfolio, and replaced by a farmer from New South Wales, Ralph Hunt. Soon, McMahon also moved Wentworth from the Aboriginal Affairs portfolio. The cabinet shake-up had the potential to break the deadlock between the CAA and Interior, not because any of the new personalities were particularly sympathetic to aboriginal land rights, but because the CAA might be able to persuade Prime Minister McMahon to become personally active in the aboriginal affairs file.

The change in personalities around the cabinet table was quickly followed by the decision of the Northern Territory Supreme Court in the Gove land case. On April 27th, 1971, Justice Blackburn ruled that the Yolngu action failed, finding that aboriginal title did not exist in the common law.[69] The finding that aboriginal people had no legal rights to land was well publicized, and evoked a general editorial opinion that, regardless of the court's decision, the Commonwealth should change the law to recognize aboriginal connections to country.[70] While editorial opinions agreed that the Commonwealth had a moral obligation to recognize aboriginal land rights in some way, opinions differed on how. It also must be noted that while Australian editorial opinion thought aboriginal people should have access to more land, approval for land rights was limited to those aboriginal people who could develop land economically. There was no widespread acceptance of the principle that aboriginal people had rights to lands of their own choosing. The editorial press had accepted, however, that the widespread goal of aboriginal economic advancement would founder as long as aboriginal people had no control over the land's development.

Two days after the court decision, the Prime Minister faced questioning in Parliament, and responded that his government would protect aboriginal "ceremonial and recreational" land rights. This was a far cry from the Yolngu position, but did indicate a small breach from the complete non-recognition language of the previous cabinet. Within a week, cabinet faced two submissions on how it should proceed on the land rights issue. The first was from the CAA, which argued that there was "widespread and deep emotional support" for land rights after the Blackburn judgment, and that on this basis, the government had an important opportunity to act "promptly and boldly," if only to forestall Labor's potential electoral gains.

The CAA submission recommended that the Commonwealth negotiate a compensation agreement with the Yolngu, while the government engaged in an internal review of its aboriginal policy.[71] The CAA advocated that a ministerial committee be appointed to consider its aboriginal leaseholds on reserves and land fund proposals.

The submission from the Minister of the Interior countered the CAA submission. Interior argued that contrary to what the CAA thought, " . . . the effect of the Gove Judgment on public opinion is not demonstrable. It is probably not great . . . [and] has been grossly overstated."[72] Neither the Minister of the Interior nor the Secretary to the Cabinet was prepared to show the boldness to which the CAA aspired. They were unwilling to move from a non-recognition position inside the Northern Territory, and were certainly not interested in picking a fight with the States by legislating in favor of aboriginal land rights elsewhere. The Minister of the Interior and the Secretary to the Cabinet both urged cabinet not to negotiate with the Yolngu in the short term, and the Interior submission accused the CAA submission as "hav[ing] a flavour of separate development and of running counter to the assimilation objective."

In a small victory for the CAA, cabinet decided to form a ministerial committee to examine the Commonwealth's overall aboriginal policy framework, a proposal for which the CAA had gained the Prime Minister's support a few weeks earlier.[73] However, cabinet refused to negotiate with the Yolngu directly, instead offering to underwrite the Yolngu's costs should they wish to pursue their case to Australia's High Court. From the formation of the ministerial committee until January of 1972, the CAA pushed internally for the government to recognize some form of traditional aboriginal leasehold to reserves in the Northern Territory, but the CAA's influence was completely dependent on having the ear of the Prime Minister in the face of concerted and bitter opposition from the Department of the Interior and the Country members of cabinet.[74] By January of 1972, cabinet agreed to establish a land fund to purchase properties off reserve, but only approved a general purpose lease for which aboriginal people on reserves in the Northern Territory could apply. The lease did not require or recognize the aboriginal person's traditional attachment to the land, but instead, would be open to aboriginal people prepared to develop the land economically, and would not distinguish aboriginal applications according to proven traditional customary occupation.

Prime Minister McMahon announced his general purpose lease initiative, and within hours, a small group of aboriginal land rights activists arrived in Canberra and pitched their tents on Parliament's front lawn.[75] Dubbed the tent embassy, the activists' central demand was a clear recognition of customary land rights and full legal ownership of aboriginal reserves. The importance of the tent embassy grew as more and more activists found their way to Canberra over the coming weeks. In July, the Liberal-Country government twice violently disbanded the embassy using police forces, a heavily publicized event which served to put aboriginal land rights squarely at the center of any Australian's discussion of aboriginal policy. On July 30th, aboriginal and non-aboriginal supporters defied the government, marched on Canberra, and re-established the embassy.[76] It was also at the tent embassy that aboriginal people would raise their newly created aboriginal flag in the full light of national publicity. Many years later, a former Labor Minister of Aboriginal Affairs recounted the key importance of the embassy for white Australians: " . . . The erection of the tent embassy showed the determination and increasingly militant tactics that the new generation of Aboriginal people were prepared to undertake to assert their rights . . . As I see it, the tent embassy and the Aboriginal flag epitomize the unity of the Aboriginal people in the fight for their rights."[77] One August 1972 editorial in Melbourne's paper, the *Age,* confirms that aboriginal unity at the embassy is not a function of contemporary reminiscence: " . . . the Government is sadly out of touch with even conservative Aboriginal opinion. . . . If any issue has the potential to draw the various Aboriginal groups together behind a common flag, it is land rights."[78]

McMahon's general lease policy and the subsequent tent embassy served to further polarize the competitive political parties on the aboriginal rights issue during a critical election year. The coalition was looking tired, and Labor was working hard to build momentum before the expected election. Opinion polls on voting intentions conducted in November 1971 gave the coalition a narrow margin of victory in nationally representative samples.[79] One series of opinion polls drawing on respondents from Sydney and Melbourne, however, gave Labor a decent margin of victory.[80] The non-aboriginal supporters of the tent embassy represented the core constituencies of the New Left, lawyers, students, and other anti-racism activists. Gough Whitlam took advantage of this emerging national issue to distance Labor from the governing parties. On February 8th, 1972, Gough Whitlam visited the tent embassy, and promised the aboriginal ambassadors that a Labor government would reverse the government's new policy and allow aboriginal tribal land ownership. In other words, Whitlam committed Labor to recognizing aboriginal customary land rights in some form. He reiterated his promise a few days later in the House of Representatives:

> My Party has stated its attitude on Aboriginal land rights in these terms:
> All Aboriginal lands to be vested in a public trust or trusts composed of

Aborigines or Islanders as appropriate. That exclusive corporate land rights be granted to Aboriginal communities which retain a strong tribal structure or demonstrate a potential for corporate action in regard to land at present reserved for the use of Aborigines, or where traditional occupancy according to tribal custom can be established from anthropological or other evidence. Aboriginal land rights shall carry with them full rights to minerals in those lands.[81]

From 1967 to 1972, the political mobilization of aboriginal and non-aboriginal opinion transformed the place of land rights within the demands for aboriginal policy reform directed to Australia's Commonwealth government. The Gurindji strike, the Yolngu demands for land ownership, and the emergence of the tent embassy had the important effects of creating new allies within the left, and subsequently, of polarizing partisan support for the recognition of aboriginal land rights. The polarization of Australia's competitive political parties would prove a double-edged sword, however. As in New Zealand, the opportunity for significant policy reform and institutional innovation under a Labor government would be mitigated by the possibility of significant policy retrenchment under a Country-Liberal reign.

Gough Whitlam, the Labor Party, and Land Rights in
the Northern Territory

For the first time in 23 years, the Country-Liberal government fell in the election of December 1972. Labor had succeeded in wooing younger, metropolitan, and white collar workers in order to edge out its competition. While aboriginal affairs was not an issue driving voting intentions, the electoral ascendancy of the Labor Party created the opportunity to make a breakthrough in aboriginal policy.[82] Especially important was the personal conviction of the new Labor Prime Minister, Gough Whitlam, that aboriginal policy reform was an important priority for his government. Whitlam moved quickly to signal the seriousness of his commitment. One of his first actions on the job was to approve the purchase of pastoral property under the Aboriginal Land Fund.[83] He also appointed Gordon Bryant, a white activist with credible links to aboriginal communities, as Minister of Aboriginal Affairs. Bryant would also oversee a new bureaucracy, the Department of Aboriginal Affairs (DAA), which would compete with, and sometimes counter the power of the Department of the Interior. Whitlam appointed Coombs' colleague Barrie Dexter as Secretary of the DAA.

By late 1972, Whitlam had said his government would recognize aboriginal land rights, but unlike Canada and New Zealand, there was no historically preferred policy option on which to build a modern land rights policy. The lack of a treaty history with Australia's indigenous peoples did not provide a historical precedent for a modern-day negotiation policy, but neither did interests within the Commonwealth bureaucracy have a history of championing an arbitration or litigation model. The policy slate was relatively wide open, and Whitlam was looking for ideas. Whitlam decided to appoint Ted Woodward, lead counsel for the Yolngu in the Gove land rights case, to investigate and recommend how the government could recognize land rights in the Northern Territory.[84] The fact that Woodward's Commission would be limited to consider aboriginal land rights mechanisms in the Northern Territory marked a shift in Whitlam's commitment expressed while in Opposition, that the Labor government would seek ways to recognize land rights across the whole of Australia.[85]

1972–1976: The Woodward Commission and Institutional Innovation in the Northern Territory

Woodward's mandate had him inquire and report on:

> The appropriate means to recognize and establish the traditional rights and interests of the Aborigines in and in relation to land, and in particular. . . . a) arrangements for vesting title to land in the Northern Territory of Australia now reserved for the use and benefit of the Aboriginal inhabitants of that territory, including rights in minerals and timber . . . b) the desirability of establishing suitable procedures for the examination of claims to Aboriginal traditional rights and interests in or in relation to land in areas . . . outside of Aboriginal reserves . . . [86]

Woodward submitted two reports, one in July 1973, and the other in April 1974. His first report warned the government that aboriginal consent to land claims processes and mechanisms was critical, and advocated against "imposed solutions": " . . . Although a result was reached, so far as possible, by a process of consultation, and agreement will undoubtedly take longer to achieve, it is far more likely to be generally acceptable and to have permanent effect."[87] Woodward's insistence on institutional land claims mechanisms which did not delegate decision-making must have been partly reflective of his and his clients' decision in 1971 not to appeal the Gove land rights decision to the Australian High Court. Part of the political fallout of that judicial decision was aboriginal activists' decision to focus their attention on political, rather than legal, strategies to pursue justice.[88] At the heart of Woodward's reports, there was an acknowledgment that land claims mechanisms were needed to build and institutionalize a new political relationship between traditional landowners and the Australian state. Having recourse to the courts and arbitrators without establishing mechanisms for consultation and bargaining in the political arena would again mean that aboriginal people would have meager means to further their claims outside of courts.

Although Woodward was clearly intent on building a consultative framework for aboriginal land claims, he rejected the importation of the then newly announced Canadian negotiation model. First, he rejected the attraction of negotiating "final settlements" which extinguished undefined rights in return for statutory rights and compensation. He argued that modern treaties would prove difficult to re-open should future conditions warrant their re-negotiation, and he proposed instead, that an Australian solution be more flexible to meet the needs of future generations.[89] Far from seeing the lack of a treaty history in Australia as negative, he felt that Australia had an enviable opportunity to establish land claims mechanisms that would respect the key principles of negotiation (consent and consultation) without conditioning these on the extinguishment of existing rights.

One structural limitation to implementing a full-fledged negotiation policy for land claims in the Northern Territory (and indeed across Australia) was the very open question of which aboriginal groups the government would negotiate with. Which aboriginal group, clan or descent group or community, would hold legal land rights once transferred? One of the legacies of Australia's historic non-recognition of aboriginal land rights was that aboriginal-state interactions did not delineate, redefine or incorporate aboriginal groups according to their customary relationships to country. As a result, the government had very little sound knowledge on appropriate land holding groups within aboriginal customary law, and it was not obvious with which group one would negotiate directly. While this was a serious obstacle to a policy of direct negotiation, it also was an impediment to the efficient work of Woodward's commission.

One of Woodward's first recommendations was for the government to create, via statute, two regional aboriginal intermediaries, the Northern and Central Land Councils. The land councils' immediate task was to facilitate consultation on future land claims policy between Woodward and traditional owners. The Whitlam government created the two land councils in 1973. Based on Woodward's positive evaluation of the land councils' role in organizing and representing traditional owners' opinions during their first few months in operation, Woodward recommended that the two land councils expand their role and become the institutional pivots on which the Woodward's land rights policy would rest. The land councils would consist of aboriginal community representatives, and would act, with those communities' consent, as legal advisors and negotiators in discussions with government and mining companies. Woodward proposed that aboriginal land be vested in another new institutional innovation, the land trusts. The land trust would become the basic landowning group recognized in Australian law. The linkages between the traditional aboriginal land holding group and the land trustees would be for the appropriate aboriginal community to decide.

Woodward's mandate allowed him to address aboriginal claims to two types of land in the Northern Territory: existing aboriginal reserves, and unalienated Crown land. He was not mandated to address how aboriginal land rights would be recognized on pastoral leases, which would leave this thorny issue for the next generation to address. Woodward recommended that the Commonwealth transfer inalienable freehold title of existing aboriginal reserves to an aboriginal trust. The most controversial recommendation of Woodward's report was that the aboriginal owners would have the right to control access to their lands. While Woodward recommended that ownership of minerals should remain in the Crown, granting aboriginal land owners the power to control others' access to their lands meant that they would have an effective veto over mining exploration and development. By granting aboriginal landowners an effective veto over mining activity, only to be overridden by the federal Minister when in the "national interest," Woodward's mining veto would structure an ongoing bargaining relationship between aboriginal people (represented by a land council), the powerful mining industry, and the Crown.

Woodward also recommended a series of institutions for aboriginal claims to unalienated Crown land. Woodward recommended that aboriginal people be able to make claims to land based on current community need and/or traditional customary connection. He argued that the Commonwealth should appoint an Aboriginal Land Commissioner under whose offices aboriginal claims would be presented and investigated. The Land Commissioner would recommend whether claims were valid and whether the lands should be transferred to aboriginal ownership. Woodward also recommended that the Aboriginal Land Commissioner maintain a register of claims relating to pastoral leases. The Aboriginal Land Commissioner model substituted an explicit bargaining model with a consultative model for Crown land, in effect replicating the role of the Canadian Indian Claims Commissioner and New Zealand's Waitangi Tribunal. Once unalienated Crown lands were transferred to aboriginal ownership, however, Woodward's veto provision would come into effect.

Woodward's report established a high standard for a Commonwealth land claims policy in the Northern Territory. The Woodward proposals represented a significant period of institutional innovation, addressing not only institutional mechanisms between aboriginal people and the state. Woodward also proposed the creation of institutions, land councils and land trusts, which would directly affect aboriginal social and political organization. It was unknown how these pieces would work together in practice, and whether these institutions would indeed give effect to aboriginal land rights, but it forced the Whitlam government to respond.

Given the personal role of the Prime Minister and his willingness to take on entrenched interests within the Department of the Interior, it is not surprising that in June of 1975, he introduced legislation in the House of Representatives that gave effect to Woodward's major recommendations. This critical piece of legislation was before the House, in November 1975, when the Governor-General dismissed the Whitlam government on an unrelated matter. The Governor-General handed the reins of power to the Country-Liberal coalition, who over the course of the next year, was the object of mobilization by the mining industry and the Northern Territory government to gut the land rights legislation of the veto provision. By 1976, however, the Northern and Central Land councils had joined the lobbying fray, and they were able to limit some of the damage. In December 1976, the coalition government passed the Land Rights (Northern Territory) Act with the all-important veto provision, but allowed for a government override, after a review by Parliament to establish whether the override would be in the national interest. The Act did not allow for aboriginal claims based on community need, therefore keeping the scope of aboriginal land claims to those aboriginal communities that could demonstrate a continuing traditional connection to land.

The Northern Territory land rights legislation created the basic Australian land claims model, a very different bargaining model from the North American. Instead of establishing a one-on-one negotiation between aboriginal people and the state, the legislation allowed aboriginal people a seat in the on-going negotiations between the government and the dominant economic industry of the region. By transferring aboriginal reserves to aboriginal ownership, aboriginal people would gain a voice over the economic development of almost 20% of the Territory. The ability of the newly constituted land councils to effectively protect aboriginal interests, given huge disparities in bargaining resources, would challenge the underlying legitimacy of the negotiation model, but the legislation remained the strongest protection for aboriginal land rights in Australia.

The legislation was the culmination of political mobilization which burst onto the public consciousness with the Gurindji strike in 1967. This mobilization had an effect on public opinion, and created important support in the Australian mainstream for Commonwealth recognition of aboriginal connections to country. At least, part of the Coalition government's weak response to the aboriginal land rights issue was a different evaluation of activists' ability to move public opinion, once the flurry of initial publicity died down. Ted Woodward, Gough Whitlam and aboriginal activists tied with the Labor Party had come to a different conclusion, and the Northern Territory land rights legislation is a product of these different calculations. The legislation was a critical advance in a country whose courts had proven unwilling to legitimate indigenous peoples' rights to land.

The Hawke Years

The next chapter in Australia's land rights drama would expose huge difficulties in transporting and implementing the Northern Territory bargaining model in the States. The first structural obstacle to such transplantation rested within Australia's constitutional division of powers. Unlike the situation in Canada, the Australian States could also legislate in aboriginal affairs. This sharing of legislative authority meant that the States could freely import or improve the Northern Territory model without Commonwealth action. In an ideal world, States would implement wise legislation that protected both aboriginal rights and allowed for harmonious economic development without arm-twisting from Canberra. Concurrent jurisdiction also meant that States could summarily legislate away land rights in defiance of Commonwealth wishes. In the presence of an intransigent or an anti-aboriginal rights State government, the Commonwealth could only forestall the erosion of aboriginal rights by imposing its own solution at the serious risk of harming intergovernmental relations.

The likelihood that such States would fight against Commonwealth attempts to impose land rights legislation was almost certain, because for the Commonwealth to do so would necessarily mean that Canberra was acting in an exclusive State jurisdiction, the use and management of State lands. The incentive for sub-national governments to protect their exclusive power in land use policy is high in Canada as well, but the balance of fiscal power between Canberra and the States makes the State protective instinct even more acute. Since State governments in Australia do not raise their own income taxes, the proceeds from the economic exploitation of lands makes up a greater percentage of State operating budgets. As a result, State governments are more likely to see their own interests aligned with major economic actors.

Outside of the Northern Territory, the aboriginal population is concentrated in South Australia, Western Australia, and Queensland. Any national land rights regime needs to include these States in order to have any substantive meaning. Of these three key states, only South Australia chose to enter into negotiations with aboriginal people at the end of the 1970s. In a significant move, the South Australian Labor government[90] negotiated with its aboriginal populations and transferred freehold ownership of its northern reserves to aboriginal people in 1981 and 1983.[91] Although the willingness of the South Australian government to enter into negotiations with aboriginal people was important, of the three critical States, the South Australian has a relatively minor mining sector, and the lands transferred were of marginal economic worth. Western Australia and Queensland, however, have significant mining sectors, and are the two States with the worst historical record of aboriginal-state relations. The culmination of these constitutional and economic factors was that the existence of a national aboriginal land rights policy rested on the Commonwealth's willingness to take on the very two governments with the motivation and resources to resist.

A window of opportunity for a national land rights regime opened when Western Australia elected a Labor government in 1983. With a Labor government in Canberra under Prime Minister Bob Hawke and Labor Premier Brian Burke in Perth, aboriginal rights activists within the Labor party pushed the Prime Minister to implement a national land rights regime that would extend the right to negotiate over Australia's economic development to aboriginal people across the country. Hawke's land rights legislation failed when Australia's mining industry targeted a public lobbying campaign in Western Australia. The decreasing support for aboriginal land rights among Western Australian voters threatened Burke's government, and hence sapped Burke's willingness to support even a minimal Commonwealth scheme. Aboriginal support for Hawke's legislation waned and then divided when Hawke began to weaken the right to negotiate provisions in the proposed legislation in order to get Burke's support. Rather than implement a weak national land rights system which would set a precedent for watering down the key provision of the Northern Territory legislation, northern land councils lobbied factions within the Labor party to drop the national land rights scheme altogether. The Northern Territory land councils were not prepared to fall on their own sword in order to win what they saw as marginal land rights concessions for aboriginal people elsewhere. Without cross-aboriginal support for the land rights legislation, in March 1986 Hawke abandoned his initiative, and vacated the field to the States.[92]

The Mabo Decision and the Native Title Act (1993)

It would not be until 1992, when the High Court recognized the validity of aboriginal title in Australian common law, that the Commonwealth Labor government would be pushed by a more cohesive coalition of aboriginal actors to implement a national land rights regime over the objections of the mining industry, pastoralists, Queensland, and Western Australia. This regime would incorporate a grab-bag of institutional mechanisms such as mediation, arbitration, and increasingly, litigation. My goal here is to show how aboriginal groups managed to cohere at the national advocacy level, and push the Commonwealth to impose a land rights framework on the States. However, I will also show, through a case study of Western Australia, how aboriginal fragmentation at the claimant level has impacted States' perceived value of negotiation as a workable strategy.

Judicial Change: The High Court's 1992 Mabo Decision

On June 3rd, 1992, the High Court handed down its judgment in the *Mabo* case. The ruling is historic in that the High Court overturned the long-established doctrine of *terra nullius,* and thereby allowed for the recognition of aboriginal title in Australian common law for the first time. The content of aboriginal title, the exact rights which an aboriginal person or group could claim, was to be determined according to aboriginal customary law, and therefore varied according to claimant and context. The *Mabo* ruling was revolutionary in that the High Court gave legal credence to aboriginal customary rights in land. The ruling was also important in protecting the existing Australian property regime by clearly stating that government grants of freehold title extinguished aboriginal title. This meant that no aboriginal person or group could legally assert a title claim over land held in freehold. Significantly, the High Court did not directly address the question of whether aboriginal title survived on pastoral leases. The Court did say, however, that the interests of pastoralists would prevail over aboriginal people in the event that their rights conflicted. The pastoral lease issue is important, as it left open the question of whether aboriginal people could legally assert a title claim to 38% of Western Australia, 42% of South Australia, 41% of New South Wales, 54% of Queensland, and 51% of the Northern Territory.[93] This silence on the part of the High Court potentially expanded the question of aboriginal land rights policy past the issue of aboriginal reserves and vacant Crown lands.

While the decision opened up the geographic scope of the lands over which aboriginal people could now legally assert rights, the Court also imposed important caveats. The High Court ruled that only those aboriginal people who had managed to maintain a continuing connection to their lands, despite two hundred odd years of government policies which made this impossible for many, could assert a title claim. The further whittling away of the substantive victory for aboriginal people came with the Court's views on the extinguishment of aboriginal title. The Court ruled that governments could unilaterally extinguish whatever aboriginal title did exist through lawful legislative action. Prior to the 1975 passage of the Commonwealth's Racial Discrimination Act (RDA), all extinguishment was lawful extinguishment, giving aboriginal people no legal leverage to seek compensation for their historic dispossession. State or Commonwealth acts which extinguished native title, possibly mining leases, for example, after 1975 were lawful if they met the provisions of the RDA. For all these reasons, the *Mabo* decision was a judicial victory for some aboriginal people, but an empty shell for others.

The Australian *Mabo* decision and the Canadian *Calder* decisions have key aspects in common. Both decisions were precedents giving common law recognition to the doctrine of aboriginal title. Both decisions left their respective governments to *infer* whether aboriginal title continued to exist in key parts of the country, importantly, in British Columbia, and in Australia, land under pastoral lease. Both decisions removed the federal government's "do-nothing" option, thereby forcing a land rights policy response and a new era in land claim politics. Prime Minister Keating said as much in October 1992: " . . . By rejecting the doctrine of *terra nullius*, the court has provided a new basis for relations between indigenous and other Australians, and given impetus to the process of reconciliation. It provides both an opportunity and a challenge."[94]

Critically, however, the *Calder* and *Mabo* decisions presented the Keating and the Trudeau governments with two very different questions. Since the Canadian federal government has sole constitutional authority over "Indians and lands reserved for Indians," resolution of aboriginal land claims required the presence of the federal government at the negotiation table. Therefore, Trudeau's decision to implement a negotiation policy was a decision to commit the federal government as a major party to negotiations across the country. In contrast, the Australian States have the jurisdiction to legislate in both aboriginal and land management issues, which are subject to the paramountcy of federal law. Given the recognition of aboriginal title in the *Mabo* decision, the critical question facing Australia's Prime Minister Paul Keating was whether he was prepared to force the *States* to negotiate by enacting a national land rights framework. Outside of the Northern Territory, federal Crown lands are marginal, limited basically to national parks and national defense installations. Moreover, given the States' authority to legislate in aboriginal affairs, the Commonwealth government wasn't legally required to sit in on aboriginal land rights negotiations. Therefore, a national land rights negotiation policy would not necessarily involve the Commonwealth government as the major government actor around the bargaining table. The biggest political question in the aftermath of the *Mabo* decision was the extent to which the Keating government was prepared to protect and advance aboriginal rights in Australia, at the cost of intergovernmental peace.

Prime Minister Keating's Response to Mabo:
The Native Title Act 1993 (NTA)

By October 1992, a key interdepartmental committee of officials (IDC) presented the Keating cabinet with a confidential options paper, canvassing a wider range of options than the Commonwealth government had entertained since the early 1970s,[95] including a specialist tribunal to adjudicate claims, a wide-ranging legislative framework, and a new negotiation model.[96] The Keating government had the option of importing the Canadian model of negotiating comprehensive regional agreements between governments and aboriginal representatives. By March 1993, the IDC recommended that the regional negotiation model be dropped from the government's option list. The IDC rejected the model as impracticable:

> . . . a very long and difficult negotiation would be inevitable, in which concepts such as self-government over native title lands, constitutional protection of title and the granting of substantial economic and other benefits would come into play as part of the 'grand bargain.' It is not therefore a practicable approach for dealing with immediate land management issues.[97]

The IDC was clearly not interested in expanding the aboriginal land rights issue into a *de facto* political settlement which would put issues other than land use on the negotiations table. I argue, however, that the social structural reality of Australian aboriginal political organization made a Canadianesque 'grand bargain' unattainable. The Labor government's Minister of Aboriginal Affairs, Robert Tickner, was acutely aware that the issue of who would negotiate for aboriginal people in a regional settlement framework was "an even tougher question" than the content of such a settlement.[98] Tickner and the other members of the Keating government were warned, during the post-*Mabo* policy debate, that a settlement negotiated between governments and regional or national aboriginal organizations would not be seen by many aboriginal people as locally binding.[99]

If claimant issues on the local and regional levels were a factor in rejecting the regional negotiation model, it was not the kiss of death for implementing *any* negotiation model. A negotiation model would need to reflect and give formal voice to the inherent localism of aboriginal land rights. Aboriginal spokespersons demanded that the Commonwealth enshrine the key principle of negotiation, aboriginal consent, within any legislation. Aboriginal leadership did recognize, however, that a negotiation policy would need to include terms defining aboriginal claimants, and establish, through federal statute, aboriginal representative bodies that would conduct title negotiations.[100] The legal definition of aboriginal claimants and the incorporation of aboriginal native title groups would be endogenous to federal legislation.

The political road, which started with the June 1992 *Mabo* decision, and culminated in the passage of the Commonwealth's national land rights legislation in December 1993, is accurately described as exhausting and "tortuous."[101] I cannot possibly recount the political drama here.[102] However, I will make the following observations. The Keating government's commitment to a land rights regime that respected the core principle of indigenous consent, and protected aboriginal land rights from State unilateralism, was sorely challenged, and at times bested by the political imperative of intergovernmental relations.[103] The critical force that limited the impact of the States' rights campaign on Commonwealth behavior was a unified, daring, and mobilized aboriginal political leadership. The then Minister of Aboriginal Affairs identifies the "incisive" turning points that cumulatively forced the Commonwealth to impose a regime on the recalcitrant States when it would have preferred to vacate the policy field: credible threats to mobilize aboriginal people should the Commonwealth not step up to the plate with the States;[104] the demonstrated ability of aboriginal political representatives from across Australia to unite behind a land rights agenda in August 1993;[105] and the ability of the aboriginal leadership to use the press and to redefine the terms of public debate in the eleventh hour.[106]

The NTA came together in a heated and hurried process of legislative bargaining. It is a highly complicated and lengthy piece of legislation born in a political maelstrom. It tried to balance the protection of newly recognized indigenous land rights with the validation of existing and future property rights, of which mining rights and pastoral lease rights were key. The basic political bargain enshrined in the NTA is summarized, if bluntly, as follows. Aboriginal leaders agreed to accept the status quo by allowing the validation of all existing legal interests in land. Aboriginal leaders therefore conceded the ability to contest the extinguishment of aboriginal title before 1993. In return, the Commonwealth would allow registered aboriginal claimants a seat at the negotiation table when future (mostly State) government acts (e.g. the issuance of mining leases for exploration and development) would have a significant impact on aboriginal title. This is what is referred to as the *future act regime*.

The NTA established a Commonwealth tribunal, the National Native Title Tribunal (NNTT), that would maintain a register of claims, determine the scope of the native title rights held, and also arbitrate a future act dispute should good-faith negotiation not yield an agreement within a six month period.[107] However, the Commonwealth could overturn an NNTT ruling if it was deemed "in the national interest." The Commonwealth legislation operated under the assumption that native title was extinguished on pastoral leases. This assumption was a strong one, given the legal advice of the day.[108] However, the NTA left the door open for aboriginal people to test this issue in the High Court by not explicitly extinguishing aboriginal title on pastoral leases.[109]

In summary, the NTA provided a national framework which forced governments, miners, and (to a lesser degree) pastoralists to pull up a chair for aboriginal people in a wider land management bargaining table. Due to the fact that the lands at issue were mostly State lands, the government party was usually a State government. The negotiation policy under the NTA is significantly different, in many ways more limited, than the negotiation policies enacted by the Canadians and New Zealanders. Firstly, the scope of the land claims negotiations conducted under the NTA (1993) are limited to land management, and cannot be seen as a wider treaty settlement. The Australian native title negotiations under the NTA have not yet extended to encompass a wider set of socio-political issues. Secondly, in keeping with the Woodward Commission's policy legacy, the truncated set of bargaining issues is contrasted with a larger set of players, since third-party economic interests are at the table, in addition to the government and all registered aboriginal claimants.

The next section of this case study addresses State-level decisions to negotiate or litigate land claims under the framework of the NTA. I will show how the NTA further exacerbated claimant fragmentation at the local level, to such an extent that State governments sought judicial solutions in key areas instead of seeking a negotiated agreement. I will focus on the case of Western Australia.

Western Australia

The State of Western Australia comprises approximately a third of the Australian land mass. Its capital city, Perth, is the most isolated major centre in Australia, sitting alone on the Indian Ocean. Settled first by prospectors and miners rushing to the Goldfields, pastoralists soon followed. The British granted the frontier colony self-governing status in 1890, and from its conception, the colonial legislature denied its aboriginal population any benefits or rights of British subjecthood.[110] The State is home to approximately

20% of Australia's aboriginal population,[111] and shares with Queensland the dubious distinction of holding the worst record in Australian's history of aboriginal oppression.

Western Australia came grudgingly into the Australian federation in 1901. On the geographic periphery, Western Australia has a well-entrenched history of anti-Commonwealth and pro-States' rights politics, complete with a separatist movement in the 1930s. The State's interest in fighting off Commonwealth encroachment in land management issues stems in large part from protecting State control over the cornerstone of its wealth. One of the key drivers of State's rights politics is its dependence on the primary resource sector, the mining sector in particular. In 1971, 62% of Australia's mining exploration occurred in Western Australia.[112] In 1994, the State Attorney-General reported that Western Australia provides 40% of Australia's mineral exports, and contributes 25% of Australia's total export income.[113] Indeed, the Western Australian mining sector has a global impact, producing 18% of the world's alumina and 14% of the world's iron ore.[114] As one State legislator said in 2000, " . . . when the mining industry sneezes, the State's economy gets pneumonia."[115]

The confluence of a significant aboriginal population, a political ethos very sensitive to Commonwealth incursions on States' rights, and the economic importance of the mining sector makes Western Australia a tough nut to crack in aboriginal land rights politics. In Western Australia, the economic value of aboriginal land rights is potentially substantial. With a large proportion of Australia's aboriginal population in the State, the success of a progressive national land rights strategy depends significantly on whether the Western Australian government is willing to recognize and protect aboriginal land rights at the perceived cost of the mining and pastoral industries.

Prior to the 1993 Native Title Act, Western Australia was the sole State not to recognize some form of traditional aboriginal land rights within its panoply of land tenures. As Labor Premier Brian Burke said in 1987, " . . . We are on the record as saying that while we are in Government in this State we will not have land rights of the Aboriginal people . . . I believe that, broadly, Australia's people accept that while they do not want Aborigines given land rights they do want them to be given a fair go."[116] The State's conception of a "fair go" was to allow aboriginal people access to lands, either through the Aboriginal Land Trust or by allowing aboriginal people to hold land under a normal freehold or leasehold like any other property owner.[117] By April 1985, 19 million hectares of land was "held for the use and benefit" of aboriginal people; an additional 7 million hectares was held by September of 1991, with 80% of the additional hectares held in the form of special purpose leases.[118] However, reserve lands (approximately 8% of the State) vested in the Aboriginal Land Trust remain Crown owned. Aboriginal leaseholds are like any other tenure in Western Australia, with minerals reserved to the Crown and no veto over mining exploration or development. Land rights activists denounced Western Australia's aboriginal land policies as woefully inadequate. "Until the Mabo decision and the subsequent [Commonwealth] native title legislation, the best Aboriginal people could hope for was a 99-year lease of the Aboriginal reserve to the local community, which gave them less security of title than a Perth suburban home-owner."[119]

Post-Mabo Land Rights Policy in Western Australia

In the aftermath of the *Mabo* decision, Premier Richard Court took a two-prong strategy against aboriginal title rights. First, Premier Court worked to defeat the Commonwealth legislation as a flagrant attempt to override States' rights:

> What is clear is that [Prime Minister Keating] seeks to ride on the back of the Aboriginal people of this country, most of whom are residents of States, in order to distort the Australian Constitution and increase, yet again, the power of the Commonwealth. His objective—one of his objectives at any rate—is to gain control for the Commonwealth of the management of land throughout a large part of Australia . . . As to its moral foundation, there is no doubt—it has none. The Commonwealth legislation is a simple play for Commonwealth power.[120]

Second, Premier Court sought to pre-empt the Commonwealth by introducing legislation in the State Assembly before the NTA became a legal reality.[121] The legislation set out to unilaterally extinguish all surviving aboriginal title in the State, and replacing aboriginal title with statutory rights of traditional usage which would be subordinate to all other land interests.[122] Claimants who could establish a claim to traditional usage would be eligible for compensation. Disputes about compensation would be litigated in the courts; once litigated, the government would restrict negotiation to the size and composition of a compensation package.[123] Western Australia enacted the legislation before the NTA came into effect, but Premier Court's victory was short-lived. In 1995, the High Court struck down the State legislation as racially discriminatory, and the State of Western Australia became subject to the right to negotiate provisions of the NTA's future act regime.

The Court government showed that negotiation was not its real preference. However, once forced by the Commonwealth and the High Court to negotiate over future acts which would impair the native title, did the Western Australian government actually negotiate? And, if not, why?

Negotiation, Claimant Fragmentation, and the NTA

Soon after the NTA came into effect, it became clear that certain provisions of the NTA interacted to create huge incentives for claim proliferation and claimant fragmentation on the ground, especially in economically important areas of the country. The reality of the post-Mabo native title framework was that the only way for aboriginal groups or individuals to benefit economically from their newly recognized rights was to access the right to negotiate provisions of the future act regime. By putting aboriginal people at a bargaining table with mining companies, the future act regime was the only way for many aboriginal people to seek reparations for loss of country, community development, or to seek old-fashioned personal gain. Aboriginal people could get a seat at the future act bargaining table if they passed the claimant registration test administered by the NNTT. Importantly, registered aboriginal *claimants* retained the valuable right to negotiate until the NNTT determined who were native title *holders*. This meant that for some claimants, the proportion of which is not possible to ascertain, there was no incentive to move through the claimant determination stage.

All rested on the NTA's threshold test that contained the criteria by which the NNTT could reject an aboriginal group's registration. As a result of last minute legislative bargaining in December 1993, the NTA's threshold test was very low. It simply required " . . . the applicant to state the belief that native title had not been extinguished."[124] In 1995, the Federal Court ruled that under the NTA, "the [NNTT] registrar had no option but to accept all claims for registration other than those that were frivolous or vexatious."[125]

Due to the relative unboundedness of the traditional claimant group and the myriad of kinship connections an aboriginal person could invoke to justify an interest over certain lands, an aboriginal group or person could make at least a *prima facie* case to be a valid claimant. The NTA also did not set out minimum claimant membership criteria, hence, claimants had the incentive to fragment into smaller family groups as each sought an independent seat at the bargaining table. The result was a situation where the level of cross-claiming, claimant fragmentation, and intra-aboriginal disputes over who were "real claimants" or just "opportunists" were directly related to the economic value of the land under claim.[126] The serious difficulties this phenomenon produced for a viable negotiation strategy were echoed by all, including key supporters of the NTA. Former Leader of the Australian Labor Party and former Governor-General Bill Hayden wrote of his attempts to reach a negotiated agreement over the Century Zinc mining project in Queensland:

> What became abundantly clear to me quite early is . . . the absence of any definition of who can be a claimant and the seemingly unlimited opportunities for people to register as such; the unrepresentativeness of some who register as claimants; the confusion and tensions which can become rampant as long-standing factional and family disputes within a tribal group manifest themselves at the expense of the issue to be settled; the jealousy and mistrust which can arise between different tribal bodies which can impair negotiation processes.[127] One key area where this phenomenon occurred was the lucrative Goldfields area of Western Australia.[128]

By 1995, the High Court had taken away Western Australia's preferred policy option, to unilaterally legislate away native title. The Court government had to decide whether to negotiate or litigate under the Commonwealth's NTA framework. Claimant fragmentation played a decisive role in the Court government's NTA-induced policy choice.[129] Convinced that negotiation with fractured, competing, and possibly illegitimate claimant groups would prove futile precisely where the economic costs of delay were high, the Court government chose a litigation strategy.[130] The Court government reportedly made this decision in 1995 without an evaluation of litigation's long-run costs.[131] Although never a fan of a negotiated response to aboriginal land rights, the Court government's litigiousness cannot be attributed to its conservative political ideology alone. The government confirmed its litigation strategy a few years later, and the reasoning behind it, in a letter to the NNTT:

> The State does not support mediation of [the south west and goldfields claims]. Based on assessment of the history since European settlement, the anthropology, the number of other valid interests, disputation in the Aboriginal community and the diversity of Aboriginal interests within the claim areas, the State does not believe it is in the position to reach definitive decisions on whether native title rights and interests have been preserved or not. Therefore the State has concluded that it is in the public interest for these claims to be referred to the Federal Court for determination.[132]

The Court government's larger strategy was to pursue amendments to the NTA in the name of workability. With the defeat of Paul Keating's Labor government in March 1996 and the ascent of the Liberal Party leader John Howard to the Prime Ministership, the political process to amend the NTA was well underway.

Negotiation, Low Indigenous Cohesion and the NTA After 1998

While the need to amend the NTA in the name of workability was real, opening up the NTA made it possible for conservative, even reactionary forces to roll back the progress achieved in aboriginal land rights since the *Mabo* decision. From 1996 to 1998, the Howard government faced extraordinary pressure from industry, pastoralists, and the States to legislate "bucket loads of extinguishment." Without a Labor government in Canberra, aboriginal activists had fewer allies in key decision-making circles, and the 1998 amendments to the NTA seriously eroded the scope of the right to negotiate provisions of the NTA.[133] The new NTA came into force on September 30th, 1998.

The Howard government did institute two new amendments which were designed to make negotiation a more workable option. The first was the new claimant registration test. The new test requires much more detail about the boundaries of the claim area, the membership of the claimant group, the nature of the rights claimed, and the extent of the group's physical connection to the claimed land. Before the claim can be registered, the applicant needs to demonstrate that he has the approval of the claimant group to act on its behalf. The registration test also disallows the previous overlapping of claim groups, although it does not disallow the overlapping of geographic claim boundaries. The new registration provisions applied retroactively to many claims already registered under the old NTA.

The claim re-registration process led to a significant redefinition process from 1998 to 2000, where claims and claimant groups, acting strategically under the new NTA, discontinued, amalgamated, and otherwise significantly redefined their claims and the claimant groups themselves.[134] The significance of this redefinition process is clear in the following figures. Of the 340 claimant applications lodged under the old Act to which the new threshold test applied, only 46% passed.[135] Of the 116 applications submitted by June 30th, 2000, under the new Act, 91% passed the registration test. Of the 1026 claimant applications submitted from January 1st, 1994, to June 30th, 2000, about half were either discontinued or combined in some way during the registration process.[136] This redefinition process was particularly marked in Western Australia.[137]

The second NTA amendment designed to facilitate negotiated outcomes was the introduction of Indigenous Land Use Agreements (ILUAs).

All registered claimants and other property rights holders in an area able to come up with an agreement can register their agreement as an ILUA.[138] Once registered, the ILUA is a legal contract that binds not just the parties to it, but any other subsequent native title claimants in that area. One possible advantage for the State of an ILUA is that once registered, its provisions prevail over the NTA's future act regime.[139] For a State government, the potential benefit of the ILUA framework is to negotiate one deal covering an area up front, rather than engaging in a series of negotiations every time a major mining development is underway or a new residential development breaks ground.

What effect did the amendments to the NTA have on Western Australia's willingness to negotiate? In March 2000, Premier Court released his government's pre-conditions for entering into any native title negotiation. Importantly, the State would negotiate only when aboriginal claimants could provide a detailed connection report which further developed the items demanded in the NTA registration test. The precedent negotiation for the Court government was with the Spinifex people, notable because the government considered the Spinifex claim legally strong, and the level of disputation among the Spinifex was also low. The Court government remained skeptical about the feasibility of reaching settlements on a larger regional scale.[140]

While announcing the pre-conditions for negotiation, the Court government continued to pursue a litigation strategy. Despite the significant amalgamation of claims in Western Australia from 1998 to 2000, the Goldfields area remained subject to 13 claims in 2001.[141] The Court government remained convinced that regional agreements were impossible due to intra-aboriginal contestation in economically vital regions, and continued to pursue those claims in the courts, rejecting a regional negotiating framework. As Premier Court stated in the State Assembly:

> The only way there will be a resolution in Kalgoorlie [the Goldfields] . . . is if a court makes a decision. The Leader of the Opposition cannot walk into this Parliament and say regional agreements are the solution to native title. He is not living in the real world. He knows that Aboriginal people are no different from other people; they have their own interests in different areas . . . the Leader of the Opposition is living in cloud cuckoo land if he believes we can have regional agreements . . . [142]

The Minister responsible for the mining and pastoral industries conveyed the same message:

The Goldfields Land Council came to me and said we should have a statewide agreement. I said, 'If you can get some heads of agreement for a statewide agreement, where you can get together people in the desert, who are small estate groups and are very jealous of their area, and urban Aboriginals, I will support it." They never came back to me. [Aboriginal leader] Pat Dodson said the same thing. I said, "I do not think you can do it. If you can, show me what you are trying to do, and I will help you work on it, if I can, to make it a reality"; but he never came back to me. It is all talk.[143]

One can argue the counterfactual that the Liberal Party government of Richard Court, with its pastoral electoral base and ideological predispositions, would never have negotiated a regional agreement in Western Australia, even if the Goldfields Land Council or Pat Dodson had actually delivered the State a cohesive regional claimant negotiating group. I remain unconvinced. The public policy challenge of implementing a negotiation policy in a context of low indigenous group cohesion remained after the fall of the Court government and the election of the Western Australian Labor Party to power in February of 2001.

The new Labor Premier, Dr. Geoff Gallop, came into office with a mandate to "mediate, not litigate." While the Labor government is confronted with the real cost of a long-run litigation strategy, it cannot run to the negotiation table without confronting the complexity of aboriginal politics across the table. Labor's negotiation policy is predicated on the same pre-negotiation conditions of its predecessor: the delivery of detailed aboriginal connection reports. The connection reports place a high burden of proof directly on aboriginal claimants and their representative bodies. During my interviews in Perth in August 2001, policy-makers inside the Labor government were coming to grips with the growing reality that while litigation is definitely expensive, mediation and negotiation are definitely not cheap. With little concrete information about the long-run financial costs of either litigation or negotiation, negotiation resources would need to be allocated according to those areas where policy-makers had reasonable expectations that settlements were politically possible.[144]

To summarize, claimant fragmentation has had important impacts in land claims politics in Australia. First, it determined which type of negotiation model was feasible. The Australian negotiation model is quite localized, with little possibility of achieving the economies of scale from larger regional agreements. When the Commonwealth legislation fragmented aboriginal cohesion even further, States chose to litigate and to lobby for change in the NTA rather than accept the negotiation framework as given.

In Western Australia, the amendments to the NTA clarified the situation. Richard Court's government indicated it would negotiate only on the condition that cohesiveness criteria were met; at the same time, it continued to pursue a litigation strategy where claims and claimants remained numerous.

REFLECTIONS ON THE AUSTRALIAN CASE

In this study, I have argued that the emergence of a land claims negotiation policy requires a government to concur with two basic propositions: 1) it will recognize the validity of aboriginal collective rights, and 2) it will not seek to insulate itself politically from the resolution of land grievances by delegating decision-making power to a third party. In each of the country case studies, the specific costs and benefits associated with each of these propositions vary according to historical legacies, political culture and partisanship. What remains constant across these cases is the following: that no government in Canada, New Zealand, and Australia agreed to negotiate indigenous land grievances without first realizing that indigenous people could unify behind a land rights agenda, credibly commit to a future strategy of protest and political disruption, and change the political landscape by influencing mainstream political opinion. In other words, the emergence of negotiation policies in these cases has been preceded by policy-makers' recognition that indigenous peoples were now players in the game of aboriginal policy development, rather than un-strategic policy takers. Indigenous people's credible threat to impose future political costs should governments not recognize their collective land rights increased the probability that negotiation would emerge as the government's policy response because the credible threat decreased the government's long-run attractiveness of a blame avoidance, "let the courts handle it" type of strategy.

In this chapter, as I had with Canada and New Zealand, I established the points in time when the Australian Commonwealth cabinet had the opportunity to choose a negotiation strategy. Drawing largely on cabinet submissions and the archival record of cabinet discussions, I examined the ideological framework in which cabinets approached indigenous land rights. I established how the political mobilization of indigenous peoples changed the terms for aboriginal policy reform in the post-war era. The mobilization of the mid 1960s was a product of underlying demographic and social shifts experienced in the Western world after World War Two: the larger phenomenon of rural depopulation created new urban centers for aboriginal activists who would be inspired by the protest repertoires of the American civil rights era. Without the capacity of indigenous peoples to act collectively behind a land rights (not just an equal rights) agenda, and the demonstrated capacity of indigenous peoples to sway mainstream public opinion, I argue that the judicial legitimation of land rights alone would not have resulted in negotiation. Indigenous mobilization, more than court decisions, changed the terms of debate within cabinet rooms. High Court decisions like the Gove land rights case (Australia 1971), the *Calder* decision (Canada 1973), and the Lands Case (New Zealand 1987), provided hugely important opportunities for significant policy change, but did not on their own guarantee that negotiation would emerge.

With indigenous people pushing the aboriginal policy reform envelope since the mid 1960s, allies within government and around the cabinet table pushed for a pragmatic re-evaluation of anti-recognition policies. In Canada, the shift in cabinet support for a pragmatic negotiation policy occurred in the lifetime of one government. In Australia and New Zealand, the respective Labor parties would differentiate themselves on the land rights issue from their more conservative competitors. In these countries where aboriginal politics would reinforce existing partisan cleavages, the support around the cabinet table for a negotiation position would depend on the party in power.

The Australian case in particular also suggests that the sequencing of political mobilization and judicial change are necessary, but insufficient conditions for the emergence of land claim negotiation policies. Other variables can come into play to mediate policy-makers' evaluations of negotiation versus other policy options. This chapter has weaved two intermediating variables of particular import to the Australian case throughout the narrative: the incentives produced by the allocation of jurisdictional power across national and sub-national governments, and the ability of local aboriginal claimants to act as cohesive negotiating parties. By making the prospect of future settlements a slim proposition, claimant fragmentation, as seen in the case of Western Australia, can significantly erode a government's relative value of negotiation versus its other policy options, such as unilateral legislation or a rush to litigation.

Chapter Six

Litigation, not Negotiation: The American Land Claims Experience in Comparative Perspective

INTRODUCTION

In April 1866, the United States Senate sat down to debate whether it would appropriate the necessary funds to allow the executive to negotiate a peace treaty with the Sioux of the upper Missouri and upper Platte rivers.[1] With settlers pushing into the American frontier and hostilities with the Sioux high, the Secretary of War had invited bands of Sioux to meet at Forts Sully, Rice, Berthold, Union and Laramie in order to negotiate a peace of sorts. Given the Sioux were invited to treat at these forts, the United States government was expected to provide the Sioux with basic provisions during the course of the negotiations. The executive was well within its rights to call for such a negotiation. Article II, section 2, of the Constitution gives the President the power to negotiate treaties "by and with the advice and consent of the Senate . . . provided two thirds of the Senators present concur . . .." In this manner, the United States, like its British predecessor, had conducted a negotiation policy with Indian inhabitants since the country's beginnings. Negotiations over land and peace formed the backbone of the United States' relations with Indians. However, in 1866, the Senate's debate over provisioning the Sioux in particular turned into a larger debate over the very merits of the United States' negotiation policy with Indian tribes in general.

Ohio's Republican Senator, John Sherman, put on record his principled objection to negotiating with Indians:

> I have always been opposed to this mode of dealing with Indians . . .
> The idea of getting together the head men of the Indian tribes and giving them pork and beans—very sensible articles of food—feeding them up and then negotiating a treaty with them, and bringing that treaty

in here to be ratified as a high negotiation with a foreign Power, has always seemed to me so ridiculous that I hope sometime or other the Senate will abolish the whole system.[2]

According to this view, the demotion of Indians from self-governing and independent tribes to weakened subjects of governance by outsiders needed to be reflected in a new federal *modus operandi*. Senator Sherman offered two alternatives to a negotiation policy:

> . . . I believe it would be wiser and better to give to the infant States and Territories of the West a portion of the money now appropriated by the Government for the support of Indians, and trust to the people of the infant States and Territories to govern those tribes, and disband our whole Indian system; or . . . to transfer this whole Indian service to the Army, and let them govern the Indians as subjects of the United States; but the present system of governing the Indians by treaty stipulations, by bribes and presents, beans and corn and pork . . . is a system that ought not to be tolerated longer.[3]

A Democratic colleague from California, Senator James McDougall, joined Senator Sherman in his opposition to negotiation, although his preferred alternative to negotiation was naked subjugation:

> I agree with the Senator from Ohio . . . They must be whipped into their place, and subjected to obedience . . . let them die out by a law established by a greater Master than confines himself to this sphere . . . Would it not be better to whip them well? . . . Is not the Government powerful, and has it not men and horses enough?[4]

Countering Senators Sherman and McDougall were a few voices in favor of negotiation. However, these voices rose in the name of expediency and humanity, rather than in recognition of Indians' property or political rights. James Doolittle, Republican Senator from Wisconsin, urged a softer hand in dealing with America's Indian problem:

> There is but one way to deal with these Indians on the plains: you must feed them or fight them[5] . . . I know, as my honorable friend knows, that dealing with these Indians is a very different thing from dealing with a great nation like England or France . . . We are dealing with a feeble people . . . they will soon pass away, and nothing will remain of the Indian tribes but the beautiful names which they gave

to our rivers and our towns. That is their inevitable destiny; but while they are passing along like sick children in our hands, it is better to deal in the spirit of humanity, to feed these dying people, than it is to turn in and slaughter them by the sword.[6]

Although the Senate granted the President his appropriation to feed the Sioux in 1866, the debate over the wisdom of a negotiation policy would grow and gain momentum. In 1871, the debate concluded when the Senate refused to ratify any more treaties with Indian tribes. The American negotiation policy came to an official end, though the executive would conclude some agreements past that date.[7] At the end of the treaty-making era, the United States had signed 370 treaties to cede Indian land rights over 95% of the United States' public domain.[8]

Even before 1871, Indians pushed forward their land claims, decrying either the federal government's unwillingness to meet its obligations under the treaties, or the circumstances in which treaties were signed. For a time, the federal government's response was to ignore these claims, later to adjudicate them. However, the United States would never again institute a formal negotiation policy. It engaged in a few *ad hoc* negotiations in the late twentieth century, but the United States government has consistently preferred to delegate the resolution of Indian land claims to its courts or to special arbitrators. It has not offered negotiation as an institutionalized alternative to litigation. Unlike Canada and New Zealand in the post-war era, the United States would not rehabilitate the negotiation precedent of its colonial past. The United States government has not negotiated, *despite* the judiciary's recognition in the nineteenth century of both native title and Indian tribes' inherent right to self-government. The inherent right to self-government is a right that the Canadian Supreme Court and New Zealand Court of Appeal have at the time of writing not directly conceded, and a right that the Australian High Court has denied. In this respect, America's indigenous communities have won a degree of latitude in the courts that remains elusive elsewhere. Why, then, do we have the paradox that the negotiation of land claims has failed to emerge in the United States?

As in the other cases in this study, I argue that the absence of a negotiation policy in the American land claims experience is due most directly to the sequencing of judicial change and indigenous political mobilization. Only in the American case did landmark judicial rulings long precede indigenous political mobilization, and therefore the American case stands as a test to this study's main argument. In Canada, the Supreme Court made its first landmark native title decision in 1973, after the political mobilization spawned by Trudeau's white paper in 1969. In the United States, the Supreme Court tackled the native title question in 1823, more than a century *before* a supra-tribal indigenous organization would get off the ground in 1944 to press for Indian rights or before the 1960s protest politics of fish-ins and occupations began.

For the majority of time that American courts have fashioned an Indian rights jurisprudence, native Americans have not had the political wherewithal to either consolidate judicial gains in the political sphere or to minimize the political impact of judicial losses. The classic statement of this problem arose in the 1830s, and did not really change until the 1970s. When Chief Justice John Marshall ruled that Indian tribes were political communities not subject to State law,[9] President Andrew Jackson is reported to have said: "John Marshall has made his decision; now let him enforce it."[10] Therefore, at the key moments when American policy-makers designed the mechanisms to deal with Indian land claims, native Americans could not credibly threaten to impose future political costs. American policy-makers were not persuaded, as were their counterparts cross-nationally, that Indian land claims represented a distinctly political problem requiring a negotiated solution. Indian land claims were defined as a primarily legal problem whose proper resolution demanded a legalistic solution.

In 1946, Congress created the Indian Claims Commission (ICC), an independent agency that acted and was accepted by all as a court. The ICC litigated Indian claims and decided the size of a monetary settlement. By the time native Americans engaged in the political protests of the 1960s and 1970s, the ICC had already dispensed with many claims, and the opportunity for a meaningful negotiation policy had already passed. In those instances where Indian land claims became politically salient, American policy-makers had a clear imperative to protect the ICC's legacy. Ad hoc negotiations would occur on those claims that would not re-open or set a precedent for negotiating the claims already concluded. Any new claims were directed to the courts.

This chapter differs from the previous national case studies in that it necessarily focuses on decision-making in both the legislative and executive branches. Although a central tenet of parliamentary systems is that the executive must maintain the confidence of the House, it is rare in these systems for the legislative branch to have any significant role in policy formulation. Cabinet is where the action is. In contrast, the American system of presidential government accords a significant, even dominant, role in policy formulation to the legislative branch. A key report on Indian policy held the ideal balance of power between the two branches to be executive subservience to Congress.[11] Indian policy outcomes in the United States are therefore a product of both legislative and executive opinion in a way unseen in the other national cases of this study. The story of Indian land claims in the United States shows a more consistent conservatism and reluctance of the legislative branch to support Indian special rights claims. The Senate is noteworthy in this regard. Again and again, the Senate would protect and promote the interest of the (especially western) States against the interests of those to whom the government owed a legal duty, the Indians.

This chapter sets out the American land claims experience against the canvas provided in the previous chapters by Australia, Canada, and New Zealand. It is only in cross-national perspective that the American experience of non-negotiation stands out as noteworthy. And it is against the American case that the central argument developed in reference to these three parliamentary cases can be tested. I trace the American land claims experience chronologically, much in the same way as I have for the three other national cases. After providing a short background on the early landmark legal cases that to this day inform federal Indian law, I examine the impact of two policy periods, known as allotment (1887–1928) and reorganization (1928–1946), on the emergence of the ICC in 1946. I show how the federal debate on how to address Indian land claims was part and parcel of a larger debate on Indians' membership in the American political community. Since access to the courts is considered a basic right of American citizenship, federal policy-makers in both the legislative and executive branches accepted a delegation strategy for those Indians considered citizens. Until 1924, however, only the "civilized" or "competent" Indian could be a citizen. Therefore, the issue of how to address land claims was entwined with notions of both citizenship and civilization.

I reiterate, as other scholars have already done, how the claims process of the ICC adhered to an assimilation policy, and how it supported the termination policy that followed (1952–1968). The ICC, a special arbitrator, was to hear and settle claims so that Indians could take their awards, the federal government could terminate its special trust relationship with tribes, and Indians could finally melt into the American mainstream. With the arrival of Indian protest politics in the 1960s, I examine through a case study of the Taos Pueblo's Blue Lake claim (1968–1970) how a key legacy of the ICC was to forestall the future emergence of a new negotiation policy that would have been more in keeping with President Nixon's renunciation of termination and his acceptance of self-determination as the guiding principle of federal Indian policy.

SETTING THE SCENE:
BEFORE THE INDIAN CLAIMS COMMISSION

*From Nations to Wards: Judicial Decision-Making, Removal, and
the End of Negotiation, 1823–1871*

Over the course of nine years, from 1823 to 1832, the United States Supreme
Court laid down three landmark cases from which American Indian jurisprudence would spring. All three cases involved balancing the political and
property rights of the States, the federal government, and Indian tribes. The
judicial decisions were also products of the political context of the time.
This period was one of American territorial expansion, with settlers moving into lands held exclusively by tribes under (what had been considered)
international treaties. As settlers created new political facts on the ground,
States sought to expand their jurisdiction over Indian lands and people,
denying both Indian sovereignty and land rights. This was in direct contravention to the thirty-year-old American Constitution, which held that
only Congress had the right to "regulate Commerce with foreign nations,
and among the several states, and with the Indian tribes." As is the case
in both Canada and Australia, the effectiveness of the States in denying
Indian rights is potentially checked by two forces: the willingness of the
federal government to act in its own constitutional jurisdiction to protect
Indian rights, and the willingness of the courts to check State and federal
encroachments on those rights.

Both forces failed America's Indian tribes. President Andrew Jackson took the oath of office in March 1829 and espoused the removal of
eastern tribes to lands across the Mississippi. Given a choice to uphold
federal treaties and constitutional responsibilities to Indians over the
expansionist interests of States, the President refused to enforce federal
law.[12] He espoused a weak federal government and supported the aspirations of States, particularly Georgia, to swallow up Indian lands. Indeed,
the Indian removal policy would become one of the founding conflicts
differentiating the fledgling Democratic Party as the party of States'
rights.[13] With Jackson as President, the protection of Indian rights rested
with the judiciary. The American Supreme Court, led by Chief Justice
John Marshall, was " . . . long reviled by states' rights partisans" and
espoused a strong central government.[14] However, the Supreme Court, in
these early years of the American Republic, was in the process of building
its own institutional legitimacy. The Supreme Court faced increasing legislative and legal challenges to its power to strike down state legislation,
should such legislation be contrary to the American Constitution.[15] John
Marshall's overriding political imperative was to carve out a meaningful

role for the Supreme Court, while shielding it from the tumult of Jacksonian politics.[16]

In the series of cases referred to as the Marshall Trilogy,[17] John Marshall fashioned a compromise of sorts. In the *Johnson v. McIntosh* decision, John Marshall invented the concept of native title at common law that would form the basis of Canadian and New Zealand law more than a century later.[18] He argued that while discovery divested Indians of ultimate fee simple ownership of the United States, the tribes did maintain rights of use and occupancy. The United States could acquire these remaining rights through agreement and consent of the tribe. Thus, the Court at once recognized and impaired Indian rights in the eyes of American law. The second decision, *Cherokee Nation v. Georgia,* addressed the political status of Indian tribes. Though they held rights in land, were they indeed foreign states according to the Constitution,[19] and thus, were land cession agreements treaties at international law? Here, Justice Marshall fashioned another legal invention. He denied tribes the status of foreign states, choosing instead to deem tribes "domestic dependent nations" whose inherent rights to self-government were limited by United States sovereignty. The relationship between the United States and the tribes was described as a "state of pupilage," similar to a relationship of a "ward to his guardian." Again, the decision recognized Indian political rights, while limiting them in the interest of the United States. This decision is the foundation of the federal government's ongoing trust responsibility to Indian tribes. Finally, in *Worcester v. Georgia,* John Marshall ruled that these "domestic dependent nations" were to be free from State jurisdiction. Indian affairs would remain under the sole legislative authority of Congress, but the alienation or extinguishment of Indian land rights could not happen through unilateral legislative fiat, but through the consent of the tribe. Thus, in the early nineteenth century, the Marshall court did what the high courts of Australia, Canada, and New Zealand have all now done: deny ultimate tribal ownership of land, but recognize occupancy rights at common law. The Marshall court also did what these other courts have yet to do: recognize a continuing inherent right to tribal self-government.

Whatever judicial protection or political leverage the Marshall Trilogy was meant to provide Indians at the time, such protection proved illusory on the ground. The political balance of power was such that Indians had little recourse to change legislative action. Andrew Jackson implemented his removal policy, which called for the exchange of Indian lands in the east for Indian territory west of the Mississippi. Despite *Worcester,* those Indians who remained in the east would be fully subject to the laws of the States and "ere long become merged in the mass of our population."[20] What was on its face a voluntary policy, Indian tribes' emigration from their traditional territories was indeed forced. The Choctaw, Chickasaw, Creek, and Seminole were followed by the Seneca, Shawnee, Delaware, Catawba and Natchez.[21] In 1839, the United States Army escorted the Cherokee, plaintiffs in the last two Marshall decisions, from Georgia to Oklahoma, a journey in which close to half of the Cherokee died.[22] The tribes in the Indian territory and across the plains faced a renewed wave of settler pressure after the Civil War. The United States government sought to secure the nation's manifest destiny through the dual strategies of war and land cession treaties to subdue western tribes, move them to reservations, and open the continent for settlement.

However, even as the executive branch negotiated land cession treaties with Indian tribes, congressional support for the expedient practice waned, and then ended entirely. In 1866, Senators McDougall and Sherman joined their predecessors, Andrew Jackson and John Marshall, in denying Indians the status of foreign powers. The Senate's refusal five years later to ratify Indian agreements as treaties confirmed Indian-U.S. relations as one of a domestic dependent to his guardian. The guardian not only waged war and ended treaty-making. It also removed whatever meager judicial remedy that remained for tribes to pursue land claims in the courts. Just as the Canadian government barred Indians from pursuing land claims in 1924, Congress passed a measure in 1863 to bar Indian tribal claims from redress in the federal Court of Claims.

Civilization, Citizenship, and Land: 1868–1928

This next section addresses how conceptions of civilization and American citizenship influenced the discussion of Indian land claims until the 1920s. To embark on a delegation strategy, by allowing courts to hear Indian land claims, federal policy-makers had to accept that Indians were indeed citizens, and had, therefore, a right to hold the government to account in the nation's courts. This acceptance did not happen overnight.

Civilization: Passport to Citizenship?

In Australia, Canada, and the United States, the political subjugation and geographic segregation of indigenous people on reserved lands begged the question of what to do next. Despite the doomed race theories of the day, indigenous people continued to exist. Canberra, Ottawa, and Washington all turned their attention to the next goal of their respective indigenous policies: civilization and assimilation of indigenous individuals into the body politic. The absorption of the indigenous individual into the dominant society necessarily involved questions about the conditions under which the individual could become a member, or citizen, of the dominant political community. Civilization, assimilation, and citizenship became the overriding themes in indigenous-settler relations. Only in New Zealand were the Maori included as citizens from the outset of colonial settlement, so the New Zealand assimilation project did not turn on questions of Maori citizenship. By contrast, in Australia, Canada, and the United States, the attainment of citizenship rights for indigenous individuals was a graduated process, conditioned on the renunciation of "savagery" and the attainment of "civilization."

The question of what to do about indigenous lands and land claims became entangled with these larger normative issues. For what rights should "domestic dependent nations" and their members have in American courts? American citizens clearly had the right to bring suit against their government, in keeping with the founding ideals of the Republic. To have your day in court is, for many, a fundamental right of American citizenship. When was an Indian "civilized" enough to assume the rights and responsibilities of citizenship? Was the renunciation of tribal life a requirement for citizenship, or should American citizenship be open to "real" Indians as an inducement to subsequent assimilation? The Americans were not alone in this debate. These were the very questions that the Canadian government would also ponder as the debate on Indian enfranchisement progressed.

The United States Constitution of 1787 held Indian tribes to be similar to foreign nations, and in keeping with that logic, individual Indians were not citizens of the Republic. When John Marshall designated tribes domestic dependents and not nations in 1831, he did not address whether this newly created status conferred American citizenship rights to Indian individuals. "Thus, the Indians were nonentities and had no legal status."[23] Congress had the opportunity to address the legal status of Indian individuals after the Civil War. In 1868, the prevailing view in Congress and the executive branch considered American citizenship fundamentally incompatible with traditional tribal life, and they sought to exclude Indians from the Fourteenth Amendment, the Amendment that extended citizenship to former slaves.[24] The Senators disagreed on the wording to accomplish its goal, but the intent of excluding Indians was clear. Civilization provided the rationale on which to exclude Indians from the American political community. Senator Howard from Michigan sums up this view rather succinctly: " . . . I am not yet prepared to pass a sweeping act of naturalization by which all the Indian savages, wild or tame, belonging to a tribal relation, are to become my fellow citizens and go to the polls and vote with me and hold lands and deal in every other way that a citizen of the United States has a right to do."[25]

If "wild" Indians, those who remained on reservations, for instance, were clearly not citizenship material, then what of those Indians who had "merged in the mass of our people"?[26] The 1870s saw the lower courts both agree and disagree with the idea that civilized Indians could become citizens. Within the executive branch, Commissioners of Indian Affairs disagreed and debated on whether Congress should extend citizenship at once or in a gradual fashion.

The debate within the executive and legislative branch received a new impetus when the case of the Ponca Indians went through the courts. The Ponca had left the Indian Territory and wanted to return to their original territories; they had been stopped by the American army and forced to turn back. The Ponca went to court to determine if the Army's interference was lawful, and the question turned on the Indians' status as persons deserving of constitutional protection. In 1879, the District Court for Nebraska held that the Ponca of South Dakota were indeed persons under the Fourteenth and Fifth Amendments.[27] The case spawned a Presidential commission investigation of the plaintiff's cause. After investigating the Ponca claim, the commission implicitly linked the resolution of land claims to the swirling debate on Indians' citizenship rights. In 1881, the commission recommended that " . . . it is of the utmost importance to white and red men alike that *all Indians* should have the opportunity of appealing to the courts for the protection and vindication of their rights of person and property."[28]

The commission's report created an opportunity. In 1863, Congress had barred Indian tribes from pursuing claims against the United States in the Court of Claims. The only way for Indians to receive redress in the courts was for Congress to allow itself to be sued by passing a special jurisdictional act. Many tribes had lobbied the House and Senate committees for years to obtain a special jurisdictional act, but were stymied by representatives for the Western states. Since the implementation of Andrew Jackson's removal policy, the Choctaw had lobbied Congress for dispensation to sue. In 1881, their request was finally granted. However, the floodgates to the Court were hardly opened. From 1881 to 1890, "tribes filed eleven claims and secured awards on two."[29] But the precedent was set. Indian tribes, if they could run the formidable Congressional gauntlet, and obtain a jurisdictional act, could take the United States government to court.

In 1884, the Supreme Court weighed into the fray to clarify Indians' legal status. In the case *Elk v. Wilkins,* the Court ruled that neither birth in the United States nor assimilation into American society could confer

American citizenship. It also stated that American statutes barred Indians from seeking citizenship through naturalization. Citizenship could only be conferred to an Indian by an Act of Congress. There was, by and large, enough support within the House and the Senate to fill the judicial vacuum and extend Indians citizenship, conditional on their education and progression towards civilization. White civil rights reformers such as the Indian Rights Association added their voices to the debate from outside the Capitol Building. So, in 1886, Senator Dawes from Massachusetts introduced the General Allotment Act in the Senate. The Act allowed " . . . an Indian who has . . . turned back upon the savage life, has adopted the modes and habit of civilized life"[30] to become an American citizen. The thought of the day, however, held that tribal collectivism hampered the civilizing process. Dawes proposed to speed up the civilization of the American Indian by carving up reservation lands and allotting parcels to Indian individuals. The granting of an allotment conferred citizenship, and after 25 years, during which time the allottee would presumably civilize, he was free to dispense with his property as any other American.[31] The General Allotment Act, also known as the Dawes Act, passed Congress and received the President's approval in 1887.

From Citizenship by Allotment to Citizenship by Birth (1887–1924)

Theodore Roosevelt would refer to the allotment policy as a "mighty pulverizing engine to break up the tribal mass."[32] The Bureau of Indian Affairs was given the authority to parcel out various sized allotments to reservation residents. Tribal land not allotted (often the best agricultural land) was deemed surplus, effectively appropriated by the federal government, and sold to settlers. Through the surplus lands provision and individual alienation, the allotment policy allowed some 86 million acres of tribal land (60% of the tribal land base of 1887) to pass out of tribal control.[33] The result was not just the diminution of the reservation land base. Allotment also allowed non-Indians to ultimately own land within reservation boundaries, creating a legacy where many reservation landowners are not members of the tribe, and do not recognize the jurisdiction of tribal governments.

The Supreme Court allowed Congress's assault on tribal sovereignty and lands by retreating from the principle of Indian consent, key in the Marshall decisions, in favor of unlimited and unilateral congressional power.[34] In this respect, the Supreme Court deferred to the actual balance of political power on the ground. From 1886 to 1903, the Supreme Court, in a series of decisions, developed the congressional plenary power doctrine.[35] The Court held that as their guardian, " . . . the [federal government's] duty to care for Indians carried with it the power to legislate *for* them."[36] Congress thus had the untrammeled legislative authority to legislate in its Indian wards' "best interest." This included the unilateral abrogation of Indian treaties. The Court also upheld Congress's power to "control and manage Indian land," including the power to allot tribal land without tribal consent.[37]

However, by the early decades of the twentieth century, the political debate on civilization, citizenship, and assimilation began to change somewhat. Organizations decrying coerced detribalization joined those that promoted the idea of Indian citizenship and assimilation. The first, though ultimately short-lived and unsuccessful, pan-tribal organization arose during the allotment era. In 1911, the Society of American Indians was founded in Columbus, Ohio. The Society was founded largely by acculturated Indians who had taken their place in American society, and were comfortable promoting Indian assimilation.[38] The Society, however, ultimately could not hold together or bridge the gap between urban and reservation communities, since it " . . . never could avoid the issues that separated tribe from tribe or that divided people within a single reservation."[39] The Society quietly ceased to function in 1923.

The promotion of Indian citizenship by the Society and social reformers was made in the context of the growing and now apparent failure of the allotment policy. The erosion of the tribal land base led to Indian impoverishment, not enlightenment or a cessation of the federal government's financial responsibility to Indian communities. White social reform groups such as the General Federation of Women's Clubs and the American Indian Defense Association (1923) joined tribal voices to help lobby for an end to allotment and an end to the eradication of tribal life. These white social reformers, anchored in the reformist politics of the Progressive era, did not challenge assimilation as the fundamental goal of Indian policy. They did, however, challenge the established generation of Indian policy reformers, represented by the "missionary-minded" Indian Rights Association,[40] by disputing the utility and morality of forcibly destroying the tribal land mass and tribal sovereignty. They disputed the causal claim that individualizing the tribal land base would create self-reliant and competent Indian citizens. Theirs was a kinder, gentler, yet still paternalistic path to Indian assimilation.

World War One proved instrumental in breaking down the perceived dichotomy between American citizenship and the maintenance of tribal affiliations. The national press recognized the valiant contributions of Indians on European battlefields, and Congress was pressed to award citizenship to those Indian veterans (acculturated or not) with an honorable discharge from the nation's service. Thus, the dichotomy between tribalism and American citizenship became less stark in policy-makers' debates.

The battles in Europe brought new attention and new debate to the membership of the Indian in the American polity, while a three-year political battle (1921–1924) in New Mexico over settler versus Pueblo land rights brought the question of land claim resolution mechanisms to national prominence for the first time. The Pueblos' land ownership stems from original land grants from Spain which were subsequently recognized by Mexico. Mexico also recognized the Pueblo Indians as Mexican citizens. In the Treaty of Guadalupe Hidalgo (1848), the United States recognized the Pueblos' citizenship and ownership rights to 700,000 acres, and the territory that is now New Mexico transferred to American control.[41] The status of the Pueblo Indians and their right to sell their lands to settlers (or other Indians) did not spur much political comment until New Mexico acquired statehood in 1910. In 1913, the Supreme Court ruled that the federal government, not the State, had jurisdiction over the Pueblos as their guardian.[42] The importance of this decision for the subsequent land claims issue was that, as wards, the Pueblos did not have the right to alienate land without the consent of the federal government. This decision clouded the title of those settlers who had acquired Pueblo lands in good faith.

With the arrival of the Harding administration in 1921, the new Secretary of the Interior, the "heavy-handed" Albert Fall,[43] sought to put his own imprint on Indian policy. Fall was committed to the allotment policy and asserted the United States' right to manage Indians lands without Indian consent. He sought to quickly validate non-Indian interests in the Pueblos, and he worked with New Mexico's Senator Bursum to introduce "an administration measure" in Congress.[44] The Bursum Bill of July 1922 allowed non-Indians to " . . . receive title to Pueblo land if they could prove continuous possession, with color of title, before or after 1848. Any non-Indian who proved continuous possession since June 29, 1900, without color of title, could claim title to Indian property."[45] The Bursum Bill was an attack on Pueblo land rights because it did much more than protect those settlers who had obtained Pueblo property in good faith. The Bursum Bill would also give Pueblo land away to the squatters and trespassers who had long encroached on the Pueblos. The issue was particularly important because squatters were a big problem on the Pueblos' irrigated land during a time of severe drought.[46]

From 1921 to 1924, the opposition to the Bursum Bill would be spearheaded by the General Federation of Women's Clubs and John Collier, a social worker and educator who first became exposed to Indian issues when on vacation at the Taos Pueblo in 1920. John Collier would found and direct the important American Indian Defense Association in 1923, at the height of the fight against the Bursum Bill. John Collier and his colleagues lobbied Congress and the Administration, utilized print media, brought new social reformers into the Indian rights issue, and helped the Pueblos to act together to fight the legislation. The campaign distanced President Harding from his Secretary of the Interior, leading to Fall's resignation in 1923. The new Secretary, Hubert Work, funded a conference of Indian reformers and sought outside recommendations for the future of Indian policy. In the Pueblo lands case, Collier opposed " . . . any measure which would settle by legislative fiat questions of Pueblo land titles now being litigated in the courts," and the conference delegates recommended that the United States create an Indian Court of Claims to deal with all other Indian land disputes.

The Pueblo land dispute ended in 1924, when Congress passed and President Coolidge signed the Pueblo Lands Act. The legislation did not create a special Indian claims court, but it did create an investigatory body to review the claims, required the Attorney General " . . . to bring suit to quiet title,"[47] and ensured the Pueblos received compensation for lands lost. The Secretary of the Interior was required to use such compensation to recover lost water and lands, and the Pueblos had the right to access the courts to review decisions on title.

In 1924, the publicity engendered by the Pueblo land question and Indian contributions to the war effort culminated in a simple legislative act that reportedly merited "little debate."[48] Congress passed the Indian Citizenship Act so that any Indian born in the United States, "competent" or not, became by right an American citizen. Indians could now vote in federal elections. They could now sue and be sued in federal and state courts. By 1928, voices in and outside of Congress and the executive branch grew louder, saying that Indian *tribes* and their claims deserved automatic access to the dispute resolution mechanisms available to all Americans.

Court or Commission? Debating Indian Claims 1928–1941

The extension of citizenship to all Indians born in the United States was a watershed event. It removed a key rhetorical reason for disallowing Indians the same rights of access to the courts enjoyed by other Americans. However, change was not automatic. Instead, the next two decades saw policy-makers in the executive and in Congress debate on what institutional mechanisms should be put in place. The two alternatives were: a special court, or an advisory commission to help the courts already in place. This next section examines the path of this debate until the opening days of World War Two.

Throughout the allotment period, tribes weathered not just attacks on their lands and sovereignty, but also the burdensome process of lobbying Congress to obtain a hearing of their land claims in the Court of Claims. The hurdle to obtain a special jurisdictional act from Congress was tremendous:

> Much depends upon the standing in Congress of the sponsors of the bill, upon the composition of the Committee on Indian Affairs, and upon the attitude of the administration. The present practice is for the Committee on Indian Affairs of the House or the Senate, as the case may be, to refer the bill to the Secretary of the Interior for report. Bills which hold possibilities of heavy payments from the treasury must also be submitted to the Bureau of the Budget, where they may receive an adverse report because in conflict with "the financial program of the President" . . . The result is that before a jurisdictional act is finally secured many years frequently must be consumed in attorneys, representatives, and witnesses, and the disappointing delays, postponements, and defeats are burdens on Indian claimants, the imposition of which may well be questioned.[49]

From the time the Choctaw first gained the right to sue the federal government in 1881 until the eve of citizenship in 1924, 39 tribal claims cases came before the Court of Claims. The 1920s, however, saw a marked increase in the number of claims sent to the Court. In the five years after the citizenship legislation, 59 cases were filed.[50] Given the federal government's increasing workload to prepare for and litigate these claims, the Indian Tribal Claims section of the General Accounting Office was organized in 1926. The press of claims applications coming before Congress would continue to mount throughout the 1930s and early 1940s.

Congress's method of dealing with Indian land claims could not be sustained, given the increase in claims. Before 1928, the preferred alternative in public debate was for Congress to allow claimants to access the Court of Claims directly. For instance, Commissioner of Indian Affairs (1905–1908) Francis Leupp recommended that Congress "[create] a special court, or the addition of a branch to the present United States Court of Claims, to be charged with the adjudication of Indian claims exclusively."[51] The necessity of providing easier access to the courts was framed in terms of the assimilation project, for as long as claims remained outstanding, Indians' "steady industry and peace of mind" would suffer.[52] In 1915, legislation allowing tribes automatic access to the Court of Claims was introduced into the Senate, but the legislation died in committee.[53]

As the Court of Claims process ground on, the debate grew on whether a new claims process was actually required, and what the alternative process would look like. In 1926, the Secretary of the Interior commissioned a study on Indian administration from the Brookings Institution. In February 1928, Brookings' chief investigator, Lewis Meriam, delivered his report. The Meriam Report addressed the whole spectrum of Indian administration, not just the process of claims resolution. The Meriam Report trumpeted the need for reform, but did not reject the basic assimilationist assumptions that continued to drive Indian policy. However, it did allow for the possibility that assimilation would be incomplete, and that those Indians who rejected American civilization still deserved humane treatment, rather than destruction.[54] This concession was a significant departure given its historical context. Thus, the Meriam Report represents the start of a shift in American Indian policy that would come to fruition with the election of Franklin Roosevelt in 1933.

In terms of Indian land claims, the Meriam Report squarely stated that both fundamental justice and the assimilation project would remain stymied as long as claims remained thwarted and unaddressed:

> The benevolent desire of the United States government to educate and civilize the Indian cannot be realized with a tribe which has any considerable unsatisfied bona fide claim against the government. The expectation of large awards making all members of the tribe wealthy, the disturbing influence of outside agitators seeking personal emoluments, and the conviction in the Indian mind that justice is being denied, renders extremely difficult any cooperation between the government and its Indian wards. Besides these practical considerations, the simple canon of justice and morality demand that no Indian tribe should be denied an opportunity to present for adjustment before an appropriate tribunal the rights which the tribe claims under recognized principles of law and government.[55]

The current process of claims resolution was "burdensome and unjust." The Meriam Report presented its views on what "an appropriate tribunal" would look like. In its recommendations, the Meriam Report presaged the contours of the debate that would bedevil Congress and the executive for the next twenty years. While the Meriam Report recommended a commission as a non-judicial fact finding body to decide the merit of claims, it also espoused the old judicial option. No consideration was given to a direct process of negotiated agreement-making with either Congress or the executive as an alternative to the judicial process. The Report's recommendation for a commission was presented so:

> The unsettled legal claims against the government should be settled at the earliest possible date. A special commission should be created to study those claims which have not yet been approved by Congress for submission to the Court of Claims. This commission should submit recommendations to the Secretary of the Interior so that those claims which are meritorious may be submitted to Congress with a draft of a suitable bill authorizing their settlement before the Court of Claims.[56]

On this reading, a claims commission would be similar to the Pueblo Lands Board. It would be tasked with investigating claims, the unfounded claims cast aside and the meritorious to still be addressed within the Court of Claims. The fundamental role of the commission would be as a fact-finder, and on this reading, its decisions would be solely of an advisory nature and without judicial functions. However, this apparent clarity between the appropriate role of a commission versus that of a court in the claims settlement process was muddled elsewhere in the text:

> Claims for which no method of settlement has yet been provided should be considered by an expert group as above recommended, and where the determination of controverted questions of fact and law is necessary, submission to the Court of Clams with opportunity to appeal to the United States Supreme Court seems the best procedure. The Court of Claims is much less likely to be influenced by political considerations than are committees of Congress and executive commissions . . . The Indians, too, like other citizens, will be satisfied with nothing less than the opportunity of presenting before the regular courts of justice provided for the settlement of such controversies, the important cases which have such a close relation to their present and future welfare.[57]

The Meriam Report added the idea of a non-judicial commission into the debate on which mechanisms the American government should adopt to resolve claims, while not dismissing the courts as part of the resolution process. From 1930 to the creation of the Indian Claims Commission in 1946, policy-makers in Congress and the executive would wax and wane between the judicial and advisory options. They would ultimately decide on a hybrid that would be called a commission, which had both investigatory and judicial functions, and operated as a court. The following section lays out in admittedly broad strokes how the Indian Claims Commission came to be.

The Court Option Dominates (1929–1935)

The Meriam Report was an important indictment of the Indian Bureau and provided Indian policy reformers with new momentum to push for change. In 1929, the ascension of Herbert Hoover brought new political possibilities. Hoover was reportedly willing to back a Meriam-inspired reform program, and his appointments to Indian Affairs were meant to signal a new openness within the executive.[58] He appointed Charles Rhoads, devout Quaker and former president of the Indian Rights Association, as the Commissioner of Indian Affairs. Although Rhoads' appointment seemed like a wind of change had arrived, such hopes soon proved over-enthusiastic. Though Rhoads denounced paternalism within the Indian Bureau, he held fast to the goal of ultimate assimilation and approved the continuation of the allotment policy. Hoover's Secretary of the Interior, Ray Wilbur, was of the same conviction.[59] Wilbur rejected the Meriam Report's acceptance of a non-assimilation option for Indians. He wrote in 1932: " . . . The Indian stock should merge with that of the Nation."[60]

Despite the long-term disappointment of Rhoads' tenure, he did present Congress with a series of reform proposals in 1929. He and John Collier, the force behind the American Indian Rights Association who had emerged from the Pueblo land dispute as the foremost critic of American Indian policy, collaborated on four reform proposals for the Indian affairs committees of both the House and the Senate.[61] One of these proposals was for the creation of a special Indian claims court. Legislation to create such a court was introduced into the House in January of 1930 (H.R. 7963), with the backing of the Interior Department. The proposed court of three judges would render judgment on claims filed within a five year period. Awards could only be monetary, and could be offset by government gratuities.[62] The key opposition to the legislation was fiscal, as representatives feared the potential liability that a court of Indian claims would present to the public purse. Commissioner Rhoads chose not to push the legislation, and it died in committee.[63] The Commissioner's unwillingness to confront congressional opposition to Indian reform measures eventually led Collier to denounce the Hoover administration as he had its predecessors.

The push for a new way to deal with Indian claims lost momentum after 1930, but a new opportunity for Indian policy reform came with the election of Franklin Roosevelt (FDR). Indian policy was not forgotten in the "storm of legislation, a hurricane of laws" that marked the arrival of FDR to the White House.[64] The irony of the Roosevelt years was that while the administration ended the allotment policy, and began the rebuilding of a tribal land base, the administration would not succeed in its attempts to create a new mechanism for Indian land claims. The reasons for this failure are diverse, including fundamental disagreements between the Departments of Justice and Interior on a new mechanism's design, and on-going disputes between Senators and Representatives on the fiscal impact of a new claims body.

For his Secretary of the Interior, Roosevelt chose Harold Ickes. Ickes was sympathetic to Indians' demands for justice. He was also a cultural pluralist in his day, though he did not escape the paternalism of his era by allowing Indians a meaningful role in the development of policy. Speaking about the person he would prefer as head of the Indian Bureau, the Indian Commissioner, Ickes said: " . . . I want someone in that office who is the advocate of Indians. The whites can take care of themselves, but the Indians need someone to protect them from exploitation. I want a man who will respect their customs and have a sympathetic point of view with respect to their culture."[65] Ickes' choice as Indian Commissioner was none other than John Collier. Roosevelt backed the choice, and the Senate deferred. Collier accepted the opportunity to shape Indian policy from within, and in April 1933, he became the head of the much maligned Bureau of Indian Affairs. To fight against an entrenched bureaucracy, he had the assistance of Nathan Margold and Felix Cohen, both legal experts who personally supported Indian land rights.[66] The new Commissioner's priority was to end the allotment policy, and in 1934, the Commissioner secured congressional endorsement for his Indian Reorganization Act (IRA). The IRA stopped the future individualization of reservation lands, created a credit fund for land purchases, and implemented a system of tribal governments with municipal-type powers of self-administration. The IRA proved problematic in its design and implementation, but it was a significant rupture with the allotment policy.[67] The battle to pass and implement the IRA was the major business on the Indian policy agenda, and it was not until 1935 that Collier and Ickes turned their attention to the question of historical Indian land claims.

The Commission Option Dominates (1935–1941)

Prior to 1935, the Department of the Interior had preferred a special Indian court of claims because of such a court's ability to hear claims and render a final ruling. The court option was Collier's stated preference, but Congress had refused to pass a provision in the IRA which would have established a special Indian court with civil and criminal jurisdiction to hear cases involving Indians and non-Indians with respect to tribal matters.[68] Although this court provision did not specifically address historical land claims,[69] the unwillingness of Congress to pass the provision could have had an impact on Collier's and Ickes' deliberations on an appropriate mechanism to address outstanding claims. Whether a strategic choice given congressional attitudes, or a fundamental re-evaluation of the special court option, Ickes and Collier reversed the traditional Interior strategy, and came to promote a commission format. In 1934 and 1935, Senator Bulow of South Dakota introduced legislation to create an Indian claims *court*, but without Interior support, the bills died in committee. Ickes argued that a new court would not solve a major cause of delay inherent in the existing claims procedure: the investigation of historical facts and the delivery of a report on gratuitous offsets by the General Accounting Office.[70] A new commission would investigate a claim's merits, and make a recommendation to Congress for a just settlement, but Congress would maintain discretion on how to proceed with the claim. This proposed commission essentially describes the Waitangi Tribunal as implemented in New Zealand in 1975. The commission proposal would essential leave the special jurisdictional act process in place.

From 1935 to 1941, Collier and Ickes tried to push legislation for a fact-finding claims commission through Congress. The proposed commission would investigate both legal and moral claims, with the commission's findings of fact to be respected in the Court of Claims. The first attempt, H.R. 6655, died with the conclusion of the congressional session that year. The second attempt in 1937 passed the Senate, and was defeated on the floor of the House. The single most important reason stifling the commission legislation was the fear that a commission might expose the treasury to serious fiscal liabilities.[71] The fact that the Court of Claims denied the majority of claims cases that came before it, and the ability of the government to significantly reduce any actual awards through gratuitous offsets, could have mollified congressional opinion on the need for a new mechanism.[72]

Two years passed before Collier and Ickes would work with officials in the Justice Department to put forward commission legislation for the third time. The relationship between Interior and Justice was always strained, with Collier and Ickes trying to promote a mechanism with some power and Justice primarily interested in fighting provisions that could harm the public purse. The Interior position was strengthened by mounting impatience regarding the special jurisdictional act process. In 1940, the Democratic Party gave voice to that frustration at its convention, and included, in its platform, a pledge to find a way for the speedy and final settlement of Indian citizens' claims.[73] Support for the principle of finality encouraged Interior to push for a commission-court hybrid (still called a commission), where it would investigate both legal and moral claims, and make binding determinations of fact and law. Justice, fearing such a commission could make indecent financial awards, demanded that legislation give Congress a final review. Interior introduced legislation in August 1940 and in 1941, but both attempts foundered due to sabotage by Justice and by continuing conflicts in Congress over one or another provision.

From 1929 to 1941, legislative and executive efforts failed to create a new mechanism to address Indian claims. Whether a court, an advisory commission, or a hybrid of the two, the creation of a new institution became the victim of the many veto points in the American legislative system. Proponents for change argued that the frustrating policy of obtaining a special jurisdictional act to sue the American government failed the standard of basic justice that, as citizens, Indians deserved. Opponents felt that the twin burdens of morality and justice did not outweigh the duty of fiscal prudence. The opponents won. By 1941, Indian policy went the way of most domestic policy, and it gave way to the overwhelming political importance of America's role in World War Two.

The bombing at Pearl Harbor made the war an American, not just a European, problem. The war was the overriding priority. Perhaps nothing indicated this priority better than the Bureau of Indian Affairs' eviction from its Washington offices so that the military could have more space.[74] The Bureau moved its administrative offices to Chicago, away from the daily cut and thrust of American politics. The early 1940s would also see John Collier's gradual demise at the head of a weakened Bureau. Indians had not embraced the IRA to the extent Collier had hoped, as the creation of band councils to administer reservation life engulfed many Indian communities into factionalism between traditionalists and the Indian New Dealers. Congress's commitment to tribal life was always thin, and it took the problems with Collier's IRA policy as reason enough to decrease congressional appropriations under the Act. "By 1940, Collier's relations with both the House and Senate Indian Affairs Committees had deteriorated so badly that several attempts were made to repeal the IRA."[75] The failures of the IRA emboldened American representatives after 1945 to gradually embrace the antithesis of Collier's legacy, the legislative termination of the federal trust responsibility to the tribes altogether.

THEIR DAY IN COURT: WORLD WAR TWO, THE NATIONAL CONGRESS OF AMERICAN INDIANS, AND THE INDIAN CLAIMS COMMISSION (1944–1946)

This next section traces the final push to create a special institutional mechanism to address Indian land claims. The Indian Claims Commission received support from Indian, executive, and legislative actors, but for different and often conflicting reasons. It was created just as an important national advocacy organization, the National Congress of American Indians, was getting on its feet. However, the long-term success of the ICC was hampered by Congress's rejection of the New Deal Indian reforms. The ICC would instead serve Congress's assimilationist policy agenda.

The World War and Pan-Tribal Organizing

While Congress and the executive paid less attention to Indian policy, particularly to Indian claims, during the Second World War, not all was quiet. Just as in Canada and New Zealand, the war restructured the Indian policy environment in important ways. It broke down tribal boundaries, and provided the initial basis for successful supra-tribal organization.[76] The demands of fighting a total war involved all sectors of the American economy. The war years accelerated the development of an industrialized and more economically diversified urban west. Indians, 75% of whom lived west of the Mississippi in 1941, became increasingly involved in the new urban economy, as did their fellow Americans. Many, however, still maintained links to their reservation communities, negotiating the urban and rural divides as part of their working and family lives.[77] The war brought 70,000 Indian men and women, approximately 20% of the total Indian population, out of reservations and into direct military service or employment in defense industries.[78] Out of this base came men and women who increasingly joined the political mainstream, and became interested in forming or supporting an effective political organization to speak for Indians, as Indians, on a pan-tribal basis. The war era marked an important time when Indians stepped apart from their white supporters to form their own distinct national organization.

Indian activists were not without aid in the pan-tribal organization effort. During the late 1930s and early 1940s, John Collier funded a series of inter-tribal conferences that served to weave together a core network of Indian pan-tribal leadership.[79] Much in the same way that the parliamentary committee investigations and reports brought Indian leaders to Ottawa immediately after the war, the Indian Bureau in the United States (though much more advertently than its counterpart in Canada) contributed to native American organizing in the 1940s. The culmination of these factors was the establishment of the National Congress of American Indians (NCAI) in Denver in November 1944.

Though it too would fight factionalism and internal policy disagreements, the NCAI started off with a degree of combined urban and reservation support that no previous Indian organization had managed to accomplish. The NCAI's immediate goal was to steer the middle road and to find common points of political action that could cement the still untested coalition of Indians. As its first lobbying effort, the NCAI focused on one issue that received widespread approval at the founding convention in Denver: the creation of an Indian Claims Commission " . . . to litigate old land claims against the government."[80] For the NCAI, a claims commission would provide a more equitable means of achieving justice. A claims commission would also serve the NCAI's larger goal of preserving tribal rights acquired in the treaties.

Congressional Support for Change

NCAI's interest in pushing for a claims commission from outside Congress corresponded with a wakening interest in Indian affairs as allied forces gained more ground in Europe and the South Pacific. However, congressional opposition to the Collier reforms was on the rise, and the very goal of tribal revitalization was under renewed scrutiny in significant quarters. In May 1943, Oklahoma Senator Elmer Thomas called for the abolition of the Bureau of Indian Affairs and wrote that the Collier reforms " . . . promoted segregation, made the Indian a guinea pig for experimentation, tied him to the land in perpetuity, and made him satisfied with all the limitations of primitive life."[81] Assimilation, not tribal revitalization, was to be the ultimate goal of federal Indian policy, and Collier's Bureau of Indian Affairs had stood in the way of what Senator Sherman had advocated back in 1866, to "disband our whole Indian system." In 1943, the House of Representatives held a committee investigation into the status of the American Indian, and it concluded, in 1944, that "it was time for complete assimilation and that one of the factors retarding this goal was the backlog of unsettled claims cases."[82] Addressing claims might cost the treasury a pretty penny, but the claims awards could also provide tribal members a basis for self-sufficiency, hence removing the raison d'être of the Indian Bureau specifically, and the federal trust responsibility to tribes generally.[83] Ironically, those in Congress most displeased with Collier's reforms were ready to back a claims commission measure Collier and Ickes had long tried to champion, but congressional support was in actuality a renunciation, not an embrace, of the Indian New Deal.

Other motivations for revisiting the claims issue existed in Congress. Some accepted the need for a new claims mechanism out of basic expedience. The Chair of the Senate's Indian Affairs Committee, Henry Jackson of Washington, was interested in a mechanism that would remove Congress from the harassments of the special jurisdictional act process.[84] He was interested in delegating decision-making over the merit of claim and the size of compensation awards to a special commission to relieve the congressional workload. Others felt that the patriotism of Indians soldiers during times of war should be rewarded.[85] A claims commission, by removing the hurdles tribes had encountered to hold the United States to some historical account, would remove the "last serious discrimination with which they are burdened in their dealings with the federal government."[86]

Consequently, by 1944, there was substantial opinion in Congress, the executive, and in the Indian policy reform community that fiscal concerns should finally bow to the need for a new claims mechanism, but for a series of often conflicting reasons. One principle united them, that any new commission should yield a *final* settlement of Indian claims. This required the delegation of some real decision-making power to this new body. As finality become more important, the proposed commission took on more judicial functions. Though called a commission, the Indian Claims Commission would become a special third-party arbitrator with judicial power.

The legislative attempt to create an Indian Claims Commission began with a few false starts. In the spring of 1944, a House bill, H.R. 4693, died in committee when Secretary Ickes reported some basic problems with its drafting.[87] Its successor, H.R. 5569, died with the conclusion of the 78th Congress. Then, in January 1945, two bills were introduced into the House. They were identical, except that H.R. 1198 stipulated that at least one Indian claims commissioner must be an Indian. H.R. 1198 was drafted by the NCAI and introduced by Representative William Stigler of Oklahoma.[88] The claims commission bills underwent four months of committee hearings, and a series of amendments. The committee dropped the mandatory Indian as commissioner clause, but the NCAI shouldered this significant loss, and continued to fight for the legislation.

Secretary Ickes pushed for further changes to the bill in the name of finality, specifically the inclusion of a fact-finding division, broad jurisdiction to hear both legal and moral claims, and with review of commission decisions by the Court of Claims and ultimately the Supreme Court.[89] Despite an attempt by the Justice Department to gut the legislation of these measures,[90] the House committee accepted the Interior amendments and when legislation passed the House committee, it also allowed for all future claims to pass automatically to the Court of Claims. When the bill passed muster during the House debate, Representative Francis Case of South Dakota sent the bill off to the Senate with this benediction: " . . . with these old claims passed upon, the road will open for a new day in the life of the Indians of this nation; now they will know where they stand . . . either the claims will be marked as good for settlement or good for nothing."[91] Though the Justice Department mounted an offensive against the Interior amendments in the Senate, Interior Solicitor Felix Cohen and claims lawyer Ernest Wilkinson managed to negate most of the Justice Department's offensive during the subsequent conference committee.[92]

In August 1946, the Indian Claims Commission bill was ready for President Truman's signature. The Secretary of the Interior called on the President to endorse "the most important Indian legislation enacted in more than a decade." The Secretary identified the key substance of the legislation as follows:

> The bill emancipates our Indian citizens from an outworn and discriminatory statute which, since 1863, has barred them from general access to the Court of Claims. For the future they will be permitted to sue on the same basis as their fellow citizens of other races to vindicate contract and property rights. In order to clear up the accumulation of past claims, the bill sets up an adjudicatory commission.[93]

On the advice of his Secretary, President Truman signed the Indian Claims Commission act into law on August 13th, 1946. In his statement marking the event, the President closed with these words:

> I hope that this bill will mark the beginning of a new era for our Indian citizens. They have valiantly served on every battle front. They have proved by their loyalty the wisdom of a national policy built on fair dealing. With the final settlement of all outstanding claims which this measure ensures, Indians can take their place without special handicap or special advantage in the economic life of our nation and share fully in its progress.[94]

The ICC and Its Operation in Comparative Perspective

The Indian Claims Commission bill allowed tribes to file legal and moral claims based on unconscionable dealings by the United States Government before August 13th, 1946. The tribes had five years to file such historical claims with the commission, or be forever barred from the courts. The Commission was given five years, after the filing period, to complete its work. Claims arising from actions after August 1946 were given clear access to the Court of Claims. By the end of the mandatory filing period, most of the 176 federally recognized tribes filed about 600 historical claims. The workload proved enormous, and Congress extended the ICC's life five times until its final demise in 1978. In September 1978, the Indian Claims Commission closed its doors, handing 68 remaining dockets to the Court of Claims for final adjudication. Over the course of the ICC's lifespan, the United States government spent $215 million (and the tribes $100 million) to produce $800 million in claims awards.[95]

The Commission's basic task was deceptively simple, yet involved enormous historical and ethnographic research. First, the Commission was to determine the merit of the claim based on the evidence presented by the tribal claimant or disputed by the Attorney General, who represented the federal government. This was the title phase, where the tribes demonstrated their recognized title or native title to a definable territory based on exclusive use or occupancy. Secondly, if the tribe could prove their title, the claim progressed to the valuation stage. Here, the Commission determined the value of the government's liability, involving the value of the land at the time of taking. The third stage was to determine the amount of allowable offsets, resulting in the final determination of a claims award.[96] The award could only be monetary. No land would be returned as part of the ICC process. The final award could be appealed to the Court of Claims and to the Supreme Court. If the award stood on appeal, Congress appropriated the money, which was held by the treasury until " . . . Congress directed how it should be distributed among the various members of the tribes."[97]

Despite the ICC's final price tag, the ICC process proved disappointing for tribes. The ICC operated as an adversarial arena for tribal litigation, and its commission-type investigation and mediation functions quickly became irrelevant. In 1958, Chief Commissioner Edgar Witt communicated as much to the Chair of the House Committee on Interior and Insular Affairs: "The Commission is a judicial body and the administrative or investigative action directed in Sec. 4 would be entirely foreign to the existing duties or facilities of the Commission."[98] In 1975, its chief commissioner described the ICC as " . . . an independent judicial body which functions solely as a court."[99] The ICC never acquired the legitimacy among the American tribes as the (judicially weaker) Waitangi Tribunal has among Maori in New Zealand. The ICC used court-based standards for evidentiary proceedings, pitted claimants against the Justice Department which refused to negotiate a claim during the critical title phase, and pitted tribes against tribes during the title phase of the claims. Claims dismissed by the ICC had no other mechanism of redress. Also, the limitation of any redress to cold hard cash is a central issue in the failure of the ICC to dispense long-term justice:

The tribes have been embittered by having to acknowledge that their title to such lands has forever been extinguished whenever they have accepted judgment funds. If Indians continue to be aggrieved over the wrongful taking of land, it is not just because so little land has ever been regained, but because the litigation process—once perceived as their only recourse—has not fully met their expectations of an honorable resolution.[100]

The ICC proved an unsatisfactory day in court, but a day in court nonetheless. It was a product of lobbying by NCAI, but even more so, it was an institution meant to serve the goals of the executive and legislative branches. The legislative machinations of the American political process produced an institution which gave some recognition to the underlying merit of Indians' historical property rights, but it also undercut the special political status of Indian tribes by delegating the responsibility for tribal grievances to a third party. Time and time again, policy-makers in the Capitol and the executive justified delegation to a court or a commission-court as a central right of American citizenship, *not* as a recognition of tribal sovereignty. But American policy-makers were not alone in using the dialogue of equal citizenship to promote a delegation strategy. In this, America was not exceptional. At points of their own political narratives, Canada and Australia in particular shared this dialogue.

It is worth reviewing the United States' choice of a delegation strategy in 1946 with a wider lens.[101] In 1950, the Canadian Minister of Indian Affairs recommended to cabinet that Indians no longer be barred from pursuing their claims against the Crown in the courts. Such a restriction was "an unnecessary interference in personal liberty" and "practical use of the legal system would advance the process of Indian integration into mainstream society." Cabinet lifted the restriction, but created no special body to hear a backlog of claims cases. Although, in 1962, the question of creating a Canadian claims commission arose again, and the Indian Affairs Branch uttered almost the same opinion as South Dakota's Francis Case in the ICC legislation's final House debate: " . . . if a claim is good, then it should be settled. Equally important, if a claim is bad the Indians should know about it so they can put it aside." In this sentiment, Francis Case and Canada's Indian Affairs Branch were joined by Australia's Minister of the Interior, Peter Nixon, who argued in 1971 that the Commonwealth should not negotiate with the Yolngu of the Northern Territory. Rather, he argued for litigation, saying that "if Aborigines have no legal rights to the land then they should be told so by the courts." Negotiation, for Peter Nixon, was "running counter to the assimilation objective."

As I outlined in previous chapters, the key ingredient which persuaded the Canadian, New Zealand, and (to its lesser and halting extent) Australia to back away from delegation and embrace a negotiation strategy was the political mobilization of indigenous peoples. When policy-makers in these countries changed their expectations of indigenous people's ability to politically demonstrate, change general political opinion, and impose future political costs through protest, the delegation strategy lost its long-run appeal. As Jean Chrétien argued to Prime Minister Trudeau in 1971 on the Treaties 8 and 11 issue, the government could no longer afford the delays of litigation once Indians showed their political muscle in 1969. This is precisely the ingredient which is missing from the entire debate leading up to the creation of America's Indian Claims Commission in 1946. While NCAI demonstrated its ability to back a piece of legislation in Congress, no reading of the situation shows that policy-makers were worried that the new NCAI was a serious *political* threat, or that Indians could collectively engage the street and impose serious political costs. Rather, the founding assumption of America's ICC was that once claims were dismissed by an independent arbitrator, the claims and the Indians would for all intents and purposes go away.

The post-World War Two era of marked Indian political resurgence would arise in the 1960s, just as indigenous political resurgence did in Canada, Australia, and New Zealand. But by then, the Indian Claims Commission had been operating for nigh twenty years, and the American debate on how to address land claims in the presence of Indian political resurgence had to contend with the continuing operation and legacy of a claims mechanism that protected settler interests. Had the Indian Claims Commission not been created in 1946, perhaps the United States would have also turned to a negotiation policy in the early 1970s. The next section of this chapter examines this idea's plausibility. Through a case study of the Taos Pueblo Blue Lake claim and its treatment by the Nixon Administration, I will outline how the ICC's legacy was to stifle the introduction of a land claims negotiation policy in the United States.

FROM TERMINATION TO SELF-DETERMINATION

The Emergence of Protest

In January 1945, Collier wearied of his battles with Congress, and resigned his office. Later that April, Franklin D. Roosevelt died and President Truman came into office. The change in administrations swept aside Secretary Ickes, and while the ICC was coming into being under new stewardship, the executive branch began a transition in players that would eventually rid itself of Collier loyalists and bring in a new set of faces who were at once deferential to Congress's role in policy formation and sympathetic to the final revocation of Indian tribes' special legal status as "domestic dependent nations." Collier's successor as the head of the Bureau of Indian Affairs, William Brophy, had "no reservations about following congressional policy," seeing his role as "implementing," not shaping, Congress's will.[102] In 1950, the new Bureau chief, Dillon Myer, not just deferred to Congress, but wholeheartedly embraced its vision. The congressional vision for the next fifteen to twenty years would be dominated by the Senate Interior Committee. Known as the terminationists, the very conservative Senate leadership in Indian policy was dominated first by Senator Arthur Watkins (R.-Utah), who put the termination policy in place. Termination's stern guardians under the Eisenhower, Kennedy and Johnson administrations were Senators Allott (R.-Colorado), Clinton Anderson (D.-New Mexico) and Henry Jackson (D.-Washington).

Termination became the name for the policy that identified tribes as ready for liberation from federal supervision and control, and can be seen as the old allotment policy's next step. The policy called for Congress to disperse tribal assets (read reservation land and claim settlement awards) among tribal members, dissolve the tribal trust status, and send Indians into the mainstream. Indians would then be under the jurisdiction of the States. Until its end in the later 1960s, termination affected 1,365,801 acres of land and 13,263 Indians.[103] For Congress and the executive during this conservative Cold War era, termination was all about advancement and freedom from government (and collective) control. Though the policy received its official expression in House Concurrent Resolution 108 in August 1953, the movement toward termination had begun, as I have outlined, during the Second World War. A former assistant to the Secretary of the Interior during the Johnson administration writes: "What really happened in 1953 and 1954 is that an incubation process underway for at least a decade finally hatched some chicks."[104] The first tribes identified for termination were the Flathead of Montana, the Klamath of Oregon, the Menominee of Wisconsin, the Potawatomie of Kansas and Nebraska, some Chippewa of North Dakota, and the tribes of California, Florida, New York, and Texas.[105]

The policy itself was not without support in some Indian quarters. Not many in Indian Country were in love with the Bureau of Indian Affairs, and a decrease in federal supervision was needed for meaningful self-management. Also, the individualization of tribal assets and claims awards made sense for urban Indians or those on reservations without power on the band councils.[106] These tensions manifested themselves in NCAI, which had a challenge to manage internal factionalism on the issue. However, by 1954, NCAI managed to develop an internal opposition to the policy's coerciveness and the intent of Congress to impose the policy on the unwilling. The fight against termination forced the largely acculturated NCAI leadership to build deeper networks with particularly Western reservation communities. NCAI would come out of the 1960s as a decently representative intertribal voice for federally recognized tribal communities.[107] Termination would also encourage the NCAI to start becoming more political in its strategies, such as encouraging its membership to register as voters and otherwise become involved in American electoral politics.[108]

Growing Indian fears about and opposition to termination pushed the development of Indian activist networks through NCAI, but these were not the only activist networks that were being built during the late 1950s and early 1960s. Just as in the other countries in this study, post-war urbanization brought soldiers and increasingly young indigenous people from reservations together in the work force and in college. Native American college clubs became a new basis for activism. From 1954 to 1960, Indian students organized and held a series of conferences in the southwest to discuss common experiences and specifically Indian issues.[109] The new young urban Indian activist was inspired by the demonstrations and protest strategies of the civil rights movement, but was left cold by the civil rights movement's denial of Indians' special (not equal) rights claims.[110] When, in 1961, the NCAI and the University of Chicago helped organize the largest intertribal conference of Indian people in Chicago in 1961, youth delegates who met at previous youth conferences joined more established Indian leadership. The young delegates found their senior counterparts too moderate and shy of political protest action.[111] The response was the National Indian Youth Council (NIYC), established in 1961. More militant groups would eventually follow, largely supported by young urban Indians: the American Indian Movement (AIM, 1968) and the Indians of All Tribes (1969).

The mid 1960s began to see, really for the first time in Indian politics, a sustained "street factor" coinciding with more institutionalized politicking. This is not to say that the more moderate and the more militant sectors of Indian activism were able to work together, as they had in New Zealand during the 1975 Land March. Instead, activists in the NIYC and AIM were highly critical of tribal leadership.[112] In the United States, in the 1960s, there was no Matakite or Dame Whina Cooper to bridge the moderate with the militant in one undeniable demonstration of collective action. In this respect, the indigenous resurgence in the United States was less effective than similar movements outside its borders. Nonetheless, in the 1960s, protest joined lobbying in the native American political repertoire. In 1964, the NIYC held a series of "fish-ins" in the Pacific Northwest to protest the restriction of treaty-based fishing rights. Resistance spread to include hunting rights.[113] Slowly, picketing greeted Bureau officials when visiting tribes, like in Minneapolis in 1966.[114] The most important demonstration that yielded national publicity was the November 1969 occupation of Alcatraz. The occupation lasted 19 months, and it " . . . provid[ed] many Indians with a dramatic symbol of self-assertion."[115]

Through the lobbying efforts of NCAI and individual tribes, growing opposition within Congress to coercive termination eroded (but did not eradicate) the influence of the Senate Interior Committee's conservative vanguard. In 1960, support for a kinder, gentler termination grew in the executive branch when President Kennedy selected former Arizona Congressman Stewart Udall as his Secretary of the Interior. Though Udall did not disavow the central goals of termination, he seemed sympathetic to the need for gradualism. When push came to shove, however, the Kennedy administration did not challenge Senator Clinton Anderson and the Senate Interior Committee.[116]

President Johnson came into the White House after the Kennedy assassination, and he decided to keep Secretary Udall and the head of the Bureau, Philleo Nash, in place. Like previous Presidents, Johnson was never particularly interested in Indian Affairs, and he was never directly involved in policy formulation or strategy.[117] As a result, he never brought his considerable knowledge of Senate politics to bear on his former Senate colleagues to rethink the basic goals of federal Indian policy. Instead, the Johnson era slowed the termination policy down by focusing on the step prior to termination: reasonable economic development. Johnson's cherished War on Poverty programs provided a renewed focus and more institutional resources to address Indian economic underdevelopment. Interesting as well, the War on Poverty funds were administered through the new Office of Economic Opportunity (OEO). This provided Indians with an opportunity to reach federal funds directly, without having to rely on the Bureau of Indian Affairs. Indians' abilities to establish a separate relationship with the OEO began to nibble away at their dependence on the Bureau of Indian Affairs as their main conduit in the executive branch.[118]

The later 1960s also marked a time when Indian leadership demanded a meaningful role in policy formulation. Under the leadership of Vine Deloria Jr., NCAI became less ridden by factional disputes and more assertive of its role in the policy process. The NCAI of the mid to late 1960s was a much more sophisticated creature in Washington than the NCAI in 1946. Indians began to have an influence in the policy process by using publicity and building allies in the House to counteract the Senate Interior Committee.[119] If Indians did not have a role in forming legislation, they were making a point of obstructing its passage. They stopped heirship legislation in 1961, and in 1967 the NCAI was important in stopping a bill that Secretary Udall pushed for, the Indian Resources Development Act. One result of the combination of protest and successful legislative obstruction was a grudging Presidential nod that the days of termination were numbered. In his Special Messages on Indian Affairs in 1968, President Johnson said that federal policy should recognize " . . . right to freedom of choice and self-determination."[120] By executive order, President Johnson also created the National Council for Indian Opportunity within the executive. The Council, to be chaired by the Vice President, created an Indian policy network within the White House. Like in Canada, New Zealand, and Australia, Indian protest had built some allies on the inside. Soon thereafter, Johnson announced he would not run for re-election.

A Precedent for a Future Negotiation Policy?
The Taos Pueblo Blue Lake Claim and the Nixon Administration

Although such a thought surely did not cross his mind at his inauguration, Richard Nixon's presidency would mark the formal repudiation of the federal government's termination policy. On July 8th, 1970, President Nixon addressed Congress and did what his predecessor had refused to do. He advised Congress in no uncertain terms to revoke and repudiate House Concurrent Resolution 108 and replace termination with self-determination as the guiding principle of federal Indian policy. At the time of his address to Congress, the President's staff was directly involved in one particular Indian land claim. The Taos Pueblo of New Mexico had litigated their claim for Blue Lake with the Indian Claims Commission, but were petitioning Congress and the President for the restoration of Blue Lake to the Pueblo rather than accept a monetary settlement. The Blue Lake claim represented Nixon's opportunity to make his administration's mark in Indian policy.

The puzzle arising from the Blue Lake claim is this. The Blue Lake restoration was supposed to showcase a fundamental change in how Indian-government relations were to be conducted in the future.[121] The Blue Lake claim was interlinked with this new commitment to self-determination, yet it did not spark a re-examination of the United States' existing claims policy under the ICC, nor did it mark a shift to negotiate Indian land claims in the future. In the other cases in this study, negotiation and self-determination went hand in hand. Negotiation, with its formal recognition of Indian consent as necessary to the resolution of the underlying grievance, would have been a more consistent strategy in this new era of self-determination. Why was a negotiation policy not a legacy of the Blue Lake claim? This next section delves in a case study of this one claim, because it could have marked a greater turning point in the history of land claim resolution in the United States. The case study shows that any future strategies to deal with outstanding Indian land claims would have to protect the legacy of the ICC. Any new formal policy, as opposed to ad hoc consideration of claims on a one by one basis, would have reopened old claims in a far different political situation than when they were settled, and this the United States has never been willing to do.

The basis of the Taos Pueblo claim is as follows. Situated in northern New Mexico, Blue Lake is considered sacred to the Taos Pueblo. It is a site of religious observance and was described to Vice President Spiro Agnew in the following way:

> This watershed area is considered by the Indians as the source of all life, is known in their language as the Home of the Great Souls, and is a natural cathedral containing the shrines, holy places and altars of their ancient religion, which remains the central force of their culture. The oldest living religion in North America, its survival depends upon the protection of the Indians' religious privacy and the preservation of the area in its natural state as a wilderness.[122]

In 1906, the Department of Agriculture extinguished Pueblo title over 130,000 acres, including Blue Lake, by transferring the lands via executive order to the Carson National Forest. In 1918, the Forest Service allowed grazing permits in the area, making the Taos Indians " . . . unhappy with the loss of exclusivity that would normally be accorded a people utilizing a religious shrine."[123] The Taos Pueblo filed a claim over the lost 130,000 acres with the ICC in 1951. In 1965 the ICC confirmed the Pueblo's original title to the lands, and also held that the Pueblo was due compensation for their loss. The ICC held off on starting the valuation stage of the claim hearings while the Pueblo appealed to Congress for land restoration as part of an overall claim settlement. The Pueblo was seeking more than a special permit to guarantee its exclusive use of Blue Lake. It was seeking the return of 48,000 of the original 130,000 acres to Indian trust status, therefore outside the management purview of the Forest Service.

The Pueblo enlisted the help of Rep. James Haley, Chair of the House Sub-Committee on Indian Affairs. Haley's control of the sub-committee was a thorn in the side of Senators Anderson and Jackson, as Haley worked against their termination program. Senator Anderson, however, was identified as the most important obstacle to the restoration of Blue Lake. The main strategy devised by the Pueblo's chief counsel, William Schaab, was to mobilize support for the House bill in order to hopefully weaken Anderson's position in the Senate:

> My general impression was that Haley had the power to obtain favorable Committee action on any bill he recommends, and that the House will pass any bill favorably reported by the Committee. The most essential factor will be to maintain Haley's interest and his continuing support . . . If a clear and convincing memorandum of the Pueblo's position is prepared and circulated, I believe that Haley's interest will be aroused to the point that the hearings will produce a favorable result . . . House approval of the bill should substantially strengthen the Pueblo's hand in dealing with Senator Anderson. However, Anderson remains the key person who must be convinced or persuaded . . . [124]

In April 1968, Senator Anderson completely opposed setting such a land restoration precedent, but was mindful of the need to be at least minimally sensitive to the issue of religious freedom. He offered a compromise of 3,150 acres containing the most sacred shrines and a special use permit over an additional 30,000 acres.[125] The Pueblo rejected the offer, and would continue to reject any other compromise offers.[126] During the process of shepherding the legislation through the House, the Pueblo mobilized support from churches in particular. By the summer of 1968, the National Committee on the Taos Blue Lake Lands, led by Corinne Locker, had mobilized important press support for the land restoration. On July 17th, 1968, the New York Times wrote that the House bill " . . . gives the Senate a clear opportunity to correct one of the multitude of tragic mistakes of the past." The Albuquerque Journal wrote the day before: " . . . we hope has changed his mind and will support the House measure." On July 30th, 1968, the Washington Post weighed in: " . . . it seems inexcusable to suppress a bill of this kind."

The legislation was indeed stalled in the Senate, and interest waned as the federal election loomed. In January 1969, Richard Nixon took over the White House. The Taos Blue Lake restoration legislation was once more introduced into the House, where it was passed a second time and furthered to the Senate. The fight to get H.R.471 out of the Senate and ready for the President's signature took all of 1970.

In November 1969, Indian militants occupied Alcatraz, and the renewed effort to pass the Blue Lake legislation through Congress the second time brought a new bout of support for the Taos Pueblo. The Indian issue caught the interest of the younger, more liberal Republicans of the White House domestic policy staff, and this coterie of younger aides kept the Blue Lake issue on the administration's radar screen over the next months.[127] In a policy field that usually languishes from the disinterest of the Oval Office, the White House became directly involved in the Taos Pueblo issue in January 1970. Nixon had inherited President Johnson's creation, the National Council on Indian Opportunity, and Nixon maintained the Vice President, Spiro Agnew, as its chair.[128]

At the end of January, Vice President Agnew received a memo from his assistant pointing out the benefits of getting involved:

> Both Senate seats in New Mexico are held by Democrats whose terms will expire within the next two years. Close contests are expected and the seats can be won by Republicans. The Indian position is popular . . . There are approximately 70,000 Indians in New Mexico, and there is a wide-spread movement among them for the first time to become involved in state and national politics. This vote is seen as primarily a bloc vote which is large enough by itself to swing an election. Administration support for Taos Pueblo is critical to winning this bloc vote. HR 471 provides a method for the Administration to demonstrate without cost its support for minority group rights on a publicly non-controversial issue receiving wide-spread attention . . . Administration support would also tend to indicate that we mean what we say with regard to our policy of non-termination.[129]

Another memo soon after read:

> I cannot stress enough the serious need to get this thing moving. Blue Lake has become a national symbol to American Indians and its significance is felt by those who are urban residents as well as those who live on the reservations. If we begin again with a new bill, the momentum for passage may well be lost and the Administration will suffer serious damage to its credibility . . . The Administration should get some positive exposure out of this. If we support H.R. 471 (and I think we should), then why not issue a statement saying so and place the blame for inaction where it really lies–i.e., in the Senate Committee.[130]

Opposition within the executive branch to the Blue Lake restoration centered on one substantive issue, the precedent such an action would set for claims already settled by the Indian Claims Commission and for those claims still pending.[131] The Department of Agriculture and the Bureau of the Budget were the two main sources of opposition. The issue was primarily fiscal:

> Regardless of how hard we try to distinguish this case it still could be
> used as a precedent for using . . . Federal lands as payment in kind,
> and using current value as a basis for making awards . . . As of June
> 30, 1969, the Indian Clams Commission had disposed of about half its
> cases, awarding $305 million based on land value at time of taking—
> possibly averaging $2 per acre. If the Taos case were to be used as a
> precedent for current value in the remaining cases . . . the awards for
> claims still pending would total $3 billion instead of $300 million to
> $400 million. There is additional risk that the tribes with settled claims
> would have an argument for reopening their cases—perhaps costing
> another $2 billion to $3 billion.[132]

The Administration took this precedent issue quite seriously, and through March and April 1970, the Vice President, the Bureau of the Budget, the Secretary of Agriculture and the Secretary of the Interior worked on amendments to H.R. 471 that would stress the Blue Lake claim's uniqueness as a religious issue to limit any precedent effect on other claims. An agreement among these parties was reached in mid April.

Aside from the precedent issue, the key obstacle to the Administration's support for H.R. 471 had nothing at all to do with the merit of the Blue Lake claim. It had everything to do with maintaining the support of conservative Democrats in the Senate on the Administration's military and foreign policy goals. In this time of SALT negotiations with the Soviets and diminishing support for the Vietnam War in Congress, the President needed "a coalition of conservative Democrats and Republicans."[133] In the spring and summer of 1970, the Administration needed Senate support for its anti-ballistic missile (ABM) program. The two most ardent terminationists in the Senate, Clinton Anderson and Henry Jackson, were closely involved in defense issues. Anderson was the Chair of the Senate Committee on Aeronautical and Space Sciences. Henry Jackson, Chair of the Interior Committee, was a highly respected member of the "congressional elite" with well-honed political skills and was actually Nixon's first choice for the Secretary of the Defense.[134] From April until November, the Taos Blue Lake Restoration bill would get caught up in the ABM issue as the Administration weighed the wisdom of "pushing for the Indians" when the ABM program was at stake.

Senator Anderson also convinced his colleagues on the Interior Committee that H.R. 471 would provide a huge precedent problem in more states than New Mexico. He would commit his objection on paper in this way a few months later:

> In my opinion, H.R. 471 would establish a landmark precedent which would upset the Indian Claims Commission Act of 1946 and even more importantly could affect the status and land resource management of our National Parks, National Forests and public lands which might be subject to Indian claims. In addition, it could become a basis for reconsidering many Indian land claims settled by the Indian Claims Commission over the past 20 years.[135]

Clinton Anderson, a senior Senator, was owed "a lot of courtesy," and in face of his opposition, Senators Harris, McGovern and Kennedy were unprepared to voice their support for Blue Lake.[136] Senators Allott (the ranking Republican on the Interior committee) and Fannin demurred to Anderson as well, while Henry Jackson refused to move the bill out of committee without Anderson's "ok."[137] On April 21st, Jackson communicated to the White House that "now was not the time to rock the boat" and that the White House had a clear choice: the ABM or the Taos Indians.[138]

The White House staff felt they had handled the precedent issue with their proposed amendment, and the time had come to call Anderson's bluff. Len Garment, a senior Nixon advisor and former law partner, wrote the memo to the President. In it, Garment outlined the President's options, and made his recommendation:

> To be very candid, the question before you is not what happens to the bill; with the kind of opposition Ken BeLieu has reported, the answer seems to be: little chance. The question, however, is what position you as President should take, for both moral and political reasons. Here the dilemma is: to risk arousing the ABM vote *vs* to risk embarrassment in New Mexico and in fact to pass up an opportunity to seize this unique issue . . . , even if the bill itself never moves out of the full Jackson-Allott committee. A new Indian policy needs a starting point. Blue Lake is just that—— strong on the merits, and powerfully symbolic.[139]

The President followed Leonard Garment's lead and chose to call Senator Anderson's bluff. On July 8th, 1970, Nixon sent his message on Indian Affairs to Congress. The message asked that Congress end the termination policy by revoking House Concurrent Resolution 108. In his statement, the President also announced his support for the Blue Lake Restoration as a significant first step in a policy of Indian self-determination. Substantive action on the Blue Lake file, however, did not happen until after the critical ABM votes in August 1970. In October, just before the congressional mid-term elections, Senator Anderson managed to win a weakening amendment to H.R. 471.

The congressional elections of November 1970 had an important effect on the future progress of the Blue Lake legislation. The alignment of military votes in the Senate had changed, and long-time Nixon loyalist and assistant director of the White House domestic staff, John Whitaker, recognized an opportunity for the Blue Lake file.[140] White House aide Barbara Kilberg writes of Whitaker's insight:

> John Whitaker was chatting with me this afternoon and asked about Blue Lake. His view was that our military votes are not in danger, especially given the new alignment in the Senate which is more conservative on international and military affairs. He thinks that if we do not fight for the original Blue Lake bill, we gain no public relations advantage and simply look bad. However, if we fight, win or lose, we look good and are right. . . . we are out in front on this issue but stand to get it snatched away . . . [141]

The White House managed to prevail on Senators Harris, Kennedy and McGovern to finally vote against the Senate patriarch, Clinton Anderson.[142] In December 1970, Blue Lake was restored as tribal trust land to the Taos Pueblo. The 48,000 acres was to be used only for traditional purposes, and cannot be developed economically.

The Blue Lake land restoration illustrates a couple of important points. First, the White House only came to intervene once it understood that the issue brought together urban and reservation opinion in a climate of both Indian militancy and Indian coalition-building. Blue Lake activists succeeded in bringing together significant non-Indian support because of its resonance with religious freedom, an important founding principle of the American republic. Because of its symbolism and its support, the Blue Lake claim became a highly visible issue on which a new federal policy of self-determination could be built, and more importantly perhaps, for which the Nixon Administration could get clear credit.

Compared to Canada, New Zealand, and Australia, however, the policy of self-determination signaled by the Blue Lake restoration was not accompanied by a new process of hearing land claims based on negotiation and the formal recognition of Indian consent. Instead, the Taos Blue Lake claim achieved Administration support only after the executive had reasonable assurances that it could not undo the Indian Claims Commission process. The fiscal and political costs of undoing twenty years of claims determinations were too high to contemplate seriously. Instead, Nixon and Congress supported the extension of the ICC's life and an increase in its resources. Nixon's policy of self-determination did not begin on a clean page, and any future consideration of Indian land claims under the new policy principle had the constraining imperative to protect the ICC's fiscal legacy. Claims would be handled by the ICC until its closure in 1978, and the American court system after that. Any other claims would obtain congressional or executive attention on a strictly ad hoc basis, and usually after many rounds of litigation.

REFLECTIONS ON THE AMERICAN CASE

Some may disagree with my characterization that the United States did not implement a negotiation policy in the Nixon era. Has the American federal government embarked on a negotiation policy after Nixon's repudiation of termination and seeming embrace of self-determination? Some point to the 1971 Alaska Native Claims Settlement Act (ANCSA) as a key negotiated settlement. ANCSA extinguished native title and any future claims over the State of Alaska in return for 45 million acres under native control and a cash settlement near $1 billion. The settlement was a landmark agreement in that Congress, not the courts, developed the settlement. It remained, however, a strictly legislative agreement, and it did not accord Alaska natives a formal role as veto players in the agreement-making process, as the Canadian and New Zealand policies do. There was no ratification requirement for native communities, and in the final analysis, Congress (and the President) were the only veto players. In this important sense, ANCSA was a legislative settlement, but not a negotiated one.

The role of Indian consent in the Alaska settlement process did not go unnoticed in the Senate debate on the legislation in June 1970. Senator Ted Kennedy challenged his colleagues to ensure that Indian participation was required in such huge issues concerning their future:

> There is a real question that comes to my mind about altering and changing the relationship between Alaska Natives and the BIA as dramatically as this bill would do. While we are trying to say to the Natives that we want them to decide their destiny and their future, actually what we are doing in the Senate is to change this important relationship and, once again, to change it without the kind of thoughtful, deliberate, and careful consideration of the views of these groups who are going to be most dramatically affected by it . . . we

are changing, *unilaterally*, the relationship between the Natives and the Government.[143]

Senator Gravel (D.-Alaska) answered: " . . . We have a right to vote on that. We make decisions all the time that affect them." Senator Gravel later denied an amendment to the legislation that would make native involvement in decision-making under the Act a statutory requirement.[144] Though the Alaska Federation of Natives and other native groups played an important lobbying role in the development of the settlement, Congress never accorded them the status of equal parties whose consent to an agreement was necessary to make it lawful.

The United States' government has preferred delegation to the courts as its primary means of addressing native land rights and historical claims. The choice to delegate decision-making power over these grievances is underpinned by an understanding of how the American government should relate to Indians as citizens, and as citizens only. Like all American citizens, Indians should take their place in the courtroom to take the American government to account. The fact that the era of self-determination did not bring with it a return of a negotiation policy, as it had elsewhere, sets the United States apart. I have presented in this chapter a narrative as to why that is. I have shown that the landmark judicial rulings on Indian rights occurred far before Indian political mobilization and the ability to influence political decision-making. The long congressional debate on the creation of a special claims mechanism was devoid of the ingredient that proved so critical to the eventual emergence of a negotiation policy in Canada, New Zealand and Australia: the demonstrated ability of indigenous people to use the street and public opinion to impose significant political costs on policy-makers if Indian claims were dismissed in the courts. By the time native political protest and sophistication in the corridors of Congress became significant forces in the 1960s, many claims had already been closed down through the ICC, and the long run benefit of negotiation over continued delegation was eroded.

Chapter Seven

Beyond Negotiation

NEGOTIATION: FROM EQUAL RIGHTS TO SPECIAL RIGHTS

The framing of indigenous grievances has undergone an evolution since World War Two. Originally anchored in the rhetoric of human rights, desegregation and the extension of equal citizenship, the rhetoric has moved to put forth more forcefully arguments of inherent indigenous sovereignty, as well as the related recognition of indigenous economic and political rights. In the language of Charles Taylor,[1] this evolution reflects a change from a politics of equal dignity among individuals to a politics of difference, a politics claiming explicit cultural and collective recognition. Within this context, the issue of land rights has been increasingly framed within the politics of cultural identity and self-determination rather than a more traditional and less controversial argument for a just redistribution of property rights and economic goods to benefit historically disadvantaged communities. This changing relative weight in the framing of indigenous grievances over time speaks to some of the most interesting interstices in contemporary political science, that between 1) the post-modernist politics of cultural recognition[2] and identity politics of post-materialist social movements, and 2) the age-old politics of economic distribution and materially-defined interest group politics.

While the framing of land rights politics may have developed over recent decades, what has remained steady is the core place of land rights in the pantheon of grievances and policy demands that indigenous peoples have put to states around the world. Since the arrival of colonial powers on New World shores and the subsequent patterns of indigenous dispossession, indigenous peoples have pressed states to respond to their land grievances. Their ability to organize politically and to press forth a land rights agenda varies across time and space, but the underlying demand has always existed. What is at play in this demand for states to respond to indigenous land rights?

Each claim to land "is an expression of parochial property rights . . . and each is an instance of the more abstract claim for the recognition of Aboriginal sovereignty."[3] The basic actionable claim for land is wrapped up in the languages of reparative and distributive justice. The particular claim-making process is contingent on the institutions and histories of nation states, but a basic assertion cross-cuts national narratives. Indigenous peoples assert that a proper indigenous-state relationship cannot begin without recognition of past grievances, grievances based in the historical and continuing imposition of colonialism and forced assimilation. The land rights issue is not only about the recognition of and compensation for past transgressions, but also about reconfiguring current property rights regimes so that they accommodate indigenous land interests, and allow for indigenous systems of law in the management of those interests.

This study has examined how negotiation policies emerged as part of indigenous' peoples demands for the recognition of their special rights as the New World's original inhabitants. I have shown how governments' decisions to let courts resolve these grievances were based on a normative view of the indigenous as equal citizens carrying no particular rights. I have argued that the mobilization of indigenous protest in the late twentieth century challenged policy-makers to recalculate the costs of a delegation strategy. Indigenous political mobilization changed policy-makers' expectations of the future political costs of not recognizing special rights claims, and negotiation policies emerged out of these new calculations. In Australia, Canada, and New Zealand, high court decisions created a climate of urgency which facilitated significant policy change, but the negotiation outcome is more directly caused by the political mobilization already underway. Into this basic dynamic, other factors come into play, conditioning policy-makers' reassessments. I have identified two, the impact of each varying in each case: political norms about the appropriateness of courts in the policy-making process, and the decentralization of legislative jurisdiction inherent in federalism. I have examined the conditions under which new institutions can emerge by focusing on the normative bases on which they rest and the changing expectations of those actors with the power to effect change.

CHANGING SOCIETY?

The negotiation choice is critically distinguished from other patterns of state-society relations in the policy-making process, particularly the pattern of policy consultation. Negotiation with the executive establishes social actors as veto-players in a process where the outcome is a contractual agreement which has legal or moral force only with that group's explicit consent. I thus distinguish negotiation from the usual processes of legislative bargaining, where the choice of a non-state actor to walk away from the policy consultation process does not ensure that the policy development process will stop. The choice for a government to institute a negotiation policy involves a calculation where any constraint on the government's policy-making function arising from the non-state actor's veto position is outweighed by the government's need for the other party's consent.

This study explores the reasons that bring liberal democracies to implement land claim negotiation policies in the first place, and I have left for another day a detailed examination of the actual outcomes of the negotiation policies now underway. The importance of land claims negotiations rests not only in theories of recognition and the symbolic politics of sovereignty, but in the material and social consequences attributed to the negotiation process and its outcomes. Do land claim negotiations actually deliver all that they can? Ideally, land claim negotiations and agreements arising from these processes address and resolve underlying grievances of indigenous peoples and are seen to deliver justice. Ideally, the achievement of a settlement agreement correlates positively with the resolution of the underlying grievance and yields an easy to way to measure a decrease in uncertainty. It is important to understand why settlement agreements come to be. However, it is another story to treat the settlement agreement as an independent variable, and evaluate its impact on the indigenous and non-indigenous communities it is supposed to serve.

Difficulties associated with measuring such a vague public good as justice are many, and the literature on land claim negotiations contains no systematic empirical study to determine whether this outcome has indeed been delivered. If justice is hard to measure, then so too is the legal and political certainty that policy-makers hope settlement agreements will provide. Indeed, in its 1998 report on Canada's comprehensive claims policy, the Auditor General of Canada noted that " . . . we recognize that certainty can mean different things to different parties. And, without a consensus on interpretation, it becomes more difficult to determine what exactly is being achieved through negotiated settlements."[4] The challenges associated with measuring and quantifying the outcomes of settlement agreements are reflected in the fact that almost 30 years after its implementation, the Canadian government has not systematically evaluated the economic, political, and social benefits accruing from these agreements.[5]

The difficulties in pointing to clear and concise impacts of settlement agreements do not preclude a presentation of the extent of monies or lands at issue. In Canada, thirteen settled comprehensive[6] claims have involved approximately $1.2 billion Cdn in compensation and the transfer in full ownership of approximately 550,000 square kilometers of settlement lands to 55,000 indigenous beneficiaries. The settlement to 2002 of 227 specific claims has involved compensation of $987 million Cdn. Budgetary annual expenditures on the research, negotiation, and litigation of claims have reached approximately $350 million annually. Through loan funding from the federal government, Canadian indigenous communities are spending $50 million a year to negotiate their claims. Under the auspices of the American Indian Claims Commission (1946–1978), $775 million US in monetary compensation was disbursed to claimants, with subsequent disbursements up to 1985 increasing that total to $1.2 billion. In New Zealand, the government, under its 1994 fiscal envelope proposal, allocated $1 billion NZD for the negotiation and settlement of indigenous claims, a budgetary ceiling revoked by a subsequent government. Current opinion considers the full financial price tag to far exceed that number once all negotiations are concluded. While these numbers are but a fraction of what indigenous peoples claim, and what many feel they are owed in order for full compensation to be met for the economic, social, and cultural detriments resulting from land loss, the point remains that the costs to respond to indigenous land grievances are not insignificant, in terms of the financial and human resources allocated to the effort by all parties.

The achievement of settlement agreements is not the sole outcome of negotiation processes. There are important outcomes of a negotiation process which are realized whether or not a settlement agreement is achieved. When pressing forward a political agenda vis-à-vis the government, the operational challenge for any social group is to maximize the appearance of internal consensus by underplaying how ideological, material, or institutional factors have created real and perhaps enduring divisions which militate against obtaining a consensus. However, once a government chooses to respond to a generalized indigenous land grievance, the particularization of that grievance takes place. In the researching, filing, negotiation, or litigation of a land claim, indigenous interests are not only identified, but reshaped, and this has implications for how the claimants group identifies itself, whether it chooses to include or exclude members from its community, and how it will resolve disputes arising from the claiming process itself. This process can create new divisions or aggravate old ones; it can highlight instances where the material and cultural interests of the community may collide.

The issue of the overlapping claim illustrates how the negotiation or litigation of land claims can pit indigenous groups against each other, increasing the cross-cutting incentives which make it more difficult to achieve a larger degree of consensus within the whole indigenous rights movement. In so far as negotiation or litigation processes seek to identify exclusive indigenous and non-indigenous interests over a defined space of land, a dynamic is created where indigenous groups have competing material incentives, and negotiation or litigation is no longer a simple picture of indigenous versus settler society, but rather an indigenous versus indigenous versus settler society. Just as indigenous-settler interests over a given space of land can be either competitive or cooperative, indigenous interests in excluding other indigenous interests can exist historically or arise due to contemporary interests. The process of negotiation or litigation can serve to exacerbate these divisions, be they rooted in historical or modern circumstance.

While the ability to press forward a national land claims agenda and the ability for indigenous communities to engage the government in a negotiation process are not the same, they are often correlated. Funds made available by governments for the researching of claims can be used to strengthen indigenous organizational capacity or can establish counterproductive incentives. For instance, significant monies for the researching of claims in Canada were channeled through provincial-level indigenous rights advocacy organizations, which were then responsible for the further disbursement of funds. This funding helped establish much more effective organizations capable of lobbying not only in Ottawa, but provincial governments as the need to do so arose. While the strengthening of the provincial level of indigenous organizational activism may have made it difficult for the national umbrella organization to speak with one voice,[7] my interview results show how important strong indigenous regional advocacy organizations are in establishing legitimate negotiation structures. In New Zealand, research dollars were channeled through the Waitangi Tribunal and were important in establishing the reputation and legitimacy of that organization to address indigenous claims. On the other hand, the arrival of another organization funding claims research, the Crown Forestry Rental Trust, has led some observers to decry its alleged role in fostering intra-Maori disputes and the increased filing of competing claims. In Australia, the establishment of land councils in the Northern Territory in the 1970s to deal with land transfers to traditional owners has not been without controversy, as some indigenous land interests are privileged under the land council system over others.[8] However, these land councils and others which arose in states such as Western Australia, are organizations which have proven critical in pressing forth a land rights agenda nationally and were instrumental in the consultation surrounding the establishment in

1993 of the cornerstone national Australian land rights legislation, the Native Title Act.

The negotiation process, then, has implications for the collective action of indigenous interests, both in terms of how claimant groups are constituted and how relations between them are structured. The negotiation process, like other instances of state-society interaction, is transformative of the indigenous interests and the groups which are formed to represent them. These are important consequences of a negotiation policy, and future research may be able to evaluate their full scope.

CHANGING THE STATE?

That interaction with the state transforms social forces is an important theme in this study and in the contemporary state-in-society literature.[9] The negotiation of indigenous land claims across the globe is illustrative of this point. What has garnered less attention within the literature on indigenous rights movements and their effects is whether, and to what extent, the companion argument of the state-in-society literature also holds true: that the state is also transformed by the interaction with social forces:

> The state is not a fixed ideological entity. Rather, it embodies an ongoing dynamic, a changing set of goals, as it engages other social groups . . . the formulation of state policy is as much a product of this dynamic as it is a simple outcome of the goals of top state leaders or a straight-forward legislative process. The results of the engagement with (and disengagement from) other social forces may modify the state agenda substantially; indeed, they may alter the very nature of the state.[10]

That states have been transformed by interaction with indigenous activism is demonstrable. This can be shown through ideological, judicial, and bureaucratic change. The judiciaries in the United States, Canada, New Zealand, and Australia have all developed an indigenous rights jurisprudence, exploring the fundamental nexus between Western colonial legal systems and those of these countries' original inhabitants. The development of indigenous rights jurisprudence is perhaps the most studied and best documented aspect of state transformation within the indigenous rights literature. Less studied, but clearly important, is the transformation of the organs of the executive branch.

For a government to institute a policy which privileges the negotiation of indigenous land claims is itself evidence of an important transformation. However, more critically in terms of maximizing the outcomes of this policy change is the ability for indigenous peoples to access and mold the administrative instruments that are put into place within the policy-making structure to support claims negotiation. This includes advisory capacity within the executive's central agencies, as well as newly constituted administrative centers within existing departmental structures. In most cases, the creation of administrative centers designated to deal with land claims negotiations represents the first time that public sector expertise comes together on such related issues as: 1) state obligations flowing from treaties or statutory instruments; 2) changing judicial views on land rights issues; 3) strategic indigenous policy development; and 4) knowledge of indigenous community goals. Land claim negotiation policies have had the perhaps mundane, but critically important, effect of forcing pockets of public sector expertise to talk to one another. They are forced to create information-sharing and policy-coordination protocols not only within the administrative apparatus traditionally charged with indigenous issues, but across public sector agencies involved with land use issues generally, and which have traditionally had nothing to do with indigenous peoples. The negotiation of land claims, when issues other than strict monetary compensation are involved, necessarily touches on the administrative turf of multiple executive departments, and increases the profile of indigenous land issues across the larger administrative system.

Thus, land claim negotiations have provided structured opportunities with the executive branch writ large, rather than segregating the access of indigenous actors to established indigenous affairs departments, which historically have been responsible for the promotion and administration of colonialist policies inimical to indigenous aspirations. The expansion of interest in indigenous land issues across administrative boundaries also enforces the principle that the whole executive, not simply the American Bureau of Indian Affairs, the Canadian Department of Indian and Northern Affairs or the New Zealand Ministry of Maori Affairs, has obligations and interests vis-à-vis indigenous land rights which must be taken into account within wider policy-making circles.

The coordination of policy-input across executive departments is an important aspect of state transformation. Another example is the opportunity negotiations provide to redesign those departments which have traditionally been the lead departments in indigenous affairs. The design of bureaucratic structures imparts important signals about a government's policy priorities, and these structures serve to entrench policy decisions once they are made. While bureaucratic structures are elastic, in some systems more than others, they are not infinitely so; subsequent changes in the administrative structures of the state are conditioned on the changes that came before. Once administrative bodies are created, they become more difficult to change as time wears on, particularly when the likelihood of oversight and policy change from cabinet ministers is low.

The entrenchment of policy choices is demonstrated in various ways, but key among them is how policy choices are enshrined within bureaucratic structures and within the financial reporting of public sector organizations. For instance, the Canadian federal government announced its land claims negotiations policy in 1973, and in 1974, it created the Office of Native Claims within the given structure of its designated lead department, the Department of Indian and Northern Affairs (DIAND). However, the costs in terms of human and financial resources in this new policy area were not reported as distinct claims-related items in the annual appropriations estimates cycle until the 1979–80 fiscal year. It was not until the early 1980s that this policy initiative was accorded the organizational prestige of its own division and reporting relationship[11] with DIAND's Deputy Minister, the department's chief bureaucratic officer. The rise of indigenous negotiation structures within the DIAND bureaucracy is also mirrored by the creation within Canada's key central agency, the Privy Council Office, of a section devoted to indigenous affairs issues.[12]

The hope for indigenous peoples is that the administrative transformations accompanying a land claims negotiation policy will support a newly defined relationship between the government and indigenous peoples, and will be enshrined within the bureaucratic mechanisms which conduct the daily business of indigenous-government relations. Will a culture of agreement-making take root within the administration of government-indigenous relations itself, to the degree that there are pockets of expertise within the public sector which can resist the unilateralism of other key policy actors, such as those within the conservative bastions of treasury departments? Will the consciousness-raising on the importance within indigenous communities of negotiation and compliance to those negotiated agreements be reflected within higher levels of bureaucratic structures? Will the machinery of government now in place to support negotiations be followed with machinery of government which addresses the implementation of those agreements, including mechanisms to resolve disputes arising from their implementation?

Perhaps one of the most important transformations of the executive brought on by a negotiation policy is its self-interest in supporting indigenous governing structures which are seen to be legitimate within the indigenous community itself. Governments have always been interested in the capacities of indigenous leaders to act essentially as administrators and agents of government policies, rather than as legitimate representatives of indigenous interests. The precedent of land claims negotiations is that for the first time in the history of indigenous-government relations, the government has a self-interest in whether the indigenous negotiating team does, in fact, have an accepted mandate to act on behalf of a majority of its group members. This self-interest occurs because the durability of a negotiated settlement is directly related to the level of support evidenced within the indigenous community for the settlement agreement as a product of legitimate indigenous negotiators.

Once a government commits to a negotiated option, several factors come into play so that this choice becomes institutionalized, and it is difficult for a government to back away from negotiation once it has begun. These factors include changes in bureaucratic structures which anchor policy choices, and a growing ideological commitment among government administrators that indigenous rights are appropriately "special" rights which cannot ethically be modified without explicit indigenous consent.

PARTING THOUGHTS

Land claim negotiations deal with fundamental questions about a nation's real estate and a nation's sovereignty. As Cornell writes, "land occupies center stage in the historical theatre of Indian-White relations. Around it the drama moves."[13] But a critical question for indigenous negotiators is also whether the agenda of the negotiations can be broadened to include other questions of essential importance, such as self-government agreements, redress for cultural as well as economic loss, and apologies for past wrongs. A negotiation which is constrained to haggling over a sum of money for the loss of a land base is of limited use to achieve the economic, political, and cultural revitalization which indigenous peoples seek. The challenge is to ensure that the negotiation opportunity is maximized so that it becomes an important forum to discuss issues not only linked to land, but to indigenous-state relations as a whole.

Notes

NOTES TO CHAPTER ONE

1. Michael Ignatieff, *The Rights Revolution* (Toronto: Anansi Press Limited, 2000).
2. Duncan Ivison, Paul Patton, and Will Sanders, eds., *Political Theory and the Rights of Indigenous Peoples* (Cambridge, UK: Cambridge University Press, 2000) 4.
3. Ibid., 3.
4. James L. Gibson, Gregory A. Caldeira, and Vanessa A. Baird, "On the Legitimacy of National High Courts," *American Political Science Review* 92, no. 2 (1998): 343.
   C. Neal Tate and Torbjorn Vallinder, eds., *The Global Expansion of Judicial Power* (New York: New York University Press, 1995) 5.
5. In Canada, jurisdiction over "Indians and lands reserved for Indians" is federal. Ownership over lands and natural resource development is assigned to the provinces. In Australia, the States had exclusive jurisdiction over aboriginal affairs until a constitutional amendment in 1967 gave the Commonwealth government concurrent power to legislate in this domain. Land and natural resource development is the jurisdiction of the States.
6. Kathryn Harrison, *Passing the Buck: Federalism and Canadian Environmental Policy* (Vancouver: University of British Columbia Press, 1996) 169.
7. F. M. Brookfield, *Waitangi and Indigenous Rights: Revolution, Law and Legitimation* (Auckland, New Zealand: Auckland University Press, 1999); James Sakej Youngblood Henderson, "Empowering Treaty Federalism," *Saskatchewan Law Review* 58 (1995); Patrick Macklem, *Indigenous Difference and the Constitution of Canada* (Toronto: University of Toronto Press, 2001); Christos Mantziaris and David F. Martin, *Native Title Corporations: A Legal and Anthropological Analysis* (Annandale, NSW: Federation Press in cooperation with National Native Title Tribunal (Perth, WA), 2000); Kent McNeil, *Common Law Aboriginal Title* (Oxford: Clarendon Press, 1989).

8. Noel Dyck, ed., *Indigenous Peoples and the Nation-State: "Fourth World" Politics in Canada, Australia, and Norway* (St. John's, Newfoundland: Institute of Social and Economic Research, Memorial University of Newfoundland, 1985); Sally M. Weaver, *Making Canadian Indian Policy: The Hidden Agenda 1968–1970* (Toronto: University of Toronto Press, 1981).
9. Peter McFarlane, *Brotherhood to Nationhood: George Manuel and the Making of the Modern Indian Movement* (Toronto: Between the Lines, 1993).

NOTES TO CHAPTER TWO

1. Charles Taylor, "The Politics of Recognition," in *Multiculturalism: Examining the Politics of Recognition,* ed. Amy Gutmann (Princeton, NJ: Princeton University Press, 1994).
2. Ibid., 25.
3. Nancy Fraser, "From Redistribution to Recognition? Dilemmas of Justice in a 'Post-Socialist' Age," *New Left Review* 212, July/August (1995); Nancy Fraser, "A Rejoinder to Iris Young," *New Left Review* 223, May/June (1997); Iris Marion Young, "Unruly Categories: A Critique of Nancy Fraser's Dual Systems Theory," *New Left Review* 222, March/April (1997).
4. Charles Taylor, "The Politics of Recognition"; James Tully, *Strange Multiplicity: Constitutionalism in an Age of Diversity* (Cambridge: Cambridge University Press, 1995).
5. Alan Cairns, *Citizens Plus: Aboriginal Peoples and the Canadian State* (Vancouver: University of British Columbia Press, 2000) 194.
6. Elizabeth McLeay, *The Cabinet and Political Power in New Zealand, Oxford Readings in New Zealand Politics* (Auckland: Oxford University Press, 1995); Donald J. Savoie, *Governing from the Centre: The Concentration of Power in Canadian Politics* (Toronto: University of Toronto Press, 1999).
7. R. Kent Weaver, "The Politics of Blame Avoidance," *Journal of Public Policy* 6, October/December (1986): 385.
8. Jack Knight, *Institutions and Social Conflict* (Cambridge: Cambridge University Press, 1992) 85.
9. *Calder v. Attorney General (British Columbia)* (1973) 34 DLR (3d) 145 (SC(Can))
10. Patrick Macklem, *Indigenous Difference and the Constitution of Canada* (Toronto: University of Toronto Press, 2001) 269; Arthur J. Ray, *I Have Lived Here Since the World Began: An Illustrated History of Canada's Native People* (Toronto: Lester Publishing Limited and Key Porter Books, 1996) 337; Paul Tennant, *Aboriginal Peoples and Politics: The Indian Land Question in British Columbia, 1849–1989* (Vancouver: University of British Columbia Press, 1990) 172.
11. *New Zealand Maori Council v. Attorney General* [1987] N.Z.L.R. 641
12. Mason Durie, *Te Mana, Te Kawanatanga: The Politics of Maori Self-Determination* (Auckland: Oxford University Press, 1998) 184.

13. *United States v. Sante Fe Pacific Railroad Co* 314 US 339 at 347 (1941)
14. *Mabo v. Queensland (No 2)* (1992) 175 CLR 1
15. *Milirripum v. Nabalco Pty Ltd* (1971) 17 FLR 141 (SC(NT))
16. The literature points to the empirical difficulty of measuring judicial uncertainty. See Linda Babcock and Lowell J. Taylor, "The Role of Arbitrator Uncertainty in Negotiation Impasses," *Industrial Relations* 35, no. 4 (1996).
17. In this literature courts are a subset of arbitration mechanisms.
18. The study of judicial processes and their impact on politics is most ardently pursued in the sub-field of American politics. See James L. Gibson, Gregory A. Caldeira, and Vanessa A. Baird, "On the Legitimacy of National High Courts," *American Political Science Review* 92, no. 2 (1998).
19. Kathleen Thelen, "Historical Institutionalism in Comparative Politics," *Annual Review of Political Science* 2 (1999).
20. Ibid., 397.
21. Avinash Dixit and John Londregan, "Fiscal Federalism and Redistributive Politics," *Journal of Public Economics* 68 (1998).
22. Knight, *Institutions and Social Conflict.*
23. C. Neal Tate and Torbjorn Vallinder, eds., *The Global Expansion of Judicial Power* (New York: New York University Press, 1995) 5.
24. *Johnson v. McIntosh,* 8 Wheat 543l 5 L Ed 681 (1823)
25. Marco Guigni, Douglas McAdam, and Charles Tilly, eds., *How Social Movements Matter* (Minneapolis: University of Minnesota Press, 1999); Sidney G. Tarrow, *Power in Movement: Social Movements and Contentious Politics,* 2 ed. (New York: Cambridge University Press, 1998).
26. Hanspeter Kriesi and Dominique Wisler, "The Impact of Social Movements on Political Institutions: A Comparison of the Introduction of Direct Legislation in Switzerland and the United States," in *How Social Movements Matter,* ed. Marco Guigni, Doug McAdam, and Charles Tilly, *Social Movements, Protest, and Contention* (University of Minnesota Press, 1999).
27. Antonia Maioni, *Parting at the Crossroads: The Emergence of Health Insurance in the United States and Canada* (Princeton, NJ: Princeton University Press, 1998); Michael S. Sparer and Lawrence D. Brown, "States and the Health Care Crisis: The Limits and Lessons of Laboratory Federalism," in *Health Policy, Federalism, and the American States,* ed. Robert F. Rich and William D. White (Washington, D.C.: The Urban Institute Press, 1996).
28. The possible exception is the State of South Australia.
29. See Nancy Bermeo, "The Import of Institutions," *Journal of Democracy* 13, no.2 (2002).
30. Gibson, Caldeira, and Baird, "On the Legitimacy of National High Courts," 343.

NOTES TO CHAPTER THREE

1. The terminology used to indicate indigenous peoples has developed extensively and varies across countries. "Indigenous" is the term which has

recently emerged internationally to indicate those peoples which first occupied the New World before the arrival of colonialism. In Canada, "indigenous" has been used interchangeably with "native" and "aboriginal." The
word "Indian" in the Canadian context refers to a specific subset of indigenous peoples who have a particular legal status, and are under the jurisdiction of the federal government. Not all indigenous people in Canada are
"Indians," such as the Métis and the Inuit. Since the 1970s, the term "First
Nations" has become accepted and widely used among Indian communities. In New Zealand, the indigenous peoples are Maori. The government
used the term "native" until the late 1940s. In Australia, the term "aboriginal" is widespread, but in the Australian context, it refers to the black
peoples of the Australian continent. The other indigenous group in Australia is the people of Polynesian descent traditionally living in the islands
north of Queensland, in the Torres Strait. In Australia, the term "native"
was used in the late 19th century and early 20th to designate a person
born in Australia, and was not necessarily a term restricted by race. See
John Chesterman and Brian Galligan, *Citizens without Rights: Aborigines
and Australian Citizenship* (Melbourne: Cambridge University Press, 1997)
88. In this study, I use the terms "indigenous," "aboriginal" and "native"
interchangeably.

2. Pierre Elliott Trudeau, *The Essential Trudeau*, ed. Ron Graham (Toronto:
   McLlelland & Stewart, Inc., 1998) 74.
3. The French did not recognize indigenous rights to land, and unlike the
   British, were more interested in New France for the fur trade than for
   settlement. Therefore, agreements which were signed between indigenous
   peoples during the French regime were more peace and friendship or trade
   treaties than land cession agreements.
4. The transfer of title from the federal to provincial governments happened
   in stages, and usually included some clause which made provinces respect
   existing indigenous land rights. Two examples are the Québec Northern
   Boundaries Extension Act (1912) and the Natural Resources Transfer Act
   (1930) involving Manitoba, Saskatchewan and Alberta. Part of the reason
   for small reserves was the obstruction of provincial governments. The segregation of Indian communities on reserves occurred where the demand
   for agricultural land by settlers was high, so there were no or few reserves
   established in the northern areas of the country.
5. Jill St. Germain, *Indian Treaty-Making Policy in the United States and
   Canada, 1867–1877* (Toronto: University of Toronto Press, 2001) xix.
6. Ibid., 97.
7. See Ibid. For a detailed look at the creation of reserves in British Columbia, see Cole Harris, *Making Native Space: Colonialism, Resistance, and
   Reserves in British Columbia* (Vancouver: University of British Columbia
   Press, 2002).
8. The Judicial Committee of the Privy Council is Britain's top court of appeal,
   and during the colonial period it was automatically the highest court of
   appeal for Britain's colonies. In 1949, Canada abolished appeals to the Privy
   Council. The Privy Council remains New Zealand's top court of appeal.

9. St. Catherine's Milling Company v. The Queen [1888] 14 App. Cas. 46 (PC). This concerned a dispute between the federal government and the province of Ontario on the northwestern boundary of the province. The jurisdictional dispute between the governments rested on the ability of the federal government to dispose of the lands ceded to it by the Saulteaux in Treaty Three (1873). The federal government argued that the lands it had acquired through treaty were previously held by the Saulteaux, and that title had been transferred to Canada, who then had the unencumbered right to grant licenses to log on Crown lands. The provincial government argued that indigenous title was not a creature in law. The province won its case through three appeals. In 1888, the Privy Council sided with the province of Ontario.

10. Olive Patricia Dickason, *Canada's First Nations: A History of Founding Peoples from Earliest Times* (Norman: University of Oklahoma Press, 1992) 342.

11. The restriction on organizing stated that "without the [federal] minister's approval, no Indian or person acting for [an Indian organization] could now request or receive from any registered Indian any fee for legal or other services or any money for postage, travel, advertising, hall rental, refreshments, research expenses, legal fees, or court costs. The amendment quite simply made it impossible for any organization to exist if pursuing the land claim was one of its objectives." Paul Tennant, *Aboriginal Peoples and Politics: The Indian Land Question in British Columbia, 1849–1989* (Vancouver: University of British Columbia Press, 1990) 112. Indian leaders in British Columbia regained interest in a judicial strategy in 1921 when the Judicial Committee of the Privy Council recognized aboriginal title in a Nigerian case. *Amodu Tijani v. Secretary, Southern Nigeria (*1921) 2 AC 399. The federal government's decision to starve an Indian litigation strategy to its financial death meant that a British Columbia test case would not make it through the Canadian appeal process and hence, never to the Privy Council.

12. Alan Cairns, *Citizens Plus: Aboriginal Peoples and the Canadian State* (Vancouver: University of British Columbia Press, 2000) 17. The Indian Act contained the compulsory enfranchisement provision in 1920, but the provision was repealed in 1922. It reappeared in 1933.

13. John Franklin Leslie, "Assimilation, Integration, or Termination? The Development of Canadian Indian Policy, 1943–1963" (PhD, Carleton University, 1999) 150.

14. By 1947, those status Indians who had fought in Canada's defense were granted federal voting rights without having to relinquish their Indian status.

15. As quoted in James Rodger Miller, *Skyscrapers Hide the Heavens: A History of Indian-White Relations in Canada,* 3rd ed. (Toronto: University of Toronto Press, 2000) 282.

16. Mary Jane Norris et al., "100 Years of Aboriginal Demography: An Analysis within the Canadian Context" (Paper presented at the Canadian Population Society, Congress of the Social Sciences and Humanities, University of Alberta, Edmonton, AB, May 28–30, 2000).

17. Tennant, *Aboriginal Peoples and Politics,* 120.
18. Memorandum to cabinet, 12 November 1948, as cited in Leslie, "Assimilation, Integration, or Termination?," 187.
19. As indicated in ibid., 194.
20. To illustrate, in 1942, the Catholic Church accounted for 34 per cent of the hospital beds in Canada. Terence J. Fay, *A History of Canadian Catholics: Gallicanism, Romanism, and Canadianism* (Montreal and Kingston: McGill-Queen's University Press, 2002) 147.
21. Ibid., 147–48. Antonia Maioni, *Parting at the Crossroads: The Emergence of Health Insurance in the United States and Canada* (Princeton, NJ: Princeton University Press, 1998) 70.
22. Jean Hamelin, *Histoire du Catholicisme Québécois: Le XXe Siècle, Tome 2, De 1940 À Nos Jours,* vol. 2 (Montréal: Boréal Express, 1984) 32.
23. NAC (National Archives of Canada), RG2, Records of the Privy Council Office, series A-5-a (cabinet conclusions), vol.2642, reel T2366.
24. NAC, RG2, series B2, vol.137, file C-20–5. Cabinet document 133–50 (undated).
25. NAC, RG2, series A-5-a, vol.2645, reel T2366.
26. Canada, House of Commons Debates, 21 June 1950, p.3938.
27. Leslie, "Assimilation, Integration, or Termination?," 206.
28. NAC, RG2, series B2, file C-20–5. Cabinet document 278–50, titled "Proposed Changes in Bill 267 (An Act Respecting Indians)," 5 December 1950.
29. NAC, RG2, series B2, file C-20–5. Cabinet document 295–50, titled "Proposed Changes in Bill 267 (An Act Respecting Indians)," 19 December 1950.
30. NAC, RG2, series A-5-a, vol.2647, reel T2367. Underline in the original.
31. Leslie, "Assimilation, Integration, or Termination?," 233.
32. Dennis Smith, *Rogue Tory: The Life and Legend of John G. Diefenbaker* (Toronto: MacFarland, Walter & Ross, 1995) 158–64.
33. Ibid., 46.
34. Ibid., 279.
35. Leslie, "Assimilation, Integration, or Termination?," 308.
36. Ibid., 391.
37. The Oka land question is a native title dispute in Québec involving the transfer in the 19th century of lands to a Catholic order. The disputed lands were to be sold to expand the Oka golf course, and set in motion the Oka protest in 1990 which brought the land claims issue to international attention.
38. NAC, MG 32, series B1, vol.100, file 1A-653, 1961–62.
39. Interview, Ottawa, Ontario, 17 October 2001.
40. NAC, MG 32, series B1, vol.100, file 1A-653, 1961–61, Memorandum to cabinet, Indian Claims Commission, 7 March 1962.
41. NAC, RG2, series A-5-a, vol. 6192. Cabinet conclusions of 19 March 1962.
42. NAC, RG2, series A-5-a, vol. 6192. Cabinet conclusions of 6 February 1962.
43. NAC, RG2, series A-5-a, vol. 6192. Cabinet conclusion of 6 February 1962.

44. NAC, RG2, series A-5-a, vol. 6192. Cabinet conclusion of 29 March 1962.
45. NAC, RG2, series A-5-a, vol. 6193. Cabinet conclusion of 16 October 1962. It is unclear from the documentary record to date regarding the true position of the Indian Affairs Branch on the adjudication versus advisory options at this time. The support of the Branch for adjudication kick-started the development of commission legislation, but it was clear that cabinet opinion was split earlier in 1961. The Branch may well have backed the advisory position in 1962, knowing that the Department of Justice and the Prime Minister were not in favor of adjudication. This speculation of strategic positioning on the part of the Indian Branch bureaucracy is unconfirmed, but the first cabinet memo prepared after the fall of the Diefenbaker government from Citizenship and Immigration puts forward adjudication once more.
46. A preliminary discussion was held on October 15th, 1962, which indicates that not all of cabinet was behind the advisory option. Cabinet deferred a decision, as the Prime Minister was not in attendance. The next day, the Prime Minister *in situ*, the advisory decision acquired cabinet approval, suggesting that opponents deferred to the Prime Minister.
47. Indian Affairs Branch memo, 30 May 1963, as cited by Sally M. Weaver, *Making Canadian Indian Policy: The Hidden Agenda 1968–1970* (Toronto: University of Toronto Press, 1981) 39.
48. NAC, RG2, series B2, vol. 6258. Memorandum to cabinet, Indian Claims Commission, 10 December 1963.
49. This is interesting because the cabinet memorandum does indeed indicate that the Commission would have jurisdiction to hear claims "based on the failure of the Crown to extinguish the so-called Indian interest in lands in certain parts of Canada."
50. Weaver, *Making Canadian Indian Policy*, 38.
51. Although the Indian Affairs Branch saw that Indian cooperation was necessary to achieve the greater policy goal of social and economic "advancement," it had a very limited view of the role of Indian consultation in the policy making process. During the time that the claims commission proposal was submitted for comment in 1964, a major initiative for the Branch was a federal-provincial conference on the delivery of welfare services to the Indian population. A difficult issue which arose was whether Indians should be consulted on the issue of which government should provide what services. The Chief of Federal-Provincial Relations wrote to the Director of the Branch stating the government's general position: "It may be politically expedient to have discussions with the Indians . . . I see this as achieving little more than explaining the basic principles to the Indians, allaying the fears they may have concerning loss of rights, treaty or otherwise, and establishing a climate of goodwill" (NAC, RG10, vol.8573, file 1/1-2-2-8-1 pt.1, letter from L.L. Brown to Director, Indian Affairs Branch, 14 April 1964). Given this context, it should be of little surprise that the 1965 version of the claims commission bill would not address Indians' fundamental concerns.
52. A "white paper" is a statement of official government policy. It is a term common to parliamentary systems.

53. The Privy Council Office (PCO) is cabinet's secretariat. It is the apex of the pubic service, and led by the Clerk of the Privy Council.
54. For a detailed account of this policy review exercise, see Weaver, *Making Canadian Indian Policy*.
55. Trudeau, *The Essential Trudeau*, 161.
56. Ibid., 84.
57. Weaver, *Making Canadian Indian Policy*, 114.
58. NAC, RG2, series A-5-a, vol. 6340. Cabinet conclusions, 13 February 1969.
59. NAC, RG2, series A-5-a, vol. 6340. Cabinet conclusions, 13 February 1969.
60. Weaver, *Making Canadian Indian Policy*, 115.
61. Ibid., 120.
62. Ibid., 133.
63. Ibid., 139.
64. Ibid., 149.
65. Ibid., 162.
66. NAC, RG2, series A-5-a, vol.6430. Cabinet conclusions 17 June 1969.
67. NAC, RG2, series A-5-a, vol.6340. Cabinet conclusions, 6 November 1969.
68. The title "The Unjust Society" alluded to Trudeau's famous speech the year before when he accepted the Liberal Party leadership, where he called on Canada to be a "just society."
69. Memorandum to cabinet, Consultative Mechanisms—Indian Policy Proposals, cabinet document 950/70, 22 July 1970. Note that, at the time of my research, cabinet documents after 1969 were not yet held or catalogued by the National Archives of Canada. Access to these documents was achieved through the Access to Information Program, Privy Council Office.
70. Memorandum to cabinet, cabinet document 950/70, 22 July 1970.
71. Cabinet conclusions, meeting no.44–70, 30 July 1970.
72. Letter from Jean Chrétien to Pierre Trudeau, 30 April 1971, included as Annex A to cabinet document 733–71, Memorandum to cabinet, Role of the Indian Claims Commissioner.
73. Letter from Jean Chrétien to Pierre Trudeau, 30 April 1971.
74. NAC, RG 33–115, Records of the Indian Claims Commissioner, vol.1, file 10-1-1.
75. NAC, RG 33–115, vol.1, file 10-1-1, in a letter (4 February 1970) from Barber to Professor Wilson Duff of the University of British Columbia, Barber writes: " . . . I am coming to the conclusion that an error may have been made in excluding [aboriginal title claims from his mandate] because of the fact that the Indians of British Columbia, the Maritimes, and many parts of Québec are not covered under treaty."
76. Chrétien drafted a letter for Trudeau's signature stating that Barber could investigate any claims that came before him, rather than explicitly changing the Commissioner's legal mandate to include claims based on aboriginal title. This is a fine point of strategy, perhaps, but it does demonstrate Chrétien's appreciation of the need to manage concrete DIAND's policy goals within the context of Trudeau's objection to the recognition of special rights claims on principle.
77. Cabinet conclusions, cabinet meeting 43–71, 29 July 1971.

78. Memorandum to cabinet, Indian Rights and Treaties Research, cabinet document 770/72, 21 June 1972.
79. Barber indicated the limitations of courts in their witness and evidentiary constraints in letter to a Blackfoot band seeking action on ammunition provisions of Treaty 7. NAC, RG 33–115, vol.1, file 10-1-2.
80. NAC, RG33–115, vol.5, file: Inuit—General, letter from Inuit Tapirisat to Barber, 9 December 1971.
81. Memorandum to the Chairman of the Interdepartmental Committee on Indian Policy, Indian Treaties 8 and 11, cabinet document 416/70, 10 February 1970.
82. Cabinet conclusion, meeting 29–70, 7 May 1970.
83. Memorandum to cabinet, Treaties 8 and 11, cabinet document 456/72, 18 April 1972.
84. Memorandum to cabinet, Treaties 8 and 11, cabinet document 456/72, 18 April 1972.
85. Cabinet Committee on Social Policy, Record of Committee Decision, 8 May 1972, confirmed by cabinet on 23 May 1972.
86. Statement by the Indians of Québec Association, included as Annex A to Memorandum to the cabinet, Proposed James Bay Hydro Electric Project, cabinet document 1010/71, 21 September 1971.
87. A few months earlier, the Québec provincial government under Premier Robert Bourassa rejected the first proposal for constitutional renewal, the Victoria Charter, reached through negotiations with the Trudeau government and the Canadian provinces. This era marks an attempt by Ottawa to manage demands within Québec for a more decentralized federal system, particularly in the area of social policy, during the beginnings of the province's separatist movement. The James Bay project was the province's "project of the century," and was linked to Québécois aspirations to be "maîtres chez nous." The James Bay power project was a political symbol of the extension of provincial power into its hinterland. Federal intervention in the James Bay project would be seen as Canadian interference in the basic political project of the Québec state. Given Bourassa's rejection of the constitutional proposals in June of 1971, the Trudeau government needed to be wary of appearing to retaliate.
88. Cabinet conclusions, meeting 59–71, 21 October 1971.
89. Cabinet conclusions, meeting 3–72, 27 January 1972.
90. Memorandum to cabinet, James Bay Project, 6 July 1972.
91. Addendum to Memorandum to cabinet of February 15 Regarding James Bay Hydro Electric Project, 8 May 1972.
92. Memorandum to cabinet, Position of the Federal Government with regard to the Indian people affected by the James Bay Hydro-Electric Project, cabinet document 517–72, 8 May 1972.
93. Memorandum to cabinet, James Bay Project, cabinet document 809/72, 6 July 1972.
94. Cabinet conclusions, 14 July 1972.
95. Calder v. Attorney-General (British Columbia) (1973) 34 DLR (3d) 145 at 200.

96. Cabinet minutes, Claims of Native Peoples, 8 February 1973.
97. Government action on aboriginal land rights was also conditioned by the results of the October 1972 federal election. The Trudeau government had been barely re-elected to a minority government. The Trudeau Liberals held two more seats in the House of Commons than their Conservative rivals, and were depending on the leftist New Democratic Party as their coalition partner.
98. For instance, he delivered a speech on the Implications of Indian Claims for Canada on the value of negotiation in March at the Banff School of Advanced Management.
99. NAC, RG 33–115, vol.1, file 9-1-3. Meeting at DIAND, March 23, 1973. In a letter to the Prime Minister in June 1974, he continued to push the government to turn away from the courts or special adjudicators " . . . I think that it would be most unfortunate if the issue is left to the courts for resolution . . . If [claims] are taken to court, they might inadvertently establish the adjudicatory process as the preferred approach, without sufficient testing of the process of negotiation . . . The negotiation process is inherently superior . . . In short, it can produce viable future oriented results while judges must concentrate on the past." RG 33–115, vol.3, file Minister-DIAND.
100. I was barred from reading the Department of Justice's memorandum and related documents under the solicitor-client privilege exemption of the federal Access to Information Act. References to the Justice position in the DIAND memorandum were similarly deleted.
101. Memorandum to cabinet, Indian and Inuit Claims Policy, cabinet document 570–73, 5 June 73.
102. Memorandum to cabinet, Indian and Inuit Title and Claims, cabinet document 667–73, 27 June 1973.
103. Cabinet minutes, 19 July 1973.
104. Ministerial Statement, Jean Chrétien, 8 August 1973. Interestingly, at the July 19 cabinet meeting, cabinet agreed to immediately announce a policy where the government recognized aboriginal title and would engage in negotiations to extinguish that title in return for various forms of compensation, including land. In this statement, the Government backpedals, indicating that the Government would *not* recognize title at the outset of negotiations, yet seek its extinguishment, and this is the policy which the Government has followed to this day. This has been a serious critique of the policy by Indian people in Canada, and emphasizes that government recognition of title is really one of the government's strongest cards. Further research should trace how and why the government moved away from this policy from July to August 1973.

NOTES TO CHAPTER FOUR

1. Andrew Sharp, *Justice and the Maori: The Philosophy and Practice of Maori Claims in New Zealand since the 1970s*, 2 ed. (Auckland: Oxford University Press, 1997) 15.

2. R. P. Boast et al., *Maori Land Law* (Wellington, New Zealand: Butterworths of New Zealand Ltd, 1999) 68.
3. Ibid., 99.
4. Alan Ward, *An Unsettled History: Treaty Claims in New Zealand Today* (Wellington, NZ: Bridget Williams Books, 1999) 159. The conclusion that the majority of Maori held lands was unsuitable for agricultural use is contradicted by a report to cabinet by the Minister of Maori Affairs in 1952, who estimated that " . . . of the approximately 4,000,000 acres of Maori land in New Zealand . . . 2,500,000 are considered to be capable of being reasonably successfully farmed." Archives New Zealand (hereafter ANZ), AAFD 811, file 144/9/1/, Maori Land—General 1950–56. Memorandum to cabinet, Maori Land Development, undated, but considered at cabinet meeting held on 29 February 1952.
5. Ibid., 22.
6. Boast et al., *Maori Land Law,* 48.
7. Unlike Canada, Australia and the United States, New Zealand's Court of Appeal has not yet had a case testing the proposition that aboriginal title has been extinguished over New Zealand's land mass. The legal argument is very strong that aboriginal title has been extinguished, but one interviewee (a senior Treasury official) in 2001 noted that both the government and Maori have not as yet been interested in proceeding with a test case, firstly because the extent of the uncertainty about what the court would decide (neither party is able to even guess a probability), and also because the political ramifications of a court decision are largely unknown. Interview, 19 March 2001, Wellington, New Zealand.
8. Wi Parata v. The Bishop of Wellington and the Attorney General (1877) 3 NZ Jur (NS) SC 72
9. Alex Frame, *Salmond: Southern Jurist* (Wellington, NZ: Victoria University Press, 1995) 114–15.
10. Letter from James Fitzgerald to J.C. Richmond, 25 August 1865, as cited by Claudia Orange, *The Treaty of Waitangi* (Wellington: Allen & Unwin New Zealand Ltd, 1987) 176.
11. In 1967, the Electoral Act was amended to allow Maori to stand as candidates for general seats in Parliament. In 1975, the fourth Labour government allowed a Maori voter the option of choosing the Maori or the general electoral roll.
12. Lindsay Cox, *Kotahitanga: The Search for Maori Political Unity* (Auckland: Oxford University Press, 1993) 135.
13. The Maori Councils Act of 1900 established 19 Maori councils which dealt with issues such as sanitation, among others. The 1900 Maori Land Administration Act was passed to allow the land councils to control the leasing of reserved lands, but the power of Maori on these councils with respect to land use and leading issues was circumscribed by the 1905 Maori Land Settlement Act. While the power of these councils to determine critical issues regarding land use was eroded by state action in the interest of settlers, these institutions, created through legislative action, were important building blocks of modern Maori political organization.

14. Orange, *The Treaty of Waitangi*, 233.
15. Richard Hill, "Enthroning "Justice above Might"?: The Sim Commission, Tainui and the Crown," (Wellington, NZ: Treaty of Waitangi Policy Unit, Department of Justice, 1989), 3.
16. Orange, *The Treaty of Waitangi*, 239.
17. One scholar writes that the Maori War Effort Organization was a compromise solution, where Maori would organize and mobilize voluntary support for the war within their communities rather than face conscription. Angela Ballara, *Iwi: The Dynamics of Maori Tribal Organisation from c.1769 to c.1945* (Wellington, NZ: Victoria University Press, 1998) 318.
18. Ibid.
19. R.S. Milne, *Political Parties in New Zealand* (Oxford: Oxford University Press, 1966) 58.
20. Hill writes that the government's attention to claims during the war period " . . . was driven by circumstances both proactive ('rewarding' the great contribution by the Maori to war effort) and more, especially, reaction—viz. Maori pressure as a quid pro quo for that war effort. On 16 June [1943], the four Maori Members of Parliament . . . met with the Acting Native Minister HGR Mason. It was decided that the Ngai Tahu claims should be the pioneering settlement." Richard Hill, "Settlements of Major Maori Claims in the 1940s: A Preliminary Historical Investigation," in *Department of Justice unpublished manuscript* (Wellington: 1989), paragraph 1.
21. Mai Chen and Geoffrey Palmer, *Public Law in New Zealand : Cases, Materials, Commentary, and Questions* (Auckland: Oxford University Press, 1993).
22. Three oft-cited references to Maori claims do not mention that the government engaged in a limited process of claims settlement during this period. Orange, *The Treaty of Waitangi*; Andrew Sharp, *Justice and the Maori: The Philosophy and Practice of Maori Claims in New Zealand since the 1970s*, 2 ed. (Auckland: Oxford University Press, 1997); Ward, *An Unsettled History*.
23. Hill, "Settlements of Major Maori Claims in the 1940s," paragraph 35.
24. Interview, Victoria University of Wellington, 20 February 2001.
25. Significantly, this is a result of the embryonic nature of cabinet record-keeping in this early period. The first time a cabinet secretary was allowed in a cabinet meeting was in January of 1948 (as indicated by Elizabeth McLeay, *The Cabinet and Political Power in New Zealand*, (Auckland: Oxford University Press, 1995) 148). Although McLeay indicates that cabinet minutes and agendas were formalized by 1949, the Archives of New Zealand only have cabinet agendas on file since 1952. This means that finding supporting cabinet documents during this early period in New Zealand cabinet history is very much a hit and miss proposition. I was able to find a few sporadic documents relating to Maori land issues starting from 1949.
26. The following remarks are based on the documents found in the cabinet's file on Maori claims from 1950–56 (ANZ AAFD 811 266/2/1). These range from 1949 to 1954, and include documents on the Lake Waikaremoana,

Wanganui River, "surplus lands," Waiuku, Hauraki Goldfields, Rotorua Township, Patutahi, and Aorangi claims.

27. ANZ, AAFD series 811, file 262/1/2 box 113b, cabinet paper (50)778, 1 August 1950.

28. ANZ, AAFD series 811, file 262/1/2 box 113b, note confirming cabinet decision from the Secretary of the Cabinet, Foss Shanahan, to the Minister of Internal Affairs, 9 August 1950.

29. ANZ, AAFD series 811, file 262/1/2 box 113b, cabinet paper from Minister of Internal Affairs, 4 June 1957.

30. Orange, *The Treaty of Waitangi*, 240. Orange suggests that the Labour Prime Minister, Walter Nash, was a roadblock to further action on the Maori file. The Prime Minister held the Maori Affairs portfolio, with Tirikatene holding an associate Maori Affairs portfolio and the Minister of Forests portfolio.

31. The National Party counted no Maori among its parliamentarians until 1975.

32. Wellington Department of Statistics, *New Zealand Official Yearbook 1961* (Wellington, New Zealand: New Zealand Government Printer, 1961) 51–61. Urban areas are towns in excess of 1000 people. Prior to the 1990s, the New Zealand census used a descent-based definition of "Maori." "Quarter-caste" Maori were excluded from the Maori census population.

33. Wellington Department of Statistics, *New Zealand Official Yearbook 1975* (Wellington, New Zealand: New Zealand Government Printer, 1975) 67.

34. *Tangata whenua* means "people of the land."

35. Department of Statistics, *New Zealand Official Yearbook 1961,* 61.

36. Mason Durie, *Te Mana, Te Kawanatanga: The Politics of Maori Self-Determination* (Auckland: Oxford University Press, 1998) 98.

37. John Williams, *Politics of the New Zealand Maori: Protest and Cooperation 1891–1909* (Seattle: University of Washington Press, 1969) 163.

38. Milne writes in 1966: "When the first New Zealand rugby team visited Britain the news of the tour was cabled direct by the High Commissioner in London to the Prime Minister in New Zealand, and he sometimes interrupted debates in the House to read the results aloud. A few years ago the annual conference of the National Party was partially disrupted by the broadcast of a rugby international." Milne, *Political Parties in New Zealand,* 16.

39. Orange, *The Treaty of Waitangi,* 242.

40. The first was the Hunn Report of 1960 which reviewed the activities of the Department. The second was the Prichard-Waetford report of 1965, authored by a Justice of the Maori Land Court and an official at the Department.

41. Boast et al., *Maori Land Law,* 98–100.

42. Sharp, *Justice and the Maori,* 7.

43. D. Tabacoff, *The Role of the Maori M.P. in Contemporary New Zealand Politics* (Madison: University of Wisconsin, 1972) 95.

44. Ian Hugh Kawharu, *Maori Land Tenure: Studies of a Changing Institution* (Oxford: Oxford University Press, 1977) 291.

45. Pakeha is a Maori term referring to New Zealanders of European descent. Sharp, *Justice and the Maori*, 41–69.
46. Michael King, *Maori: A Photographic and Social History* (Auckland: Heineman Publishers, 1983) 269.
47. Mark Sheehan, *Maori and Pakeha: Race Relations 1912–1980* (Auckland: The Macmillan Company of New Zealand Ltd., 1989) 51.
48. ANZ, AAFD 811 w4198/91 file 244/1/1 part 2, cabinet minutes for 8 February and 1 March, 1971.
49. ANZ, AAFD 811 file 244/1/1 part 2, cabinet paper (71) 517, 27 May 1971.
50. ANZ, AAFD 811 244/1/1/ Part 2, Note from the Secretary of the Cabinet to the Minister of Maori Affairs, 3 October 1972.
51. I know of only one survey of the 1972 election. It was conducted by Prof. Nigel Roberts of Canterbury University in Christchurch. The survey consisted of 106 respondents in one electoral district in the Christchurch area.
52. Stephen Levine, "New Zealand's Political System," in *New Zealand at the Polls: The General Election of 1978*, ed. Howard R. Penniman (Washington, D.C.: American Enterprise Institute for Public Policy Research, 1980), 16.
53. This account of Rata's early career relies heavily on a more detailed description found in Hazlehurst, *Political Expression and Ethnicity: Statecraft and Mobilisation in the Maori World*, 43–44.
54. In Labour governments, the caucus votes on the composition of cabinet. In National governments, this prerogative remains that of the Prime Minister. McLeay, *The Cabinet and Political Power in New Zealand*, 62.
55. ANZ, AAFD 811 5/1/2 part 1, minute of a meeting of the Cabinet Committee on Policy and Priorities, 10 January 1973.
56. ANZ, AAFD 807 5/1/1 part 1, minute of the Cabinet Committee on Policy and Priorities, 19 March 1973.
57. McLeay writes that Labour cabinets are much more constrained than their National counterparts by the need to maintain participatory and inclusive linkages with caucus. The long review of caucus of this legislation would suggest that the ratification issue, despite the appearance of party unity conveyed by the Manifesto, was still potentially divisive. Unfortunately, I have no documents that trace how caucus factions digested Rata's ratification proposal.
58. ANZ, AAFD 811 5/1/2 part 2, minutes of the Cabinet Committee of Policy and Priorities, 18 March 1974.
59. The long delay is also explained by the untimely death of Prime Minister Kirk in August, the subsequent leadership race and re-election of cabinet by caucus.
60. ANZ, AAFD 807 cm(74) 45, Treaty of Waitangi Bill, P.C.O. 103/4, Draft, Clause 6(1)c.
61. ANZ, AAFD 811 w3738 Box 632 22/4/1/ part 3, Committee on Legislation and Parliamentary Questions, Minutes, 31 October 1974.
62. ANZ, AAFD 807 cm(75)29, Memorandum for cabinet, Treaty of Waitangi Bill, CP (75) 499, 16 July 1975.

63. The Maori Affairs Amendment Act 1967, the Public Works Act, the Town and Country Planning Act, and the Rating Act were all statutes under which the Crown could appropriate land.
64. Michael King, *Whina: A Biography of Whina Cooper* (Auckland: Hodder & Stoughton, 1983) 207.
65. A marae is a traditional tribal meeting place, and represents the centre of the community's social and political life.
66. King, *Whina*, 209.
67. Ibid., 219.
68. Hugh Templeton, *All Honourable Men: Inside the Muldoon Cabinet 1975–1984* (Auckland, NZ: Auckland University Press, 1995) 12. Hugh Templeton was a member of the Muldoon cabinet for its duration.
69. Data are from polls conducted by the New Zealand marketing firm, the National Research Bureau. The trend I report here is reported in Brian Murphy, "Polling and the Election," in Penniman, *New Zealand at the Polls*, 173.
70. Ibid., 172.
71. Alan McRobie, "The Electoral System and the 1978 Election," in Penniman, *New Zealand at the Polls*, 72.
72. Templeton, *All Honourable Men*, 224–25.
73. McLeay, *The Cabinet and Political Power in New Zealand*, 76.
74. Robert Muldoon, *My Way* (Wellington, NZ: A.H. & A.W. Reed Ltd, 1981) 7.
75. Ibid.
76. In 1868, the Ngati Whatua held approximately 700 acres of land in the Auckland area. In 1898, the government designated the Ngati Whatua trustees the legal owners of this land, and over the next twenty five years, the trustees sold the land to Europeans. By 1930, only three acres of land remained under Ngati Whatua ownership. The Bastion Point protesters challenged the authority of the trustees to sell off this most basic of tribal assets.
77. Parliamentary Petition no.1976/6: W Cooper and 1760 Others.
78. Cabinet minute 78/8/41, 12 March 1978, in reference to cabinet paper (78) 217, 9 March 1978.
79. Muldoon, *My Way*, 134.
80. Couch's responsibilities did increase in 1980, when he was also given the Minister of Police portfolio.
81. The Beehive is the building in Wellington housing the executive branch. It has a distinctive round shape, hence its moniker.
82. Hazlehurst, *Political Expression and Ethnicity*, 51.
83. Ibid., 55.
84. Mana Motuhake would take 15% of the Maori vote in 1981, but only 9.6% in 1984. Figures are for the Maori seats.
85. Jack Vowles and Peter Aimer, *Voters' Vengeance: The 1990 Election in New Zealand and the Fate of the Fourth Labour Government* (Auckland: Auckland University Press, 1993) 50.
86. Mana Motuhake has not live up to its early promise. It proved to be a vehicle for Rata, but once he left politics, the party did not make significant inroads into the Labour support among Maori.

87. Geoffrey Palmer, *New Zealand's Constitution in Crisis: Reforming Our Political System* (Dunedin, NZ: John McIndoe Ltd, 1992) 75–76.

88. McLeay, *The Cabinet and Political Power in New Zealand*, 6. In 1993 New Zealanders voted via referendum to change electoral systems from the first-past-the-post system. They opted for a mixed member proportional electoral system, and the 1996 election was the first general election held under the new electoral rules.

89. Palmer, *New Zealand's Constitution in Crisis*, 80.

90. Ibid., 77.

91. Government of New Zealand Minister of Justice, A Bill of Rights for New Zealand: A White Paper, (Wellington, NZ: P.D. Hasselberg, Government Printer, 1985), 6.

92. Palmer, *New Zealand's Constitution in Crisis*, 77.

93. The refrain that talent in the New Zealand bureaucracy is unevenly distributed is a common one. See McLeay, *The Cabinet and Political Power in New Zealand*, 106; Palmer, *New Zealand's Constitution in Crisis*, 81; and Jonathan Boston, "The Cabinet and Policy Making," in Holland and Boston, *The Fourth Labour Government*.

94. Cabinet document CS (86) 292, Treaty of Waitangi: Implications of Recognition, 18 June 1986.

95. I have seen no detailed analysis of these parliamentary submissions which analyzes differences in Maori opinion. One scholar notes that one ground for Maori objection was the inclusion of the Treaty in a Bill of Rights which could be amended via referendum. Richard Mulgan, *Politics in New Zealand*, 2 ed. (Auckland, NZ: Auckland University Press, 1994) 164. I find the lukewarm reception among Maori to the Bill of Rights proposal surprising, given it responds to the traditional Maori demand for the recognition of the Treaty within domestic law. Although the importance of recognizing Maori rights was the common and almost unchallenged refrain among Maori political voices, the difficulty in gaining cross-Maori support for specific policy proposals to give effect to that recognition is a more complicated issue.

96. Palmer, *New Zealand's Constitution in Crisis*, 78. New Zealand passed an un-entrenched Bill of Rights in 1990 which did not allow for courts to disallow legislation, nor does it incorporate the articles of the Treaty.

97. Cabinet minute 84/51/54 (caucus), Treaty of Waitangi Amendment Bill, 17 December 1984.

98. New Zealand Maori Council v. Attorney General [1987] N.Z.L.R. 641

99. Sharp, *Justice and the Maori*, 80.

100. Ibid.

101. Palmer, *New Zealand's Constitution in Crisis*, 88.

102. *Te Weehi vs. Regional Fisheries Office* [1986] NZLR 682. The High Court delivered the judgment in this case on 19 August 1986.

103. Interview, Wellington, New Zealand, 20 March 2001.

104. Peter H. Russell, "High Courts and the Rights of Aboriginal Peoples: The Limits of Judicial Independence," *Saskatchewan Law Review* 61 (1998).

105. Chen and Palmer, *Public Law in New Zealand*, 354.

106. New Zealand still maintains the Judicial Committee of the Privy Council in the British House of Lords as its final court of appeal. Canada did away with the Privy Council as its final court of appeal in 1949.
107. Palmer, *New Zealand's Constitution in Crisis*, 90.
108. Ibid.
109. The Tribunal experienced a brush with government disapproval when it recommended that privately-held lands be returned to Maori for compensation. The Minister of Justice and Minister Responsible for Treaty Affairs, Sir Douglas Graham, sent a shot over the Waitangi Tribunal's bow when he amended the Treaty of Waitangi Act, disallowing the Tribunal to make recommendations with respect to privately held assets.
110. Palmer, *New Zealand's Constitution in Crisis*, 92.
111. Author interview, Auckland, 6 April 2001.

NOTES TO CHAPTER FIVE

1. Citation downloaded from www.whitlam.org/collection on 2 September 2003.
2. 1976 census data records 23751 out of 160915 aboriginals and Torres Strait Islanders living in the Northern Territory. R.J. Cameron, *Year Book Australia, No.64, 1980* (Canberra: Australian Bureau of Statistics, 1980) 100.
3. The Gove land rights case, unlike the *Calder* case in Canada, was not appealed to the High Court.
4. These are Western Australia, South Australia, Victoria, New South Wales, Queensland, and Tasmania.
5. Maureen Tehan, "Customary Title, Heritage Protection, and Property Rights in Australia: Emerging Patterns of Land Use in the Post-Mabo Era," *Pacific Rim Law and Policy Journal* 7, no. June (1998): 776.
6. For an account of pastoralists' understandings of the importance to the aboriginal workforce of connection to country, see Tim Rowse, *White Flour, White Power: From Rations to Citizenship in Central Australia* (Melbourne: Cambridge University Press, 1998) 123–27.
7. The Northern Territory was originally under the jurisdiction of South Australia, but South Australia transferred control to the Commonwealth in 1907.
8. Much of the remote and huge cattle and sheep operations are not owned outright, but leased under a variety of lease agreements, where the Crown holds ownership of the lands and retains all mineral rights. The percent of lands held under pastoral lease are: Western Australia 38%, South Australia 42%, New South Wales 41%, Queensland 54%, Victoria 0%, Tasmania 0%, Australian Capital Territory 0%. Figures are as cited in Richard H Bartlett, *Native Title in Australia* (Sydney NSW: Butterworths, 2000) 50. The conditions of these leases as well as their duration vary.
9. The non-aboriginal social reform coalition was based in church or missionary groups, and included such groups as the Western Australian Modern Women's Club, the United Churches of Victoria, the National

Missionary Council of Australia, and the Native Welfare Council. NAA (National Archives of Australia), A431, 1948/1494, 69051.

10. NAA, series A431/1, item 48/1494, letter from George Tulloch, President of the Native Welfare Council, to Prime Minister John Curtin, 29 March 1945.

11. Heather Goodall, *Invasion to Embassy: Land and Aboriginal Politics in New South Wales, 1770–1972* (Sydney: Allen & Unwin Pty Ltd, 1996) 230.

12. NAA, series A431, item 49/1591, letter from W. Cooper, Honorable Secretary of the Australian Aborigines' League, to the Prime Minister, 23 May 1938.

13. NAA, series A431/1, item 48/1494. Department of the Interior memorandum 44/1/4339, Administration of Native Affairs: Australia, 11 July 1945. This memorandum states: "The Commonwealth Government, and all Commonwealth Departments will be more than fully occupied with post-war problems for several years to come and any question of assuming additional responsibilities which are at present adequately catered for by the State governments, should . . . be deferred until legitimate Commonwealth responsibilities arising out of the war have been coped with."

14. The Country Party changed its name to the National Country Party in 1974. I will use its original name in this chapter.

15. Tim Rowse, *Obliged to Be Difficult: Nuggett Coombs' Legacy in Indigenous Affairs* (Oakleigh, Australia: Cambridge University Press, 2000) 18.

16. The following summary on the mining industry relies on Coal and Mineral Industries Division Department of Industry, "Special Article—a Century of Mining in Australia," in *Year Book Australia, 2001* (Australian Bureau of Statistics, 2001).

17. These included uranium, bauxite, iron ore, nickel, lead, zinc, copper, and gold.

18. The dynamics of this shift are carefully laid out in, Rowse, *White Flour, White Power*, particularly in chapter 8 titled "The Crisis of Managed Consumption."

19. Ian Castles, *Year Book Australia 1995. ABS Catalogue No. 1301.0* (Canberra: Australian Bureau of Statistics, 1995) 96. These figures are based on the 1991 census.

20. Kate Ross, *Occasional Paper: Population Issues, Indigenous Australians, 1996. ABS Catalogue No. 4708.0* (Canberra: Australian Bureau of Statistics, 1999) 29.

21. Goodall, *Invasion to Embassy*, 322.

22. Section 96 of the Australian Constitution (1900) holds that "During a period of ten years after the establishment of the Commonwealth and thereafter until the Parliament otherwise provides, the Parliament may grant financial assistance to any State on such terms and conditions as the Parliament thinks fit."

23. NAA, series A4940/1, item C4257, Notes on cabinet submissions nos. 46 and 64: Constitutional amendment: Aborigines, Prime Minister's Department, 22 February 1967.

24. NAA, series A432/70, item 67/3321 Pt1, draft submission to cabinet, Constitution s.51(xxvi), 22 July 1965.

25. NAA, series A4940/1, item C4257, submission no. 64, Constitutional Amendment: Aborigines: Comments on Cabinet Submission no. 46 by the Attorney-General, signed C.E. Barnes, Minister for Territories, 31 January 1967.

26. NAA, series A4940/1, item C4257, cabinet submission no. 75: Referendum Proposals, joint submission by the Attorney-General's Department, the Department of the Interior, and the Prime Minister's Department, 10 February 1967.

27. NAA, series A4940/1, item C4257, cabinet minute, decision no.80, 22 February 1967.

28. Rowse, *Obliged to Be Difficult*, 20.

29. Goodall, *Invasion to Embassy*, 327; David Alastair Kemp, *Society and Electoral Behaviour in Australia* (St. Lucia, Queensland: University of Queensland Press, 1978) 296–97.

30. Rowse, *Obliged to Be Difficult*, 42.

31. Wentworth's lack of serious standing at the cabinet table was apparent to the director of the Office of Aboriginal Affairs, Barry Dexter. Dexter's evaluation of Wentworth is cited in ibid., 43.

32. As reported in a letter to the editor by Frank Hardy, Sydney Morning Herald, 9 April 1968.

33. NAA, series A452/54 item NT 67/5674, memo to the Secretary, Prime Minister's Department, titled Representation from the Amalgamated Engineering Union Concerning the Gurindji Aborigines, 13 September 1967.

34. Goodall, *Invasion to Embassy*, 325.

35. Sydney Morning Herald, 19 March 1968.

36. NAA, series A5872/1, vol. 1, cabinet minute, 19 March 1968, decision no.81. The wording reads: "The Cabinet took the view that any such statement would need to have its careful consideration and decision and that the Minister might bring forward a submission for this purpose. In the meantime, if questioned in the House as to Commonwealth policy on Aborigines, the Minister should not go beyond saying that policy issues are in the course of being referred to Cabinet."

37. Colin A. Hughes, "The Electorate Speaks—and After," in *Australia at the Polls: The National Elections of 1975*, ed. Howard R. Penniman (Washington, D.C.: American Enterprise Institute for Public Policy Research, 1977), 286.

38. NAA, series A1209/43, item 67/7512, letter to the Prime Minister's Office from Bill Wentworth, 31 May 1967. Wentworth writes immediately after the constitutional referendum: "I think it is absolutely essential that we should be taking the initiative in this rather than leave all the running to Labor . . . in terms of money, this is quite a minor matter, but in terms of prestige, it could be quite important." In a follow-up note to the Secretary of the Prime Minister's Department, a Department official wrote: "The P.M. commented, . . . , 'Bill W. seems to think there's some mileage in the aborigines, doesn't he? . . . that may be. .'"

39. The Age, 19 April 1968, "Their Own Land."
40. The portfolio "Minister of the Territories" is changed to "Minister of the Interior" early in 1968, when C.E. Barnes leaves cabinet and Peter Nixon, both of the Country Party, takes over in his stead.
41. A former government whip would comment that "the Menzies government is ninety percent Menzies." As cited by Michelle Grattan, "The Liberal Party," in Penniman, *Australia at the Polls,* 105.
42. Leon D. Epstein, "The Australian Political System," in Penniman, *Australia at the Polls,* 20.
43. Patrick Weller and R.F.I. Smith, "The Rise and Fall of Whitlam Labor: The Political Context of the 1975 Elections," in Penniman, *Australia at the Polls,* 54–55.
44. Epstein, "The Australian Political System," 21.
45. Kemp, *Society and Electoral Behaviour in Australia,* 17.
46. Don Aitken, *Stability and Change in Australian Politics* (Canberra: Australian National University Press, 1977) 186; Kemp, *Society and Electoral Behaviour in Australia,* 302.
47. Hughes, "The Electorate Speaks—and After," 290–91.
48. Ibid., 286.
49. Weller and Smith, "The Rise and Fall of Whitlam Labor," 53.
50. Margaret Bridson Cribb, "The Country Party," in Penniman, *Australia at the Polls,* 147.
51. NAA, series A2354/83 item 68/58, letter from the Northern Territory Cattle Producers Council to the Minister of the Interior, 22 April 1968. The Council wrote that it was authorized to speak for the Australian Woolgrowers & Graziers Council, the United Graziers Association of Queensland, the Stockowners Association of South Australia, and the Pastoralists & Graziers Association of Western Australia. Interestingly, correspondence between the OAA and the Deputy Secretary of the Interior suggests that the Minister of the Interior encouraged the pastoralists' lobbying (note from the OAA Director on Wattie Creek, 26 April 1968) to strengthen his position around the cabinet table.
52. NAA, series A2354/83, item 68/58, note for the file sent to the Prime Minister's Department from W.E.H. Stanner of the Office of Aboriginal Affairs, 3 May 1968. Stanner writes: "A single (especially an initial) instance of an aboriginal claim being exploded as badly based will provide pastoralists and others with an outwardly-respectable means of blocking better claims and be a rod for the back of Commonwealth policy."
53. NAA, series A2354/83, item 68/58, note for the file sent to the Prime Minister's Department from W.E.H. Stanner of the Office of Aboriginal Affairs, 3 May 1968.
54. Rowse, *Obliged to Be Difficult,* 44.
55. NAA, series A5872/1, vol.1, cabinet minute ad hoc committee, draft decision, Northern Territory. Land for "Gurindji" People, 2 May 1968.
56. The OAA also set out to develop a policy paper on aboriginal affairs, but the submission was stalled by Wentworth and never sent to cabinet (as cited in Rowse, *Obliged to Be Difficult,* 35).

57. NAA, series A2354 item 68/58 pt1, Draft cabinet submission, "Northern Territory—Land for Gurindji People—Policy and Financial Implications; undated, but definitely written in June 1968, para.17 and 18. This appears to be the OAA's draft submission which Wentworth did not forward to cabinet.

58. NAA, series A2354 item 68/58 pt 1. These views of Nixon and the Department of the Interior are cited in an OAA draft submission to Wentworth on the Wattie Creek issue dated 6 November 1968.

59. NAA, series A5882/1 item CO80 Pt 1, cabinet minute, 2 July 1968, Decision no.314, paragraphs 1 and 2.

60. "Cattlemen to oppose grants to Aborigines," The Northern Territory News, 15 July 1968.

61. NAA, series A1209/43 item 67/7512, statement for the press by the Minister for the Interior, the Honorable P.J. Nixon, 9 August 1968.

62. NAA, series A2354/83, item 68/78/ pt3. Letter dated 21 October 1968.

63. It must be noted that mineral rights are held by the Crown, and an Australian (aboriginal or not) land owner or lessee has not the right to stop mineral exploration or development on her lands. In the event of mining development, existing property rights holders would have a right to monetary compensation to the degree that their rights were compulsorily acquired or infringed.

64. Rowse, *Obliged to Be Difficult*, 51.

65. NAA, series A43/16, item 68/649 pt 7, letter to Bill Wentworth from W.E.H. Stanner, 1 April 1969.

66. NAA, series A432/145, item 68/649 pt24, memo to the Attorney-General from the Solicitor-General, R.J. Ellicott, 11 June 1970. The Solicitor-General identifies Nixon as a key player in the government's legal strategy, writing: "In a past conference with Ministers, the Minister for the Interior has emphasized the desire of the Commonwealth that this action should not, if at all possible, go off on some technical ground without the question of aboriginal rights to the land being determined."

67. NAA, series A432/16, item 68/649 pt 2, "Gove writ—arguments against settlement," paper submitted to C.L. Hewitt, Secretary, Prime Minister's Department from P.J. Nixon, August 1969 (exact date illegible).

68. NAA, series A432/16, item 68/649 pt 7, letter to Bill Wentworth from P.J. Nixon, 5 May 1969.

69. *Milirrpum v. Nabalco Pty Ltd* (1971) 17 FLR 141 (SC(NT)).

70. NAA, A5619, C136 Pt2, Annex to cabinet submission #82, Analysis of Editorial Comment of Blackburn Judgment, 1 May 1971.

71. NAA, A5619, C136 Pt2. Cabinet submission #76, 1 May 1971.

72. NAA, A5619, C136 Pt2. Cabinet submission #82, 1 May 1971.

73. NAA, A5619, C136 Pt2. This file contains the Prime Minister's statement on aboriginal policy at an April meeting with State aboriginal affairs ministers in Cairns. The speech, drafted by the CAA, mentions McMahon's intention to form a Commonwealth ministerial committee.

74. For a detailed account of these deliberations, see Rowse, *Obliged to Be Difficult*, 59–67.

75. Goodall, *Invasion to Embassy,* 338.
76. Ibid., 351.
77. Robert Tickner, *Taking a Stand: Land Rights to Reconciliation* (Crow's Nest, N.S.W.: Allen & Unwin, 2001) 11–12.
78. The Age, 15 August 1972.
79. Malcolm Mackerras, *Australian General Elections* (Sydney: Angus & Robertson (Publishers) Pty Ltd, 1972) 240.
80. Ibid.
81. House of Representatives, Debates, 23 February 1972, p.127.
82. In a September 1972 Gallup Poll, respondents answered that welfare-state issues (free medical services, pensions, education) and economic issues (unemployment, inflation, overseas ownership, and industrial unrest) were the most important issues driving their vote choices. Colin A. Hughes, "The 1972 Australian Federal Election," *Australian Journal of Politics and History* 19, no. April (1973) 11.
83. Ian Palmer, *Buying Back the Land: Organisational Struggle and the Aboriginal Land Fund Commission* (Canberra: Aboriginal Studies Press, 1988) 27.
84. Since Commonwealth cabinet documents are closed for a 30 year period, my access to cabinet submissions and conclusions ends in 1971. The remainder of this chapter will rely solely on published sources.
85. Whitlam stated in the House of Representatives on 23 February 1972, that a commission's work would " . . . [cover] the whole of the Commonwealth and not just the Northern Territory" (p.128, Debates). In July 1973, Woodward's mandate was expanded so that he could make recommendations regarding adjacent aboriginal reserves in South Australia and Western Australia.
86. Letters Patent, as cited in A.E. Woodward, *Aboriginal Land Rights Commission, Second Report* (Canberra: The Government Printer of Australia, 1974) 1.
87. From Woodward's first report, as cited in Ibid., 3.
88. Goodall, *Invasion to Embassy,* 337. Conclusion also supported in author interview, former Minister of Aboriginal Affairs, Adelaide, March 2000.
89. Woodward, *Aboriginal Land Rights Commission, Second Report,* 6.
90. South Australia has a history of leading the edge of political innovation, including such initiatives as the Torres land tenure system, the secret ballot, and female suffrage (the first colony in the world to extend full voting rights to women). It is far beyond this project to pin point why South Australia is such a remarkable innovator, but in the aboriginal rights field, this overall pattern of innovation is upheld.
91. Pitjantjatjara Land Rights Act 1981 (SA) and the Maralinga Land Rights Act 1984 (SA).
92. Queensland did enact a statutory land rights regime after the failure of the Hawke initiative. The Queensland regime did set up a claimant procedure with respect to aboriginal reserves similar to the Northern Territory, but significantly, the Queensland legislation did not include the critical veto provision, rendering (by my definition) the Queensland policy a "consultation" policy, but not a "negotiation" policy. Bradley Selway, "The Role of Policy

in the Development of Native Title," *Federal Law Review* 28, no. 3 (2000): 413.

93. Bartlett, *Native Title in Australia,* 50.
94. Tickner, *Taking a Stand,* 92.
95. Ibid.
96. Bartlett, *Native Title in Australia,* 33.
97. Ibid., 34.
98. Tickner, *Taking a Stand,* 29, 38.
99. Ibid., 112.
100. The head of the Aboriginal and Torres Strait Islander Commission, Lois O'Donoghue, submitted such policy proposals to Keating in March 1993. Ibid., 110.
101. Bartlett, *Native Title in Australia,* 39.
102. For a blow-by-blow account of this critical period, the following sources are particularly informative: Ibid., 33–44; M.A. Stephenson, ed., *Mabo: The Native Title Legislation* (St. Lucia, Qld: University of Queensland Press, 1995); Tickner, *Taking a Stand,* 83–220.
103. Ibid., 100, 21, 82.
104. Ibid., 114.
105. Ibid., 153.
106. Ibid., 190.
107. The High Court ruled in 1995 that governments could not delegate judicial functions to non-court actors. This decision stripped the NNTT of its role as a third-party arbitrator, and reserved its judicial functions to the federal court. *Brandy v. Human Rights and Equal Opportunity Commission* (1995) 183 CLR 245.
108. Frank Brennan, *The Wik Debate: Its Impact on Aborigines, Pastoralists, and Miners, Frontlines* (Sydney: University of New South Wales, 1998) 38–39.
109. Tickner, *Taking a Stand,* 196.
110. John Chesterman and Brian Galligan, *Citizens Without Rights: Aborigines and Australian Citizenship* (Melbourne: Cambridge University Press, 1997) 65.
111. Cameron, *Year Book Australia, No.64, 1980,* 100. This is according to 1971 census figures.
112. Ronald T. Libby, *Hawke's Law: The Politics of Mining and Aboriginal Land Rights in Australia* (Nedlands WA: University of Western Australia Press, 1989) 127. This figure is in terms of meters drilled ('000), and is derived from data provided by the Australian Mining Industry Council.
113. State Assembly, 7 April 1994, p.11681.
114. These global figures are cited in the biography of Clive Brown, Western Australian legislator and current Labor government member.
115. Legislative Council, 14 November 2000, p.2763.
116. Legislative Assembly, 15 December 1987, p.8092.
117. The State government reported in November 1991 that approximately 10.5 million hectares of Aboriginal Trust Land was leased to individual aboriginal persons. Legislative Assembly, 5 November 1991, p.6071.

118. Legislative Council, 17 September 1991, p.4681. 19 million hectares is approximately 73,000 square miles.
119. Tickner, *Taking a Stand*, 23.
120. Legislative Assembly, 4 November 1993, p.6328.
121. Land (Titles and Traditional Usage) Act 1993 (WA).
122. Bartlett, *Native Title in Australia*, 42.
123. Legislative Assembly, 4 November 1993, p.6330.
124. Brennan, *The Wik Debate*, 21.
125. Ibid.
126. Peter Sutton, "Atomism Versus Collectivism: The Problem of Group Definition in Native Title Cases," in *Anthropology in the Native Title Era: Proceedings of a Workshop Conducted by the Australian Anthropological Society and the Native Titles Research Unit, Australian Institute of Aboriginal and Torres Strait Islander Studies*, ed. Jim Fingleton and Julie Finlayson (Canberra: Australian Institute of Aboriginal and Torres Strait Islander Studies, 1995). This pattern was also confirmed in an interview with an official at the NNTT, Perth WA, 13 August 2001.
127. Brennan, *The Wik Debate*, 25.
128. The reported number of claims in the Goldfields varies. Frank Brennan Ibid.,19, cites 17 claims were filed over the Goldfields. In a conference I attended in Perth WA in August 2001, Dr. Bertus de Villiers of the Goldfields Land Council stated that approximately 85 claims were active in the Goldfields from 1993 to 1998.
129. Confirmed in interview with an official in the Department of Premier and Cabinet, Perth WA, 10 August 2001.
130. Interview, former Western Australia cabinet member, Perth WA, 11 August 2001.
131. Interview, Department of Premier and Cabinet, Perth WA, 10 August 2001.
132. As reported in the Legislative Council, 14 December 1999, p.4098.
133. For example, the right to negotiate no longer applied to leases for mining exploration. For a list of future acts for which the right to negotiate no longer applied after 1998, Bartlett, *Native Title in Australia*, 58–61.
134. Interview, National Native Title Tribunal, Perth WA, 13 August 2001.
135. National Native Title Tribunal, *National Native Title Tribunal Annual Report 1999–2000* (Perth,WA: National Native Title Tribunal, 2000) 4.
136. Ibid., 6.
137. Ibid., 4.
138. There are three types of ILUA agreements under the NTA: body corporate agreements, area agreements, and alternative procedure agreements. I refer here mainly to area agreements.
139. Bartlett, *Native Title in Australia*, 406.
140. Native Title and Strategic Issues Division, "General Guidelines: Native Title Determinations and Agreements," (Perth WA: Ministry of the Premier and Cabinet, Government of Western Australia, 2000) 8–9.
141. Dr. Bertus de Villiers, Goldfields Land Council, remarks made at Butterworths' conference Negotiating Native Title, Perth WA, 8 August 2001.

142. Legislative Assembly, 21 December 1999, p.4219. Another member of the Court cabinet echoed the Premier when he stated: "the Leader of the Opposition stands in this place and in his electorate and says all we need to do is negotiate; if we sit down and talk, we will get through it. How can we do that when in many cases, we cannot even get the claimants to go to a meeting?" Legislative Council, 14 November 2000, p.2761.

143. Remarks of Hon. Mark Neville, Legislative Council, 14 November 2000, p.2769.

144. The ability of the Labor government to back away from Court's litigation strategy was also questionable, given the reluctance of the Federal Court to stop litigation already in progress to suit the State's new administration. (Interview, Department of Premier and Cabinet, 10 August 2001). The Federal Court of Australia has emerged since 1998 as an increasingly strategic player. In 2001, the Federal Court refused the Gallop government's request to suspend native title litigation while the State developed a mediation process. *Bolton & Ors v. State of Western Australia & Ors* [2001] FCA 1074 at 8.

NOTES TO CHAPTER SIX

1. Wilcomb Washburn, *The American Indian and the United States: A Documentary History. Volume 2* (New York: Random House, 1973). I will cite the debate as reprinted in the Washburn text.
2. Ibid., 1389.
3. Ibid., 1403.
4. Ibid., 1391–2.
5. Ibid., 1393.
6. Ibid., 1399.
7. Executive agreements, unlike treaties, do not require Senate ratification. The legal difference between treaties and executive agreement is highly ambiguous. Robert J. Spitzer, *President and Congress: Executive Hegemony at the Crossroads of American Government* (Philadelphia: Temple University Press, 1993) 194–210. Spitzer suggests that on a practical level, Presidents pursue executive agreements when the questions are not highly political, or when they do not anticipate such action will raise the ire of the Senate. The continuation of executive agreement-making with Indian tribes after 1871 suggests that the executive branch did not reject Indian's political rights as starkly as the legislative branch at the time.
8. Harvey Daniel Rosenthal, *Their Day in Court: A History of the Indian Claims Commission,* (New York: Garland Publishing Inc., 1990) 7.
9. *Worcester v. Georgia* (1832) 6 Pet 515.
10. A.J. Beveridge, *The Life of John Marshall,* vol. 4 (Boston: Houghton Mifflin, 1919) 551.
11. Lewis Meriam, *The Problem of Indian Administration: Report of a Survey Made at the Request of Honorable Hubert Work, Secretary of the Interior, and Submitted to Him, February 21, 1928* (Baltimore: The John Hopkins Press, 1928) 750.

12. Richard B. Latner, *The Presidency of Andrew Jackson: White House Politics 1829–1837* (Athens GA: University of Georgia Press, 1979) 90.
13. Ibid., 97.
14. Jill Norgren, *The Cherokee Cases: The Confrontation of Law and Politics* (New York: McGraw-Hill, Inc., 1996) 104.
15. Ibid., 97.
16. Ibid., 101–03.
17. These are: *Johnson v. McIntosh* 8 Wheat 543 (1823*)*, *Cherokee Nation v. Georgia* 5 Pet 1 (1831) and *Worcester v. Georgia* (1832) 6 Pet 515.
18. Richard H Bartlett, *Native Title in Australia* (Sydney, NSW: Butterworths, 2000) 5.
19. Article III, section 2.
20. Latner, *The Presidency of Andrew Jackson,* 88.
21. Norgren, *The Cherokee Cases,* 142.
22. Ibid., 143.
23. Jill E. Martin, ""Neither Fish, Flesh, Fowl, nor Good Red Herring": The Citizenship Status of American Indians, 1830–1924," in *American Indians and U.S. Politics: A Companion Reader,* ed. John M. Meyer (Westport, CT: Praeger Publishers, 2002), 52.
24. The Fourteenth Amendment, section 1 reads: "All persons born or naturalized in the United States and subject to the jurisdiction thereof, are citizens of the United States and of the State wherein they reside." The second section reads: "Representatives shall be apportioned among the several states according to their respective numbers, counting the whole number of persons in each state, excluding Indians not taxed."
25. Martin, ""Neither Fish, Flesh, Fowl, nor Good Red Herring," 54. Martin writes that only one Senator thought the Indians should be granted citizenship under the Amendment.
26. *Dred Scott v. Sanford.*
27. *Standing Bear v. Crook.*
28. Rosenthal, *Their Day in Court,* 15. Italics added.
29. Ibid., 16.
30. Martin, "Neither Fish, Flesh, Fowl, nor Good Red Herring," 66.
31. In 1906, Congress amended the citizenship provisions of the Allotment Act. The so-called Burke Act conferred citizenship 25 years after the time of allotment. This meant that the federal government could still regulate Indian allottees as wards. Allottees could be granted citizenship before the 25 year period if the Secretary of the Interior found them to be "competent."
32. Norgren, *The Cherokee Cases,* 145.
33. Stephen Cornell, "The New Indian Politics," in *American Indians and U.S. Politics: A Companion Reader,* ed. John M. Meyer (Westport, CT: Praeger Publishers, 2002), 95.
34. In 1914, the Supreme Court ruled that congressional action was lawful if "reasonable" and not "arbitrary." In 1955, the Supreme Court would also rule that Indian lands were not considered property under the Fifth Amendment, and that the federal government did not have to pay compensation for its taking.

35. The first decision to turn away from the principle of tribal consent was *United States v. Kagama,* 118 U.S. 375 (1886). The plenary power doctrine was fully developed in *Lone Wolf v. Hitchcock,* 185 U.S. 553 (1903).
36. Nell Jessup Newton, "The Judicial Role in Fifth Amendment Taking of Indian Land: An Analysis of the Sioux Nation Rule," *Oregon Law Review* 61 (1982): 245–46. Italics not in the original.
37. Ibid., 246.
38. Thomas W. Cowger, *The National Congress of American Indians: The Founding Years* (Lincoln: University of Nebraska Press, 1999) 17.
39. Roger L. Nichols, *The Indians in the United States and Canada: A Comparative History* (Lincoln: University of Nebraska Press, 1998) 271.
40. Kenneth R. Philp, *John Collier's Crusade for Indian Reform 1920–1954* (Tucson: University of Arizona Press, 1977) 55.
41. Ibid., 28.
42. *U.S. v. Sandoval,* 231 U.S. 28 (1913).
43. Lawrence C. Kelly, "Charles Henry Burke (1921–1929)," in *The Commissioners of Indian Affairs, 1824–1977,* ed. Robert M. Kvasnicka and Herman J. Viola (Lincoln and London: University of Nebraska Press, 1979) 252.
44. Philp, *John Collier's Crusade for Indian Reform 1920–1954,* 32.
45. Ibid.
46. Ibid., 30.
47. Ibid., 53.
48. Martin, ""Neither Fish, Flesh, Fowl, nor Good Red Herring," 70.
49. Meriam, *The Problem of Indian Administration,* 806.
50. Rosenthal, *Their Day in Court,* 98, footnote 17.
51. Ibid., 50.
52. Ibid., 51.
53. S. 1542, 64th Congress, 1st session.
54. Meriam, *The Problem of Indian Administration,* 86 and 88.
55. Ibid., 805.
56. Ibid., 48.
57. Ibid., 811.
58. Lawrence C. Kelly, "Charles James Rhoads (1929–33)," 264.
59. Ibid., 266.
60. T.H. Watkins, *Righteous Pilgrim: The Life and Times of Harold L. Ickes* (New York: Henry Holt and Company, 1990) 534.
61. Kelly, "Charles James Rhoads (1929–33)," 264.
62. "Gratuitous offsets" were funds the American government had spent "for the benefit of Indians." This issue of offsets was a huge thorn in the side of Indian claimants, as the types of gratuities used to decrease claims awards were not allowable in claims involving non-Indians. In a June 1945 letter to D'Arcy McNickle of the National Congress of American Indians, Felix Cohen (former Interior Department solicitor and key legal expert) summarized the central issue regarding gratuitous offsets: " . . . I don't think that it is fair to set off gratuities against debts, in Indian or other cases. If I sue

the United States in the Court of Claims on a construction contract, the United States does not deduct from a just recovery the sums it has spent on the education of my children, social security benefits, work relief, etc. I see no reason why it should adopt a different policy towards Indians. Prejudice may make such a special policy inevitable . . .." United States National Archives and Record Administration (NARA), Washington D.C., RG 48, Entry 810, Box 42.

63. Kelly, "Charles James Rhoads (1929–33)," 265.
64. Watkins, *Righteous Pilgrim*, 327.
65. Ibid., 331.
66. Nathan Margold acted as a legal adviser on the Meriam Report, and Felix Cohen had been involved in the Pueblo land campaign that defeated the Bursum Bill. Ibid., 329.
67. Collier's initial legislation, the Wheeler-Howard bill, was weakened by a series of amendments during the legislative process. For instance, the following provisions were deleted: the mandatory return of individual allotments to collective ownership, and heirship clauses to stop the fractionalization of allotments to multiple heirs. Senator Elmer Thomas of Oklahoma also ensured that his State was excluded from the provisions of the IRA. The tribal government provisions of the IRA also proved problematic, as the new band government regime imposed new governance rules rather than simply recognizing traditional self-government practices. Thomas Biolsi, *Organizing the Lakota: The Political Economy of the New Deal on the Pine Ridge and Rosebud Reservations* (Tucson: The University of Arizona Press, 1992).
68. Ibid., 68.
69. Biolsi's description of the provision does not include historical claims as part of the proposed court's jurisdiction, but Rosenthal does make this suggestion. Rosenthal, *Their Day in Court,* 57.
70. Ibid.
71. Michael Leider and Jake Page, *Wild Justice: The People of Geronimo vs. The United States* (New York: Random House, Inc., 1997) 60; Rosenthal, *Their Day in Court,* 64. The fear of fiscal exposure from land claims also furrowed the President's brow. In 1936, President Roosevelt refused to support a Senate measure (S.1793) that would allow the Indians of California to bring their suit to the Court of Claims. In his Memorandum of Disapproval dated June 30th, 1936, Roosevelt wrote that "Not only would such a course of action result in an incalculable financial burden to the Government, but justice to the Indians of today does not seem to require this type of reparation." NARA, RG 46, Sen 83-A-F9 [1928–1953] (new box 50) Box 43, Folder 1—General File, California 3:4.
72. Leider and Page write that from 1920 to 1939, the Court of Claims decided 73 claims cases, from which only 10 received a judgment of awards. Of the approximately $14 million awarded by the court, the tribes recovered just under $284,000. Leider and Page, *Wild Justice,* 57.
73. Rosenthal, *Their Day in Court,* 73.
74. Watkins, *Righteous Pilgrim*, 547.

75. Kenneth R. Philp, "John Collier (1933–1945)," 279.
76. Three attempts to organize on a pan-tribal basis before World War Two proved unsuccessful. I have already mentioned the Society of American Indians. The SAI was followed by the National Council of American Indians, which failed to garner widespread support in Indian Country. Another organization was the American Indian Federation, established by an acculturated Oklahoma Indian, Joseph Bruner. Bruner's AIF was formed to combat Collier's IRA policy. In favor of Indian assimilation, Bruner and the AIF attacked the IRA as a government imposed communist plot. The AIF succumbed to internal dissention. Cowger, *The National Congress of American Indians*, 22. The Interior Department acknowledged the AIF's opposition to the IRA, but did not consider Bruner a legitimate representative voice. In a letter to Bruner written in March 1937, Secretary Ickes responded to the AIF's objections to the IRA in this way: " . . . It isn't often that I pay attention to such irresponsible vapourings as these. However, I cannot forbear to express my admiration of your powers of imagination." NARA, RG 48 Entry 766 Record of Secretary Ickes, General Subject File, 1933–1942, Box #5.
77. Ibid., 26–27.
78. Rosenthal, *Their Day in Court*, 79.
79. Cowger, *The National Congress of American Indians*, 25.
80. Ibid., 44.
81. James E. Officer, "Termination as Federal Policy: An Overview," in *Indian Self-Rule: First-Hand Accounts of Indian-White Relations from Roosevelt to Reagan*, ed. Kenneth R. Philp (Salt Lake City: Howe Brothers, 1986), 116.
82. Rosenthal, *Their Day in Court*, 81.
83. Officer, "Termination as Federal Policy," 118.
84. Rosenthal, *Their Day in Court*, 81.
85. Leider and Page, *Wild Justice*, 61.
86. Rosenthal, *Their Day in Court*, 85.
87. Ibid., 79.
88. Cowger, *The National Congress of American Indians*, 55. Cowger identifies the NCAI as the architects of H.R. 1198, while Rosenthal writes that H.R. 1198 was identical (except for the mandatory Indian commissioner clause) to the bill (H.R. 5569) introduced in the previous Congress. Leider and Page identify Interior Solicitor Felix Cohen and lawyer Ernest Wilkinson as the primary authors and shapers of the bill. Leider and Page, *Wild Justice*, 63.
89. Rosenthal, *Their Day in Court*, 84.
90. Ibid., 87.
91. Ibid., 88–89.
92. Leider and Page, *Wild Justice*, 63–64.
93. NARA, RG 48 Entry 768 Box 14, Folder: Indian Affairs 1946–1947. Memo from Secretary Krug to President Truman, 1 August 1946.
94. NARA, RG 48 Entry 748, Office Files of the Secretary of the Interior Oscar Chapman 1933–53, Box 15.

95. Rosenthal, *Their Day in Court*, 255.
96. Harvey Daniel Rosenthal, "Indian Claims and the American Conscience: A Brief History of the Indian Claims Commission," in *Irredeemable America: The Indians' Estate and Land Claims*, ed. Imre Sutton (Albuquerque, NM: University of New Mexico, 1985), 48. Rosenthal writes that allowable off-sets "must have been a gratuitous expenditure made without obligation on the part of the government to make it or the Indians to repay it and must have been of benefit to the tribe rather than to the individual."
97. Ibid., 49.
98. NARA, RG 279, 11E2/032/13/03 Entry 6 Box 1. Letter to Chair Engle from Edgar Witt, 11 August 1958.
99. NARA, RG279, 11E2/032/13/03 Entry 6, Congressional Correspondence Box 4. Letter from Chairman Jerome K. Kuykendall to Rep. Bella S. Abzug, 19 November 1975.
100. Sutton, *Irredeemable America*, 5–6.
101. The following quotations have already been cited and documented in chapters 3 and 5.
102. S. Lyman Tyler, "William A. Brophy 1945–48," in Kvasnicka and Viola, *The Commissioners of Indian Affairs*, 284.
103. Cowger, *The National Congress of American Indians*, 100.
104. Officer, "Termination as Federal Policy," 124.
105. Ibid., 114.
106. Cowger, *The National Congress of American Indians*, 102–04; Nancy Oestreich Lurie, "Epilogue," in Sutton, *Irredeemable America*, 367.
107. Cowger, *The National Congress of American Indians*, 135.
108. Ibid., 129.
109. Cornell, "The New Indian Politics," 100.
110. Vine Deloria, Jr., *Behind the Trail of Broken Treaties: An Indian Declaration of Independence* (New York: Delacourt Press, 1974) 23–25.
111. Cornell, "The New Indian Politics," 100; Cowger, *The National Congress of American Indians*, 140.
112. Biolsi, *Organizing the Lakota*, 182–85.
113. Deloria, *Behind the Trail of Broken Treaties*, 27.
114. Ibid., 32.
115. Cornell, "The New Indian Politics," 102.
116. Thomas Clarkin, *Federal Indian Policy in the Kennedy and Johnson Administrations, 1961–1969* (Albuquerque: University of New Mexico Press, 2001) 49, 80.
117. Ibid., 108.
118. Ibid., 122–31.
119. Ibid., 198.
120. Ibid., 260.
121. Joseph H. Cash, "Louis Rook Bruce (1969–1973)," in Kvasnicka and Viola, *Commissioners of Indian Affairs*, 334.
122. Princeton University Seeley-Mudd Library, Barbara Greene Kilberg Papers (hereafter Kilberg), Box 1 Folder 1, Memo to the Vice President from C.D. Ward, 29 January 1970.

123. Imre Sutton, "Incident or Event? Land Restoration in the Claims Process," in Sutton, *Irredeemable America,* 217.

124. Princeton University Seeley-Mudd Library, William Schaab Papers (hereafter Schaab), Box 1 Folder 2, letter to Governor of Taos Pueblo and Taos Pueblo Council from William C. Schaab, 14 February 1968, at pages 15 and 19.

125. Schaab, Box 1 Folder 2, letter from Senator Anderson to William Schaab, 26 April 1968.

126. The Pueblo's unwillingness to bend to Senator Anderson was explained in this way: " . . . We have tried to express to Senator Anderson in the past that the Blue Lake area is not just land to be bargained with like ordinary property. It is the seat of our religion and the spiritual home of the Taos Indians, and we are fighting here to save our religious freedom and our way of life which are the principles guaranteed by the Constitution. How can you . . . compromise these things that are sacred to all Americans?." Schaab, Box 2 Folder 1, letter to Senator McGovern from Paul Bernal, Taos Pueblo Council Secretary, 22 August 1970.

127. John Ehrlichman, *Witness to Power: The Nixon Years* (New York: Simon and Shuster, 1982) 103.

128. This was not a reward. Nixon's (and others') relationship with Agnew was difficult, and Nixon was looking for ways to get Agnew out of harm's way: "Nixon decided that if Taft and the others wouldn't have Agnew, our new Native brothers might. Maybe the Native American vote could be won if pursued. 'Let's put Agnew on at least six reservations between now and November,' Nixon ordered. 'Let's tie him to Indians. And,' he said, as if to solve all his problems at once, 'Pat [Nixon] should also do Indians.'" Ibid.

129. Kilberg, Box 1 Folder 1, Memorandum to the Vice President from C.D. Ward, 29 January 1970.

130. Kilberg, Box 1 Folder 1, Memo for Brad Patterson by Bobbie Kilberg, 12 March 1970.

131. The Department of Agriculture was also concerned with third party grazing rights, but this issue was relatively easy to address. I make no further mention of it here.

132. Kilberg, Box 1 Folder 1, Memorandum for Mr. Kenneth Cole from James R. Schlesinger, Acting Director of the Bureau of the Budget, 31 March 1970.

133. Ehrlichman, *Witness to Power,* 94.

134. Ibid.

135. Kilberg, Box 1 Folder 6, Open letter to Senators from Clinton Anderson, 2 October 1970.

136. Schaab, Box 2 Folder 1, Memo for the record re: telephone conversation with Senator McGovern by Paul Bernal, Taos Pueblo Council Secretary, 21 August 1970.

137. Kilberg, Box 1 Folder 1, Memorandum for John Ehrlichman from Ken BeLieu, 17 April 1970.

138. Kilberg, Box 1 Folder 1, Memorandum for John Ehrlichman from Ken BeLieu, 22 April 1970.

139. Kilberg, Box 1 Folder 1, Memorandum for the President from Leonard Garment, 17 April 1970.

140. Ehrlichman describes John Whitaker in this way: " . . . If an issue had come to Nixon with Whitaker recommending 'yes' and seven OMB men advising 'no,' Nixon would have gone along with Whitaker because he knew he could rely on him to look out for Nixon's political success, whatever the merits of the opposite argument might be." Ehrlichman, *Witness to Power: The Nixon Years,* 92.
141. Kilberg, Box 1 Folder 2, Memo to Ken from Bobbie, 5 November 1970.
142. Kilberg, Box 1 Folder 6, Open letter from Senators of Committee on Finance, 17 November 1970.
143. Wilcomb Washburn, *The American Indian and the United States: A Documentary History. Volume 3* (New York: Random House, 1973) 2123–24. Italics added.
144. Ibid., 2126.

NOTES TO CHAPTER SEVEN

1. Charles Taylor, "The Politics of Recognition," in *Multiculturalism: Examining the Politics of Recognition,* ed. Amy Gutmann (Princeton NJ: Princeton University Press, 1994).
2. James Tully, *Strange Multiplicity: Constitutionalism in an Age of Diversity* (Cambridge: Cambridge University Press, 1995).
3. John Bern and Susan Dodds, "On the Plurality of Interests: Aboriginal Self-Government and Land Rights," in *Political Theory and the Rights of Indigenous Peoples,* ed. Duncan Ivison, Paul Patton, and Will Sanders (Oakleigh VIC: Cambridge University Press, 2000), 4.
4. Auditor General of Canada, *Report of the Auditor General of Canada* (Ottawa: Supply and Services Canada, 1998) 14.30.
5. Ibid., 14.43.
6. Canadian land claims policy distinguishes between comprehensive claims (where no previous treaties or legal agreements were signed) and specific claims (where the claim relates to a legal obligation).
7. Sally Weaver, "The Joint Cabinet/National Indian Brotherhood Committee: A Unique Experiment in Pressure Group Relations," *Canadian Public Administration* 25, no. 2 (Summer) (1982).
8. Bern and Dodds, "On the Plurality of Interests," 175.
9. Joel S. Migdal, "The State in Society: An Approach to Struggles for Domination," in *State Power and Social Forces: Domination and Transformation in the Third World,* ed. Joel S. Migdal, Atul Kohli, and Vivien Shue (New York: Cambridge University Press, 1994).
10. Ibid., 12.
11. Position of the Assistant Deputy Minister (ADM) of Native Claims was created in the early 1980s. This position was upgraded to Senior ADM after a departmental reorganization in 1992.
12. Donald J. Savoie, *Governing from the Centre: The Concentration of Power in Canadian Politics* (Toronto: University of Toronto Press, 1999) 383 fn 124.
13. Stephen E. Cornell, *The Return of the Native: American Indian Political Resurgence* (New York: Oxford University Press, 1988) 33.

Bibliography

Agius, Parry, and Jocelyn Davies. "Post Mabo Institutions for Negotiating Coexistence: Building a Statewide Negotiation Process for Native Title in South Australia." Adelaide, 2001.

Aitken, Don. *Stability and Change in Australian Politics*. Canberra: Australian National University Press, 1977.

Anderson, Terry L., and Fred S. McChesney. "Raid or Trade? An Economic Model of Indian-White Relations." *Journal of Law and Economics* 37 (1994): 39–74.

Asch, Michael, and Norman Zlotkin. "Affirming Aboriginal Title: A New Basis for Comprehensive Claims Negotiations." In *Aboriginal and Treaty Rights in Canada*, edited by Michael Asch, 208–229. Vancouver: University of British Columbia, 1997.

Auditor General of Canada. *Report of the Auditor General of Canada*. Ottawa: Supply and Services Canada, 1998.

Babcock, Linda, and Craig A. Olson. "The Causes of Impasses in Labor Disputes." *Industrial Relations* 31, no. 2 (1992): 348–60.

Babcock, Linda, and Lowell J. Taylor. "The Role of Arbitrator Uncertainty in Negotiation Impasses." *Industrial Relations* 35, no. 4 (1996): 604–10.

Ballara, Angela. *Iwi: The Dynamics of Maori Tribal Organisation from c.1769 to c.1945*. Wellington, NZ: Victoria University Press, 1998.

Barron, F. Laurie. *Walking in Indian Mocassins: The Native Policies of Tommy Douglas and the C.C.F.* Vancouver: University of British Columbia Press, 1997.

Bartlett, Richard H. *Native Title in Australia*. Sydney NSW: Butterworths, 2000.

Bates, Robert H., Avner Greif, Margaret Levi, Jean-Laurent Rosenthal, and Barry R. Weingast, eds. *Analytic Narratives*. Princeton, N.J.: Princeton University Press, 1998.

Bermeo, Nancy. "The Import of Institutions." *Journal of Democracy* 13, no. 2 (2002): 96–110.

Bern, John, and Susan Dodds. "On the Plurality of Interests: Aboriginal Self-Government and Land Rights." In *Political Theory and the Rights of Indigenous Peoples*, edited by Duncan Ivison, Paul Patton and Will Sanders, 163–79. Oakleigh VIC: Cambridge University Press, 2000.

Beveridge, A.J. *The Life of John Marshall*. Vol. 4. Boston: Houghton Mifflin, 1919.

Biolsi, Thomas. *Organizing the Lakota: The Political Economy of the New Deal on the Pine Ridge and Rosebud Reservations.* Tucson: The University of Arizona Press, 1992.

Boast, R. P., Andrew Erueti, Doug McPhail, and Norman F. Smith. *Maori Land Law.* Wellington, New Zealand: Butterworths of New Zealand Ltd, 1999.

Boston, Jonathan. "The Cabinet and Policy Making." In *The Fourth Labour Government: Politics and Policy in New Zealand,* edited by M. Holland and Jonathan Boston. Auckland, NZ: Auckland University Press, 1990.

Boston, Jonathan, John Martin, June Pallot, and Pat Walsh. *Public Management: The New Zealand Model.* Auckland: Oxford University Press, 1996.

Brennan, Frank. *The Wik Debate: Its Impact on Aborigines, Pastoralists, and Miners.* Sydney: University of New South Wales, 1998.

Breton, Albert. "Federalism and Decentralization: Ownership Rights and the Superiority of Federalism." *Publius* 30, no. 2 (2000): 1–16.

Brookfield, F. M. *Waitangi and Indigenous Rights: Revolution, Law and Legitimation.* Auckland, New Zealand: Auckland University Press, 1999.

Cairns, Alan. *Citizens Plus: Aboriginal Peoples and the Canadian State.* Vancouver: University of British Columbia Press, 2000.

Cameron, R.J. *Year Book Australia, No.64, 1980.* Canberra: Australian Bureau of Statistics, 1980.

Cash, Joseph H. "Louis Rook Bruce (1969–1973)." In *The Commissioners of Indian Affairs, 1824–1977,* edited by Robert M. Kvasnicka and Herman J. Viola, 333–40. Lincoln and London: University of Nebraska Press, 1979.

Castles, Ian. *Year Book Australia, 1994.* Canberra: Australian Bureau of Statistics, 1994.

———. *Year Book Australia 1995. ABS Catalogue No. 1301.0.* Canberra: Australian Bureau of Statistics, 1995.

Chen, Mai, and Geoffrey Palmer. *Public Law in New Zealand : Cases, Materials, Commentary, and Questions.* Auckland: Oxford University Press, 1993.

Chesterman, John, and Brian Galligan. *Citizens Without Rights: Aborigines and Australian Citizenship.* Melbourne: Cambridge University Press, 1997.

Clarkin, Thomas. *Federal Indian Policy in the Kennedy and Johnson Administrations, 1961–1969.* Albuquerque: University of New Mexico Press, 2001.

Cooter, Robert, and Thomas Ulen. *Law and Economics.* 3rd ed. New York: Addison Wesley Longman, Inc., 2000.

Cornell, Stephen. "The New Indian Politics." In *American Indians and U.S. Politics: A Companion Reader,* edited by John M. Meyer, 93–106. Westport, CT: Praeger Publishers, 2002.

Cornell, Stephen E. *The Return of the Native: American Indian Political Resurgence.* New York: Oxford University Press, 1988.

Cowger, Thomas W. *The National Congress of American Indians: The Founding Years.* Lincoln: University of Nebraska Press, 1999.

Cox, Lindsay. *Kotahitanga: The Search for Maori Political Unity.* Auckland: Oxford University Press, 1993.

Cribb, Margaret Bridson. "The Country Party." In *Australia at the Polls: The National Elections of 1975,* edited by Howard R. Penniman, 143–69. Washington, D.C.: American Enterprise Institute for Public Policy Research, 1977.

Davidson, D.S. "An Ethnic Map of Australia." *Proceedings of the American Philosophical Society* 79 (1938): 649–80.

Davis, Stephen L., and John Robert Victor Prescott. *Aboriginal Frontiers and Boundaries in Australia*. Carleton, Victoria: Melbourne University Press, 1992.

Deloria, Vine, Jr. *Behind the Trail of Broken Treaties: An Indian Declaration of Independence*. New York: Delacourt Press, 1974.

Department of Industry, Coal and Mineral Industries Division. "Special Article—A Century of Mining in Australia." In *Year Book Australia, 2001*: Australian Bureau of Statistics, 2001.

Department of Statistics, Wellington. *New Zealand Official Yearbook 1961*. Wellington, New Zealand: New Zealand Government Printer, 1961.

———. *New Zealand Official Yearbook 1975*. Wellington, New Zealand: New Zealand Government Printer, 1975.

Dickason, Olive Patricia. *Canada's First Nations: A History of Founding Peoples from Earliest Times*. Norman: University of Oklahoma Press, 1992.

Dixit, Avinash, and John Londregan. "Fiscal Federalism and Redistributive Politics." *Journal of Public Economics* 68 (1998): 153–80.

Drees, Laurie Meijer. *The Indian Association of Alberta: A History of Political Action*. Vancouver: University of British Columbia Press, 2002.

Durie, Mason. *Te Mana, Te Kawanatanga: The Politics of Maori Self-Determination*. Auckland: Oxford University Press, 1998.

Dyck, Noel, ed. *Indigenous Peoples and the Nation-State: "Fourth World" Politics in Canada, Australia, and Norway*. St. John's, Newfoundland: Institute of Social and Economic Research, Memorial University of Newfoundland, 1985.

Edmunds, Mary. "Key Issues for the Development of Regional Agreements: An Overview." In *Regional Agreements: Key Issues in Australia. Volume 2: Case Studies*, edited by Mary Edmunds, 21–55. Canberra: Australian Institute of Aboriginal and Torres Strait Islander Studies, 1999.

Ehrlichman, John. *Witness to Power: The Nixon Years*. New York: Simon and Shuster, 1982.

Epstein, Leon D. "The Australian Political System." In *Australia at the Polls: The National Elections of 1975*, edited by Howard R. Penniman, 1–48. Washington, D.C.: American Enterprise Institute for Public Policy Research, 1977.

Fay, Terence J. *A History of Canadian Catholics: Gallicanism, Romanism, and Canadianism*. Montreal and Kingston: McGill-Queen's University Press, 2002.

Fingleton, Jim, and Julie Finlayson, eds. *Anthropology in the Native Title Era: Proceedings of a Workshop Conducted by the Australian Anthropological Society and the Native Titles Research Unit, Australian Institute of Aboriginal and Torres Strait Islander Studies*. Canberra: Australian Institute of Aboriginal and Torres Strait Islander Studies, 1995.

Folds, Ralph. *Crossed Purposes: The Pintupi and Australia's Indigenous Policy*. Sydney: University of New South Wales, 2001.

Frame, Alex. *Salmond: Southern Jurist*. Wellington, NZ: Victoria University Press, 1995.

Fraser, Nancy. "From Redistribution to Recognition? Dilemmas of Justice in a 'Post-Socialist' Age." *New Left Review* 212, July/August (1995): 68–93.

———. "A Rejoinder to Iris Young." *New Left Review* 223, May/June (1997): 126–29.

Fried, Morton. *The Evolution of Political Society.* New York: Random House, 1967.

Gibson, James L., Gregory A. Caldeira, and Vanessa A. Baird. "On the Legitimacy of National High Courts." *American Political Science Review* 92, no. 2 (1998): 343–58.

Goodall, Heather. *Invasion to Embassy: Land in Aboriginal Politics in New South Wales, 1770–1972.* Sydney: Allen & Unwin Pty Ltd, 1996.

Graham, Douglas. *Trick or Treaty?* Wellington, New Zealand: Institute of Policy Studies, Victoria University of Wellington, 1997.

Grattan, Michelle. "The Liberal Party." In *Australia at the Polls: The National Elections of 1975,* edited by Howard R. Penniman, 103–41. Washington, D.C.: American Enterprise Institute for Public Policy Research, 1977.

Guigni, Marco, Douglas McAdam, and Charles Tilly, eds. *How Social Movements Matter.* Minneapolis: University of Minnesota Press, 1999.

Hamelin, Jean. *Histoire du Catholicisme Québécois: Le XXe Siècle, Tome 2, de 1940 à Nos Jours.* Vol. 2. Montréal: Boréal Express, 1984.

Harris, Cole. *Making Native Space: Colonialism, Resistance, and Reserves in British Columbia.* Vancouver: University of British Columbia Press, 2002.

Harrison, Kathryn. *Passing the Buck: Federalism and Canadian Environmental Policy.* Vancouver: University of British Columbia Press, 1996.

Hazlehurst, Kayleen M. *Political Expression and Ethnicity: Statecraft and Mobilisation in the Maori World.* London: Praeger, 1993.

Henderson, James Sakej Youngblood. "Empowering Treaty Federalism." *Saskatchewan Law Review* 58 (1995): 241.

Hill, Richard. "Enthroning "Justice above Might"?: The Sim Commission, Tainui and the Crown." Wellington, NZ: Treaty of Waitangi Policy Unit, Department of Justice, 1989.

———. "Settlements of Major Maori Claims in the 1940s: A Preliminary Historical Investigation." Department of Justice unpublished manuscript. Wellington, 1989.

Horton, David, ed. *The Encyclopedia of Aboriginal Australia: Aboriginal and Torres Strait Islander History, Society and Culture.* Canberra, ACT: Aboriginal Studies Press for the Australian Institute of Aboriginal and Torres Strait Islander Studies, 1994.

Hughes, Colin A. "The 1972 Australian Federal Election." *Australian Journal of Politics and History* 19, April (1973): 11–27.

———. "The Electorate Speaks—and After." In *Australia at the Polls: The National Elections of 1975,* edited by Howard R. Penniman, 277–311. Washington, D.C.: American Enterprise Institute for Public Policy Research, 1977.

Ignatieff, Michael. *The Rights Revolution.* Toronto: Anansi Press Limited, 2000.

Immergut, Ellen M. *Health Politics: Interests and Institutions in Western Europe.* New York: Cambridge University Press, 1992.

Ivison, Duncan, Paul Patton, and Will Sanders, eds. *Political Theory and the Rights of Indigenous Peoples.* Cambridge, UK: Cambridge University Press, 2000.

Jebb, Mary Ann. *Blood, Sweat and Welfare: A History of White Bosses and Aboriginal Pastoral Workers.* Crawley, WA: University of Western Australia Press, 2002.

Kawharu, Ian Hugh. *Maori Land Tenure: Studies of a Changing Institution.* Oxford: Oxford University Press, 1977.

Kelly, Lawrence C. "Charles Henry Burke (1921–1929)." In *The Commissioners of Indian Affairs, 1824–1977,* edited by Robert M. Kvasnicka and Herman J. Viola, 251–61. Lincoln and London: University of Nebraska Press, 1979.

———. "Charles James Rhoads (1929–33)." In *The Commissioners of Indian Affairs, 1824–1977,* edited by Robert M. Kvasnicka and Herman J. Viola, 263–71. Lincoln and London: University of Nebraska Press, 1979.

Kemp, David Alastair. *Society and Electoral Behaviour in Australia.* St. Lucia, Queensland: University of Queensland Press, 1978.

King, Michael. *Maori: A Photographic and Social History.* Auckland: Heineman Publishers, 1983.

———. *Whina: A Biography of Whina Cooper.* Auckland: Hodder & Stoughton, 1983.

Knight, Jack. *Institutions and Social Conflict.* Cambridge: Cambridge University Press, 1992.

Kochan, Thomas. *Collective Bargaining and Industrial Relations.* Homewood, IL: D. Irwin, Inc, 1980.

Kriesi, Hanspeter. "The Organizational Structure of New Social Movements in a Political Context." In *Comparative Perspectives on Social Movements: Political Opportunities, Mobilizing Structures, and Cultural Framings,* edited by Douglas McAdam, John D. McCarthy and Mayer N. Zald, 152–84. New York, NY: Cambridge University Press, 1996.

Kriesi, Hanspeter, and Dominique Wisler. "The Impact of Social Movements on Political Institutions: A Comparison of the Introduction of Direct Legislation in Switzerland and the United States." In *How Social Movements Matter,* edited by Marco Guigni, Doug McAdam and Charles Tilly: University of Minnesota Press, 1999.

Latner, Richard B. *The Presidency of Andrew Jackson: White House Politics 1829–1837.* Athens GA: University of Georgia Press, 1979.

Leacock, Eleanor. "Ethnohistorical Investigation of Egalitarian Politics in Eastern North America." In *The Development of Political Organization in Native North America (1979 Proceedings of the American Ethnological Society),* edited by Elisabeth Tooker, 17–31. Washington, D.C.: The American Ethnological Society, 1983.

Leider, Michael, and Jake Page. *Wild Justice: The People of Geronimo vs. the United States.* New York: Random House, Inc., 1997.

Leslie, John Franklin. "Assimilation, Integration, or Termination? The Development of Canadian Indian Policy, 1943–1963." PhD Dissertation, Carleton University, Canada,1999.

Levine, Stephen. "New Zealand's Political System." In *New Zealand at the Polls: The General Election of 1978,* edited by Howard R. Penniman, 1–33. Washington, D.C.: American Enterprise Institute for Public Policy Research, 1980.

Libby, Ronald T. *Hawke's Law: The Politics of Mining and Aboriginal Land Rights in Australia.* Nedlands WA: University of Western Australia Press, 1989.

Lurie, Nancy Oestreich. "Epilogue." In *Irredeemable America: The Indians' Estate and Land Claims,* edited by Imre Sutton, 363–82. Albuquerque, NM: University of New Mexico, 1985.

Mackerras, Malcolm. *Australian General Elections.* Sydney: Angus & Robertson (Publishers) Pty Ltd, 1972.

Macklem, Patrick. *Indigenous Difference and the Constitution of Canada.* Toronto: University of Toronto Press, 2001.

Maioni, Antonia. *Parting at the Crossroads: The Emergence of Health Insurance in the United States and Canada.* Princeton, NJ: Princeton University Press, 1998.

Mantziaris, Christos, and David F. Martin. *Native Title Corporations: A Legal and Anthropological Analysis.* Annandale, NSW: Federation Press in cooperation with National Native Title Tribunal (Perth WA), 2000.

Martin, Jill E. ""Neither Fish, Flesh, Fowl, nor Good Red Herring": The Citizenship Status of American Indians, 1830–1924." In *American Indians and U.S. Politics: A Companion Reader,* edited by John M. Meyer, 51–72. Westport, CT: Praeger Publishers, 2002.

McFarlane, Peter. *Brotherhood to Nationhood: George Manuel and the Making of the Modern Indian Movement.* Toronto: Between the Lines, 1993.

McLeay, Elizabeth. *The Cabinet and Political Power in New Zealand.* Auckland: Oxford University Press, 1995.

McNeil, Kent. *Common Law Aboriginal Title.* Oxford: Clarendon Press, 1989.

McRobie, Alan. "The Electoral System and the 1978 Election." In *New Zealand at the Polls: The General Election of 1978,* edited by Howard R. Penniman, 64–98. Washington, D.C.: American Enterprise Institute for Public Policy Research, 1980.

Meriam, Lewis. *The Problem of Indian Administration: Report of a Survey Made at the Request of Honorable Hubert Work, Secretary of the Interior, and Submitted to Him, February 21, 1928.* Baltimore: The John Hopkins Press, 1928.

Migdal, Joel S. "The State in Society: An Approach to Struggles for Domination." In *State Power and Social Forces: Domination and Transformation in the Third World,* edited by Joel S. Migdal, Atul Kohli and Vivien Shue, 7–34. New York: Cambridge University Press, 1994.

Miller, James Rodger. *Skyscrapers Hide the Heavens: A History of Indian-White Relations in Canada.* 3rd ed. Toronto: University of Toronto Press, 2000.

Milne, R.S. *Political Parties in New Zealand.* Oxford: Oxford University Press, 1966.

Minister of Justice, Government of New Zealand. "A Bill of Rights for New Zealand: A White Paper.." Wellington, NZ: P.D. Hasselberg, Government Printer, 1985.

Minow, Martha. "Identities." *Yale Journal of Law & the Humanities* 3 (1991): 97–130.

Moe, Terry M. "Control and Feedback in Economic Regulation: The Case of the N.L.R.B." *The American Political Science Review* 79, no. 4 (1985): 1094–116.

Molloy, Tom. *The World Is Our Witness.* Calgary, Alberta: Fifth House Ltd, 2000.

Muldoon, Robert. *My Way.* Wellington, NZ: A.H. & A.W. Reed Ltd, 1981.

Mulgan, Richard. *Politics in New Zealand.* 2 ed. Auckland, NZ: Auckland University Press, 1994.

Murphy, Brian. "Polling and the Election." In *New Zealand at the Polls: The General Election of 1978,* edited by Howard R. Penniman, 168–80. Washington, D.C.: American Enterprise Institute for Public Policy Research, 1980.

National Native Title Tribunal. *National Native Title Tribunal Annual Report 1999–2000.* Perth,WA: National Native Title Tribunal, 2000.

Native Title and Strategic Issues Division. "General Guidelines: Native Title Determinations and Agreements." Perth WA: Ministry of the Premier and Cabinet, Government of Western Australia, 2000.

Newton, Nell Jessup. "The Judicial Role in Fifth Amendment Taking of Indian Land: An Analysis of the Sioux Nation Rule." *Oregon Law Review* 61 (1982): 245.

Nichols, Roger L. *The Indians in the United States and Canada: A Comparative History.* Lincoln: University of Nebraska Press, 1998.

Norgren, Jill. *The Cherokee Cases: The Confrontation of Law and Politics.* New York: McGraw-Hill, Inc., 1996.

Norris, Mary Jane, Eric Guimond, Paula Saunders, and Dan Beavon. "100 Years of Aboriginal Demography: An Analysis within the Canadian Context." Paper presented at the Canadian Population Society, Congress of the Social Sciences and Humanities, University of Alberta, Edmonton, AB, May 28–30, 2000.

Office of Treaty Settlements. *Crown Proposals for the Settlement of Treaty of Waitangi Claims: Detailed Proposals.* Wellington, New Zealand: Office of Treaty Settlements, Department of Justice, Government of New Zealand, 1994.

Officer, James E. "Termination as Federal Policy: An Overview." In *Indian Self-Rule: First-Hand Accounts of Indian-White Relations from Roosevelt to Reagan,* edited by Kenneth R. Philp, 114–28. Salt Lake City: Howe Brothers, 1986.

O'Malley, Vincent. *Agents of Autonomy: Maori Committees in the Nineteenth Century.* Wellington, New Zealand: Huia Publishers, 1998.

Orange, Claudia. *The Treaty of Waitangi.* Wellington: Allen & Unwin New Zealand Ltd, 1987.

Palmer, Geoffrey. *New Zealand's Constitution in Crisis: Reforming Our Political System.* Dunedin, NZ: John McIndoe Ltd, 1992.

Palmer, Ian. *Buying Back the Land: Organisational Struggle and the Aboriginal Land Fund Commission.* Canberra: Aboriginal Studies Press, 1988.

Pevar, Stephen L. *The Rights of Indians and Tribes: The Authoritative ACLU Guide to Indian and Tribal Rights.* Carbondale and Edwardsville: Southern Illinois University Press, 2002.

Philp, Kenneth R. "John Collier (1933–1945)." In *The Commissioners of Indian Affairs, 1824–1977,* edited by Robert M. Kvasnicka and Herman J. Viola, 273–82. Lincoln and London: University of Nebraska Press, 1979.

———. *John Collier's Crusade for Indian Reform 1920–1954.* Tucson: University of Arizona Press, 1977.

Ray, Arthur J. *I Have Lived Here Since the World Began: An Illustrated History of Canada's Native People.* Toronto: Lester Publishing Limited and Key Porter Books, 1996.

Riker, William H. *Federalism: Origin, Operation, Significance.* Boston: Little, Brown, 1964.

Rose, Deborah Bird. *Dingo Makes Us Human: Life and Land in an Australian Aboriginal Culture.* Oakleigh, Victoria: Cambridge University Press, 2000.

Rosenthal, Harvey Daniel. "Indian Claims and the American Conscience: A Brief History of the Indian Claims Commission." In *Irredeemable America: The Indians' Estate and Land Claims,* edited by Imre Sutton, 35–70. Albuquerque, NM: University of New Mexico, 1985.

———. *Their Day in Court: A History of the Indian Claims Commission.* New York: Garland Publishing Inc., 1990.

Ross, Kate. *Occasional Paper: Population Issues, Indigenous Australians, 1996. ABS Catalogue No. 4708.0.* Canberra: Australian Bureau of Statistics, 1999.

Rowse, T. *White Flour, White Power: From Rations to Citizenship in Central Australia.* Melbourne: Cambridge University Press, 1998.

Rowse, Tim. *Obliged to Be Difficult: Nuggett Coombs' Legacy in Indigenous Affairs.* Oakleigh, Australia: Cambridge University Press, 2000.

Russell, Peter H. "High Courts and the Rights of Aboriginal Peoples: The Limits of Judicial Independence." *Saskatchewan Law Review* 61 (1998): 247.

Savoie, Donald J. *Governing from the Centre: The Concentration of Power in Canadian Politics.* Toronto: University of Toronto Press, 1999.

———. *The Politics of Public Spending in Canada.* Toronto: University of Toronto Press, 1990.

Scott, James C. *Seeing Like a State: How Certain Schemes to Improve the Human Condition Have Failed.* New Haven: Yale University Press, 1998.

Seljak, David. "Catholicism's 'Quiet Revolution': *Maintenant* and the New Public Catholicism in Quebec after 1960." In *Religion and Public Life in Canada: Historical and Comparative Perspectives,* edited by Marguerite van Die, 257–74. Toronto: University of Toronto Press, 2001.

Selway, Bradley. "The Role of Policy in the Development of Native Title." *Federal Law Review* 28, no. 3 (2000): 402–52.

Sharp, Andrew. *Justice and the Maori: The Philosophy and Practice of Maori Claims in New Zealand since the 1970s.* 2 ed. Auckland: Oxford University Press, 1997.

Sheehan, Mark. *Maori and Pakeha: Race Relations 1912–1980.* Auckland: The Macmillan Company of New Zealand Ltd., 1989.

Smith, Dennis. *Rogue Tory: The Life and Legend of John G. Diefenbaker.* Toronto: MacFarland, Walter & Ross, 1995.

Sparer, Michael S., and Lawrence D. Brown. "States and the Health Care Crisis: The Limits and Lessons of Laboratory Federalism." In *Health Policy, Federalism, and the American States,* edited by Robert F. Rich and William D. White, 306. Washington, D.C.: The Urban Institute Press, 1996.

Spitzer, Robert J. *President and Congress: Executive Hegemony at the Crossroads of American Government.* Philadelphia: Temple University Press, 1993.

St. Germain, Jill. *Indian Treaty-Making Policy in the United States and Canada, 1867–1877.* Toronto: University of Toronto Press, 2001.

Stephenson, M.A., ed. *Mabo: The Native Title Legislation.* St. Lucia, Qld: University of Queensland Press, 1995.

Sterritt, Neil J., Susan Marsden, Robert Galois, Peter R. Grant, and Richard Overstall. *Tribal Boundaries in the Nass Watershed.* Vancouver: University of British Columbia Press, 1998.

Sutton, Imre. "Incident or Event? Land Restoration in the Claims Process." In *Irredeemable America: The Indians' Estate and Land Claims,* edited by Imre Sutton, 211–31. Albuquerque, NM: University of New Mexico, 1985.

———, ed. *Irredeemable America: The Indians' Estate and Land Claims.* Albuquerque, NM: University of New Mexico, 1985.

Sutton, Peter. "Atomism Versus Collectivism: The Problem of Group Definition in Native Title Cases." In *Anthropology in the Native Title Era: Proceedings of a Workshop Conducted by the Australian Anthropological Society and the Native Title Research Unit, Australian Institute of Aboriginal and Torres Strait Islander Studies,* edited by Jim Fingleton and Julie Finlayson, 1–10. Canberra: Australian Institute of Aboriginal and Torres Strait Islander Studies, 1995.

———. "The Robustness of Aboriginal Land Tenure Systems: Underlying and Proximate Customary Titles." *Oceania* 67 (1996): 7–29.

Tarrow, Sidney G. *Power in Movement: Social Movements and Contentious Politics.* 2 ed. New York: Cambridge University Press, 1998.

Tate, C. Neal, and Torbjorn Vallinder, eds. *The Global Expansion of Judicial Power.* New York: New York University Press, 1995.

Taylor, Charles. "The Politics of Recognition." In *Multiculturalism: Examining the Politics of Recognition,* edited by Amy Gutmann, 25–74. Princeton NJ: Princeton University Press, 1994.

Tehan, Maureen. "Customary Title, Heritage Protection, and Property Rights in Australia: Emerging Patterns of Land Use in the Post-Mabo Era." *Pacific Rim Law and Policy Journal* 7, June (1998): 765.

———. "Practising Land Rights: The Pitjantjatjara in the Northern Territory, South Australia and Western Australia." *Australian Quarterly* 65 (1994): 34.

Templeton, Hugh. *All Honourable Men: Inside the Muldoon Cabinet 1975–1984.* Auckland, NZ: Auckland University Press, 1995.

Tennant, Paul. *Aboriginal Peoples and Politics: The Indian Land Question in British Columbia, 1849–1989.* Vancouver: University of British Columbia Press, 1990.

Thelen, Kathleen. "Historical Institutionalism in Comparative Politics." *Annual Review of Political Science* 2 (1999): 369–404.

Thelen, Kathleen, and Sven Steinmo. "Historical Institutionalism in Comparative Politics." In *Structuring Politics: Historical Institutionalism in Comparative Analysis,* edited by Sven Steinmo, Kathleen Thelen and Frank Longstreth, 1–32. New York: Cambridge University Press, 1992.

Tickner, Robert. *Taking a Stand: Land Rights to Reconciliation.* Crow's Nest, N.S.W.: Allen & Unwin, 2001.

Treasury Board Secretariat. *The Expenditure Management System of the Government of Canada.* Ottawa: The Planning and Communications Directorate, Treasury Board of Canada, 1995.

Treaty of Waitangi Policy Unit. *The Direct Negotiation of Maori Claims.* Wellington, New Zealand: The Treaty of Waitangi Policy Unit, Department of Justice, Government of New Zealand, 1990.

Trudeau, Pierre Elliott. *The Essential Trudeau.* Edited by Ron Graham. Toronto: McLlelland & Stewart, Inc., 1998.

Tully, James. *Strange Multiplicity: Constitutionalism in an Age of Diversity.* Cambridge: Cambridge University Press, 1995.

Turner, David H. *Australian Aboriginal Social Organization.* Canberra: Humanities Press, Australian Institute of Aboriginal Studies, 1980.

Turner, Jan, and David Brooks. "Who Are the Boundary Riders? Mapping Claims in the Ngaanyatjarra Area." In *Native Title in Perspective: Selected Papers from the Native Title Research Unit 1998–2000,* edited by Lisa Strelein and Kado Muir, 107–14. Canberra, ACT: Aboriginal Studies Press and the Native Title Research Unit, Australian Institute of Aboriginal and Torres Strait Islander Studies, 2001.

Tyler, S. Lyman. "William A. Brophy 1945–48." In *The Commissioners of Indian Affairs, 1824–1977,* edited by Robert M. Kvasnicka and Herman J. Viola, 283–87. Lincoln and London: University of Nebraska Press, 1979.

van Meijl, Toon. "The Reemergence of Maori Chiefs: "Devolution" as a Strategy to Maintain Tribal Authority." In *Chiefs Today: Traditional Pacific Leadership and the Postcolonial State,* edited by Geoffrey M. White and Lamont Lindstrom, 84–107. Stanford, CA: Stanford University Press, 1997.

Vowles, Jack, and Peter Aimer. *Voters' Vengeance: The 1990 Election in New Zealand and the Fate of the Fourth Labour Government.* Auckland: Auckland University Press, 1993.

Ward, Alan. *An Unsettled History: Treaty Claims in New Zealand Today.* Wellington, NZ: Bridget Williams Books, 1999.

Washburn, Wilcomb. *The American Indian and the United States: A Documentary History. Volume 2.* New York: Random House, 1973.

———. *The American Indian and the United States: A Documentary History. Volume 3.* New York: Random House, 1973.

Watkins, T.H. *Righteous Pilgrim: The Life and Times of Harold L. Ickes.* New York: Henry Holt and Company, 1990.

Watts, Ronald L. *Comparing Federal Systems.* 2 ed. Montreal and Kingston: McGill-Queen's University Press in association with School of Policy Studies, Queen's University, 1999.

Weaver, R. Kent. "The Politics of Blame Avoidance." *Journal of Public Policy* 6, October-December (1986): 371–98.

Weaver, Sally. "The Joint Cabinet/National Indian Brotherhood Committee: A Unique Experiment in Pressure Group Relations." *Canadian Public Administration* 25, no. 2 (Summer) (1982): 211–39.

———. *Making Canadian Indian Policy: The Hidden Agenda 1968–1970.* Toronto: University of Toronto Press, 1981.

Weller, Patrick, and R.F.I. Smith. "The Rise and Fall of Whitlam Labor: The Political Context of the 1975 Elections." In *Australia at the Polls: The National Elections of 1975,* edited by Howard R. Penniman, 49–76. Washington, D.C.: American Enterprise Institute for Public Policy Research, 1977.

Whittington, Keith E. "Once More Unto the Breach: Postbehavioralist Approaches to Judicial Politics." *Law and Social Inquiry* 25, Spring (2000): 601–34.

Williams, John. *Politics of the New Zealand Maori: Protest and Cooperation 1891–1909.* Seattle: University of Washington Press, 1969.

Woodward, A.E. *Aboriginal Land Rights Commission, Second Report.* Canberra: The Government Printer of Australia, 1974.

Young, Iris Marion. "Unruly Categories: A Critique of Nancy Fraser's Dual Systems Theory." *New Left Review* 222, March/April (1997): 147–61.

Index